THE AUTHORSHIP

AND

HISTORICAL CHARACTER

OF THE

FOURTH GOSPEL.

THE AUTHORSHIP

AND

HISTORICAL CHARACTER

OF THE

FOURTH GOSPEL

*Considered in Reference to the Contents of the Gospel
itself*

A CRITICAL ESSAY

BY

WILLIAM SANDAY, M.A.

FELLOW OF TRINITY COLLEGE, OXFORD

London

MACMILLAN AND CO.

1872

OXFORD:

By T. Combe, M.A., E. B. Gardner, and E. Pickard Hall,

PRINTERS TO THE UNIVERSITY.

IF THIS BOOK DESERVE A DEDICATION,

IT SHALL BE TO

THE PRESIDENT AND FELLOWS OF
TRINITY COLLEGE,

WHO HAVE ALWAYS BEEN

THE KINDEST OF FRIENDS TO ME,

AND FROM

WHOSE CLOSER SOCIETY

I AM NOW UNWILLINGLY PARTING.

PREFACE.

In looking back over this first attempt in the difficult and responsible field of theology, I am forcibly reminded of its many faults and shortcomings. And yet it seems to be necessary that these subjects should be discussed, if only with some slight degree of adequacy. I cannot think that it has not been without serious loss on both sides, that in the great movement that has been going on upon the continent for the last forty years, the scanty band of English theologians should have stood almost entirely aloof, or should only have touched the outskirts of the questions at issue, without attempting to grapple with them at their centre.

It is not for me to presume to do this : but I wish to approach as near to it as I can and dare ; and it has seemed to me that by beginning upon the critical side and taking a single question in hand at a time I might be not altogether unable to contribute to that, perhaps far-off, result, which will only be obtained by the co-operation of many men and many minds.

There is no limit to the efficacy of scientific method if it is but faithfully and persistently applied. If we could but concentrate upon theological questions a small part of that ability and that activity which is devoted in this country to practical pursuits, I have little doubt that in a quarter or half a century the whole position of theology, and with it necessarily of belief and practical religion, would be very different from what it is now.

In the meantime it is of importance that isolated historical or critical questions should be dealt with, and that we should either come to some definite conclusion respecting them, or else at least see how far a definite conclusion is attainable.

Until the facts of history and criticism are accurately determined, speculative systems are but castles in the air. Even if a non-religious system of philosophy should be destined ultimately to prevail, it will still have to give some account of religious phenomena, and must therefore know exactly, or with as much exactness as possible, what those phenomena are. The facts of religion (i. e. the documents, the history of religious bodies, the phenomena of contemporary religious life, &c.) are as much facts as the lie of a coal-bed or the formation of a coral reef. And, if the 'record is defective,' that is no excuse for throwing the whole problem aside as insoluble. A reasonable man will enquire *how far* the record is defective, *what portions* of the problem are insoluble, what conclusions are probable, what others may be said to reach that degree of probability which in practical matters is called certainty, and what are the legitimate and necessary inferences from them.

I propose, if I am permitted, and the judgment of critics on the present volume should at all warrant me in proceeding, to carry on the same method of enquiry, first, to investigate the origin and composition of the Synoptic Gospels, and finally, to the subject of New Testament theology.

With each of these topics I have already in the course of the present enquiry been more or less brought into contact, and upon both I have had to accept provisional conclusions.

With regard to the Synoptists these have been taken from the elaborate work of Dr. Holtzmann (Die Synoptischen Evangelien. Leipzig, 1863). It should be remembered that Dr. Holtzmann does not stand alone, but that for the greater portion of his results (e. g. as to the documentary origin of the Synoptic Gospels, the priority of St. Mark, the existence of two main documents, and the independent use of them by the Evangelists) he has the support of a majority of the best critics during the last ten or fifteen years, including among these Weizsäcker, Meyer, Ritschl, Weiss, Wittichen, and practically also the veteran Ewald. These conclusions I accept temporarily, but I hope to be able to approach the subject myself with sufficient independence.

On points of theology the reader will observe, perhaps, a certain ambiguity of language. When the time comes I hope that this may be removed. But at present I have thought it best to adhere as nearly as possible to the language of Scripture, introducing a minimum of inference or comment, until the various data have been subjected to a closer analysis and more thorough co-ordination.

Those who are acquainted with the subject will find little in this work, at least in the shape of general lines of thought and argument, that can lay claim to be considered new. Indeed, so thorough have been the labours of German critics that I doubt whether any entirely new element in the discussion is possible. If there is anything at all distinctive in the following pages, it will be found, perhaps, partly in the analysis of the discourses, partly in the attempt to consider the several hypotheses as to the authorship of the Gospel from a point of view that may be called *psychological*, i. e. constantly with reference to what in the supposed position of the author would be psychologically natural and probable. I cannot but think that through neglecting to do this, writers of great ability, like M. Wittichen, and also perhaps in a less degree Dr. Weizsäcker, have been led into conclusions which must really be seen to be untenable.

In conclusion, I would only remind the reader that the object of the present essay is critical, and nothing more. My endeavour has been to state the facts plainly and sincerely, and to draw the critical inferences from them with sobriety and care. Beyond this I have not gone, nor could I have attempted to go, without greatly miscalculating my own powers and fitness. But the work of criticism is necessary, and must be done; though in itself it is obviously incomplete. For its completion different and higher gifts are needed. And I shall be well content to wait for the time, when—non sine afflatu divino—a worthier hand shall be found to build either upon this or upon some other foundation.

I have experienced so much difficulty and inconvenience myself from not knowing the edition, date, &c., of works referred to, that I have thought it well to give a roughly-classified list of those which I have principally used, at the risk of drawing attention to its incompleteness. My object has been, not to write an exhaustive commentary upon the Gospel, but merely to determine two points—its authorship and historical character. And in order to do this, it has seemed enough to take certain representative works, so far as possible the best and latest in their respective schools. I would gladly do what I could to remedy any serious omission that might be pointed out to me; but I can hardly think that anything will have been overlooked by which the balance of the argument generally would be altered. A few brief notes are added in explanation of the position and characteristics of those writers who will be less well known in England.

I. Writers who maintain the Johannean authorship and complete authenticity of the Gospel :—

Alford, Dr. H.—Commentary on the Greek Testament. Vol. i. sixth edition, Cambridge, 1868.

Caspari, Dr. C. E.—Chronologisch-geographische Einleitung in das Leben Jesu Christi. Hamburg, 1869. Dr. Caspari (who must not be confounded with the Professor of Theology at Christiania) dates from Geudertheim, in Alsace, and apparently belongs to the Gallo-German school of Strasburg. He would seem, however, to hold more closely to the traditional position than other members of that school, such as

Reuss, Nicolas, Colani. His 'Chronological and Geographical Introduction' is a clear and careful treatise, which often throws new light on the subject discussed, and is especially valuable for Talmudic illustrations.

Ellicott, Bp.—Hulsean Lectures on the Life of Our Lord. Third edition, London, 1862.

Westcott, Professor, B. F.—Introduction to the Study of the Gospels, third edition, London and Cambridge, 1867.

Wieseler, Dr. Karl.—Synopsis of the Four Gospels, translated by the Rev. Edmund Venables, M. A., Cambridge, 1864 (the original appeared in 1843). Beiträge zur richtigen Würdigung der Evangelien und der Evangelischen Geschichte. Gotha, 1869. This work is a supplement to the preceding one ; in the main elaborately maintaining, but in some instances retracting, the views previously held. The value of Dr. Wieseler's labours is already well known to the English public, both through his translator and also through the Hulsean Lectures of Bp. Ellicott, pp. 143 n, 244 n. There are few works that more deserve to be inscribed with the German motto, 'Fleiss und Treue.'

In this class also may be placed, with slight qualification :—

Luthardt, Dr. C. E.—Das Johanneische Evangelium. Nürnberg, 1852. To this writer also Dr. Ellicott has paid a merited tribute of praise, Huls. Lect. p. 31, n. Dr. Luthardt's is not in a special sense the work of either a scholar, a critic, or a theologian ; but everywhere shows signs of thought and care.

II. Writers who maintain Johannean or mediate Johannean authorship and qualified authenticity, in the first degree :—

Bleek, Dr. F.—Einleitung in das Neue Testament, herausgegeben von Johannes Friedrich Bleek. Zweite Auflage, Berlin, 1866. The work of the late illustrious Professor at Bonn, now translated in Clark's series. I only regret that I am not in a position to refer to the work in which Dr. Bleek has dealt specially with many questions arising out of the Fourth Gospel, 'Beiträge zur Evangelien-Kritik,' published in 1846. The results, however, seem to be given in the 'Einleitung' in sufficient detail.

Lücke, Dr. F.—Commentar über das Evangelium des Johannes. Dritte Auflage, Bonn, 1843. It is unnecessary to say that this work, the author of which died in 1855, is still one of the undisputed classics of Biblical criticism ; although, when it is compared with the last edition of Meyer's Commentary, we see in some respects the advance which must be made merely by time.

Meyer, Dr. H. A. W.—Kritisch-exegetisches Handbuch über das Evangelium des Johannes. Fünfte Auflage, Göttingen, 1869. The second part of the Commentary on the New Testament. My admiration for this masterly commentary daily increases. It is a perfect mine of valuable matter of every kind—in scholarship and exegesis unrivalled. Dr. Meyer is bold in statement, perhaps almost to the verge of dogmatism : but there is something refreshing in the vigour and precision which results from this, and it is far better for the student of theology that he should know precisely from what he has to differ, than that he should find himself in the midst of vague expressions with which he may possibly be able to agree. My own obligations to Dr. Meyer are very great.

Orr, James.—The Authenticity of John's Gospel deduced from Internal Evidences, with Answers to Objections. London, 1870.

Holding a place somewhat ambiguous between this and the next class is

Ewald, Dr. H.—Die Johanneischen Schriften übersezt und erklärt. Erster Band, Göttingen, 1861. Dr. Ewald needs no commendation to an English or to any public. I had read the introductory portion of his work before beginning to write, but was accidentally prevented from consulting it while writing. Hence the references will be found to be somewhat less frequent than they should be.

III. Writers maintaining mediate or immediate Johannean authorship and qualified authenticity, in the second degree :—

Renan, M. E.—Vie de Jésus. Treizième édition, Paris, 1867. (See p. 4, n.) I will only add that the thirteenth edition generally has been largely added to and improved, and quite supersedes all former ones.

Weizsäcker, Dr. C.—Untersuchungen über die Evangelische Geschichte, ihre Quellen und den Gang ihrer Entwicklung. Gotha, 1864. Dr. Weizsäcker is, I believe, a professor at Tübingen, but is not identified with the school which takes its name from that University. He is one of the editors of a well-known review, representing moderate Liberalism in theology, the 'Jahrbücher für Deutsche Theologie.' The present work is a fine example of grave, dispassionate, able investigation.

Wittichen, M. C.—Der geschichtliche Charakter des Evangeliums Johannis in Verbindung mit der Frage nach seinem Ursprunge. Elberfeld, 1868. A terse and able little work, but encumbered by paradoxes. M. Wittichen's view is that the Gospel was written by St. John, who, however, never left Syria, and retained to the last his Jewish stand-point. In the Gospel he seems to think that real and ideal elements are mixed in almost equal proportions. As it is beside my present purpose to discuss the criticism of the Ephesian tradition, perhaps I may be allowed to refer to what is said upon the subject in the article upon Dr. Keim in 'The Academy' (July, 1871). The theory that is shared by Dr. Keim and M. Wittichen has hardly obtained foothold in Germany—at least it is rejected unhesitatingly by Ewald, Meyer and Weizsäcker, though it has recently found an adherent in Dr. Holtzmann. It is possible that I may have occasion to return to this subject.

IV. Writers who deny the Johannean authorship and authenticity of the Gospel entirely :—

Hanson, Sir Richard.— The Jesus of History. London, 1869. See p. 87 foll., below.

Hilgenfeld, Dr. A.—Die Evangelien nach ihrer Entstehung und geschichtlichen Bedeutung. Leipzig, 1854. This book has been chosen as representing the best and latest version of the Tübingen theory, and as one the plan of which ran more or less parallel to my own. It is throughout ably written.

Keim, Dr. Theodor.—Geschichte Jesu von Nazara, in ihrer Verkettung mit dem Gesammtleben seines Volkes. Band I, Zürich, 1867. I was permitted to review the first half of this most exhaustive work in 'The Academy' for July, 1871. The last part of the second and first part of the third volume did not reach me until after the manuscript had been sent to the press. A few brief references to these are inserted in brackets. I hope to do them more justice at some future time.

Scholten, Dr. J. H.—Das Evangelium nach Johannes, aus dem Holländischen übersetzt von H. Lang. Berlin, 1867. This a German translation of the work of a leading Dutch theologian, published originally in 1864. It is the one book out of those I have been led to consult, which has seemed to me distinctly inferior to its reputation. Admirably written, with perfect lucidity of exposition, the more solid qualities seem to be greatly lacking to it. It bristles with unsound reasoning, and, in spite of an apparently considerable acquaintance with the literature of the subject, must still be pronounced superficial.

Tayler, J. J.—An Attempt to ascertain the Character of the Fourth Gospel, especially in its Relation to the Three First. Second edition, London, 1870. I have hardly crossed the path of this work, as only eleven pages of it are given to the discussion of 'internal indications.'

With regard to other books, the references to Lightfoot's 'Horae Hebraicae et Talmudicae' are taken from an old folio (somewhat faultily paged) of 1684; those to Schöttgen from a Dresden and Leipsic edition of 1733; Herzog's 'Realencyklopädie für Protestantische Theologie und Kirche' is alluded to simply as 'Herzog'; Schenkel's 'Bibel-Lexicon' is indicated by the letters 'S. B. L.,' and Smith's Dictionary by 'S.D.' The articles chiefly referred to in the latter are those on geography and topography, which are excellent, and quite up to date—in this, I regret to say, a contrast to the article on the Gospel.

I am greatly indebted for valuable help and suggestions, during the passage of the book through the press, to the Rev. T. A. Eaglesim, B.A., of Worcester College, and to my friend Mr. James Beddard, of Nottingham, to whose kindness and judgment I never appeal in vain.

GREAT WALTHAM, CHELMSFORD,
February 8, 1872.

CONTENTS.

CHAPTER I.

INTRODUCTION AND PROLOGUE OF THE GOSPEL.

Necessity for critical examination of the Evangelical documents.

AMONG the lengthened discussions which have had for their object the reconstruction of the history contained in the four Gospels, one conclusion seems to have emerged with considerable distinctness; that is, the necessity of starting from a thorough critical investigation of the documents. It may, no doubt, be possible to draw a picture in rough outline and then simply to allege its consistency in proof of its truth. To a certain extent this method is a legitimate one; and it is more applicable to a subject so unique and remarkable in its character, than it would be to a more ordinary series of events, where the number of possible combinations was greater. But it is clear that such a method can only admit of vague and approximate results. As soon as we descend to particulars, it fails us altogether. The question may be raised as to whether the picture presented is really consistent, or as to whether it is the only consistent picture deducible from the premisses; and where this is the case, it is obvious that its self-evidential force at once ceases.

B

For example, to take the question of miracles: one writer produces a picture in which miracles are an essential feature; another writes a history from which they are altogether eliminated[1]. How are we to decide between them? Prior to the examination of the documents, what criterion have we that is not far too subjective to carry with it general conviction? We need to know how near the original narrators stood to the events, and what is the character of the context in which the miracles are found.

The most satisfactory method, then, is to begin at the beginning, and to work steadily upwards: first to institute a searching examination of the documents, so as to discover their true nature and value; and then, with the results of this before us, to fit their contents, so far as is possible, into a single historical frame.

Object of the Essay.

The present essay is intended as an instalment towards the first half of such an enquiry. Following the natural division, according to which the three first or Synoptic Gospels are taken as one class, and the fourth, that which goes under the name of St. John, as another, it deals only with the latter, partly as the more important of the two, — a greater divergence of opinion in respect of it being possible,—and partly because the questions raised in connection with it seem most ripe for decision.

---

[1] 'Between the astonishing design and its astonishing success there intervenes an astonishing instrumentality—that of miracles.' (*Ecce Homo*, p. 42.) 'Ce n'est donc pas au nom de telle ou telle philosophie, c'est au nom d'une constante expérience, que nous bannissons le miracle de l'histoire.' (Renan, *Vie de Jésus*, Introd. p. xcvi., 13th ed.).

Within this more limited range, however, our enquiry still does not profess to be exhaustive. It is a subdivision of a division. It is confined to what is commonly known as the internal evidence to the character of the Gospel. Several reasons seem to make this limitation of treatment desirable. The subject of the external evidence has been pretty well fought out. The opposing parties are probably as near to an agreement as they ever will be. It will hardly be an unfair statement of the case for those who reject the Johannean authorship of the Gospel, to say, that the external evidence is compatible with that supposition. And on the other hand, we may equally say for those who accept the Johannean authorship, that the external evidence would not be sufficient alone to prove it[1]. As it at present stands, the controversy may be regarded as drawn; and it is not likely that the position of parties will be materially altered.

Thus we are thrown back upon the internal evidence; and I have the less hesitation in confining

---

[1] I am aware that in making this statement I am obliged to express a different opinion from Canon Liddon (*Bampton Lectures*, p. 224 *n*). But Canon Liddon has gone almost entirely to Tischendorf, who with all his merits is a notorious partisan. Besides, he does not seem to have noticed sufficiently the qualifications to which the external evidence is subject. This side of the question will be found fairly discussed by Keim, *Jesu von Nazara*, pp. 136-146, and Holtzmann in *S. B. L.* ii. 222. 'Speaking impartially,' Dr. Holtzmann says, 'it must be confessed, that the evidence for the Synoptic Gospels hardly begins earlier than that for St. John. The use of the latter, however, was for a long time much weaker, much more cautious than that of the former.' This 'weaker and more cautious use' may be explained by other causes than doubts as to the genuineness of the Gospel. It may be partly due to the fact, that it was in any case composed later than the other three; partly also to its peculiar and almost esoteric character; partly to external accidents, which may have for a time limited its circulation.

myself to this, because I believe it to be capable of leading to a quite definite conclusion. Whether it really does so the event must show. But in the meantime the present essay is submitted to the public, as a contribution towards the solution of the problem.

Method pursued.

Its plan is not indeed unprecedented[1], but may appear to an English reader somewhat novel. In accordance with the general principle by which literary neatness has throughout been sacrificed to practical serviceableness and reliability, it has been thought well to go through the Gospel chapter by chapter and verse by verse, determining, as far as possible, the exact value of the separate data as they present themselves, and not combining the whole into a single view until the detailed investigation was complete.

Obviously such a procedure will have its disadvantages. It will involve an appearance of confusion, and a certain amount of repetition. But I cannot but think that the reader will be willing to put up with these in return for the greater security he will possess, that the facts have not been garbled, or their true bearing distorted ; inasmuch as he will be able to see each one of them in connection with its context, and if he should be led to form a different judgment from the writer, he will be able on each occasion to take note of it.

Strictly inductive.

The method is indeed in the strict sense of the

---

[1] It is practically the plan pursued by Hilgenfeld in his work, *Die Evangelien*, and also by Renan in the Appendix to the 13th edition of his *Vie de Jésus*—a somewhat slight sketch, but one that often shows the author's fine historical sense to much advantage.

word inductive. It first seeks and defines its data out of the confused mass of phenomena ; and then, when they are ready for use, groups and arranges them ; and not until that is done does it finally draw its conclusions. It may adopt the privilege of science in forming a provisional hypothesis as it proceeds ; but not until it has been tested and verified and compared with the whole sum of the phenomena, will that hypothesis venture to assert itself as established ; and even then it will still be amenable to the bar of a competent public opinion.

There will be the further incidental advantage that our enquiry itself will, in some respects, serve as a running commentary upon the fourth Gospel, and it is hoped that it may contribute something to the elucidation both of the narrative and the discourses which occur in the course of it. But this has been of course only a secondary object, and has been throughout subordinated to that announced upon the title-page ; viz. the attempt to ascertain who was the author of the Gospel, and what degree of authenticity is to be assigned to its contents. Incidental advantage.

With this object before us we proceed to the consideration of the first chapter.

THE PROLOGUE.

The Gospel opens with a prologue, which is the philosophical or theological introduction to the history that follows. In high metaphysical language the subject of the Gospel is announced as 'the Word made Flesh.' Accordingly in these first eighteen St. John i. 1–18.

verses the Evangelist sets forth the nature, functions, and successive manifestations of the Word.

1. As pre-existent. When time began the Word was already throned face to face with God (πρὸς τὸν Θεόν), and partaking of His Divine Essence. Through the Word the work of creation was accomplished. He was the Source of light and life, i. e. of all physical, moral, and spiritual well-being for man. But the Light shone in vain : the darkness of human nature was too gross to receive it.

2. As incarnate. To this incarnation the prophet John bare witness. He was not himself the Light. The functions of the True Light were not, like his, limited and subsidiary, but wide as the world itself, and extending to every man that is born into it[1]. He came ; the Creator to His creatures ; the Messiah to His people. As a people they rejected Him ; but there were some few who by the election and grace of God did receive Him ; and to them He proved to be the source of life indeed.

3. As revealing the Father. Thus the Word was made flesh, and manifested forth His glory, which as well by its own essential character, the grace and truth which flowed from it, as by the direct testimony of John, was seen to be the glory of the only-

---

[1] The one argument which seems fatal to the combination of ἐρχόμενον with ἦν is, that in that case a *series* of manifestations, the *continuous* manifestation of the word ('kam stets' Ewald), must be meant; but the context clearly points to the special and chief manifestation in the Incarnation, to which John bore witness. The antithesis is between the lesser reflected light of John, and the world-wide illumination of the incarnate Word. For the expression ἐρχ. εἰς τ. κ. there is a parallel in 2 John 7. Several others are quoted by Lightfoot from Jewish writers (*Horae Hebraicae*, p. 521). It would appear to be a Hebraism.

begotten, pre-existent Son[1]. Thus God Himself has been revealed; no longer partially as by Moses, but in the fulness of His attributes by Jesus Christ.

It is obvious that we are moving here in a region of ideas wholly different from anything that is to be found in the Synoptic Gospels. All appears to turn round this single expression, the Logos or Word. The Word is that mediatory Divine Being by whom the invisible, unapproachable God acts visibly upon the world and upon men. It is the Organ of creation, revelation, salvation, the Giver of light and life, and It was incarnate in the 'man Christ Jesus.'

Such is the Johannean doctrine of the Logos; and the question at once arises, what is the sphere of ideas to which it belongs? what is the theological or philosophical system with which it is to be correlated? The answer to this may throw some light upon the origin of the Gospel.

There are several systems into which 'the Logos' or 'Word' enters as an important factor, and with any of these it would seem that the Gospel might be connected; it might be either Gnostic, or Jewish, or Alexandrine. If we are to suppose that it was formed under the influence of developed Gnosticism, then it will probably have been written some time in the second quarter of the second century. If it grew directly out of Alexandrinism or Judaism, then it may fall any time in the last quarter of the first. In other words, the first supposition is in any case

---

[1] We are absolved from the necessity of deciding the difficult question as to the reading of ver. 18, μονογενὴς Θεός or μον. υἱός. Both are found in patristic citations as early as Irenaeus, and in the writings of Irenaeus himself (170–200 A.D.). Canon Lightfoot argues from this that the text must have been some time in existence. (*Revision of Eng. N. T.*, p. 20.)

To Gnostic
systems.

incompatible with Apostolic authorship; either of the two others are compatible with it.

But the hypothesis of Gnostic origin, e. g. in a system like the Valentinian, cannot in the present stage of critical investigation be regarded as tenable. The difference between the external evidence for the fourth Gospel and the Synoptics is now seen to be far too small for an interval of seventy or eighty years to be placed between them[1]. And on internal grounds, if the fourth Gospel had been produced in the midst of the Gnostic systems, it must have been much more explicit upon the points where it comes into contact with Gnosticism. Whether it was composed in the interest of the Gnostics or of orthodoxy, or to reconcile both, it could not have failed to declare its object much more plainly and definitely.

The Valentinian.

A brief glance at the Gnostic systems will, I think, suffice to make this clear. The Valentinian system has indeed the Logos, but it has much more besides. The Logos is only one of a series of thirty Aeons or emanations which, proceeding from the Bythos or incomprehensible central point of the Divine Being, and combined in pairs male and female, fill up the circle of the Divine attributes known as the Pleroma. Outside the Pleroma, and parted from it by the boundary Horos or Stauros, lies the Ogdoas, an abode formed for Achamoth, the abortive fruit of Sophia the twenty-eighth Aeon. Beyond that again is the Hebdomas presided over by the Demiurgus, the

---

[1] Cf. Holtzmann in *S. B. L.* ii. 222 ad fin. Dr. Holtzmann speaks of 'three to five decads;' but that is from the Tübingen point of view, according to which the last of the Synoptists would come about 100 A.D. Dr. Holtzmann's own view is more probable, that the Synoptic literature was complete by the year 80 A.D.

maker of the world and of men. Monogenes is another name for the Aeon Nous; the Aeon Logos is separated from the Aeon Christus; Christus from Jesus Soter, who is not an Aeon, but the fruit of all the Aeons, the 'Star of the Pleroma.' The Soter again is separated from the Son of Mary; and the different parts of the system are linked together by an elaborate mythology[1].

What has become of all this wild overgrowth in the Gospel? Surely it is not to be supposed, that the Evangelist has thrust his hand, as it were, into the middle of it, and drawn forth the Logos alone. Is it not much more natural to regard the Valentinian system as a corrupt heretical development of the ideas contained in the Gospel? The two are related to one another much as, in architecture, Florid Perpendicular is related to Norman. But it is a law both of thought and nature, that the simpler form precedes the more complex. Again, it seems impossible, that if the Evangelist had had these strange distortions of his own ideas before him, he should not have guarded more expressly against misconception. Would he not have told us that his Logos was not the Valentinian Logos; that with him, Monogenes, Christus, Soter were but divers appellations of a single person; that he knew nothing of Ogdoas or Hebdomas, of Achamoth or Sophia, of the Demiurgus, of Syzygies or Aeons? It would have seemed almost superfluous to argue the question, if the opposite view had not actually been maintained[2].

---

[1] Cf. Baur, *Kirchen-geschichte der drei ersten Jahrhunderte*, pp. 196–203. The original authorities are principally Irenaeus *adv. Haer.* b. i. and ii.; Hippolytus, *Philosophumena*, vi. 21 foll.

[2] e. g. by Hilgenfeld, pp. 330–334. Dr. Scholten thinks that the

Valentinus appears to have flourished about 140 A.D.; Basilides comes fifteen years earlier: but the same arguments which push the Gospel back behind Valentinus, also push it back behind Basilides. The Basilidian system starts with two main postulates, God, who represents the extreme of abstraction, none but negative predicates being applied to Him, and the primaeval chaos. In this chaos are mingled seeds of divine matter, which are designated by the name of υἱότης. Some of these fly upwards at once by their own volatility. From the rest is evolved, first, the region of the Ogdoas with its Archon or sovereign, and the son who reigns by his side, better and wiser than himself; and then the region of the Hebdomas, with its Archon and his son. These regions are filled besides with other 'principalities and powers;' and above them all, but below the highest region of the non-existent, hovers the Holy Ghost. There are still some particles of υἱότης remaining beneath among the residuum of chaos; and Christianity represents with Basilides the scheme by which these are liberated, through separation, from the matter in which they are imprisoned. A series of communications pass from the Spirit to the son of the higher Archon, from him to his father, and also to the son of the lower Archon, and finally to the son of Mary, through whom the ultimate separation takes place[1].

author of the fourth Gospel, 'penetrated by the philosophy of his time, and highly valuing the Gnostic speculations, set himself to reform the immorality and fantastic extravagance of Gnosticism, as much in the interest of Christianity as of the true Gnosis, and so produced a work by which Gnosticism is brought down from the sphere of barren abstraction to that of reality.' (p. 428.) Schwegler connects the origin of the fourth Gospel with the still later phenomena of Montanism. *Nachapost. Zeit.*, p. 345; cf. Pfleiderer, *Geschichte der Religion*, p. 481.

[1] Cf. Baur, *Kirchen-geschichte*,

We repeat the question, is it credible that the doctrine of the prologue to the fourth Gospel should have grown by any means of contact or of contrast out of systems such as these? May we not go farther and say that the interval necessary for their development out of the kind of conditions that the fourth Gospel implies, must have been a considerable one? The date of Basilides and his system is about 125 A.D.: that assigned to the fourth Gospel by those who believe it to be the work of the Apostle, is the decad 80–90 A.D. And conjecturally, taking as a basis of calculation the interval which separates Basilides from Valentinus and the number of points which they have in common, this would appear to be a not unreasonable period to place between them.

There are however, I suspect, data a degree more definite than those supplied by the system of Basilides. The Ophitic is the earliest Gnostic system of which we have sufficiently full and trustworthy information. But there is much reason to doubt whether the Evangelist would have written iii. 14 as he has done, if Ophitic Gnosticism had then been in existence, or at least if it had come within his knowledge. The serpent was the centre of this system, at once its good and its evil principle. The serpent who tempted Eve, the fiery serpent in the wilderness, the rod of Moses, the brazen serpent, represented under various forms the malevolent or beneficent powers. The good serpent is also the ἀρχή, the Logos, the Saviour who stands between God and matter, and works in its votaries that Gnostic emancipation

St. John i.
1–18.

The Ophitic.

pp. 204–212.   Original authorities, Iren. *adv. Haer.* i. 24; Hipp. *Philos.* b. vii. etc.

by which they are delivered from the thraldom of the flesh. But, this being so, it does not seem likely that the serpent would have been introduced as it is in the discourse with Nicodemus. An orthodox writer could not treat it as a harmless symbol; a writer with Ophitic leanings would have emphasized the point and enlarged upon it[1].

To the Pauline Epistles of the imprisonment.

We are thus brought by a negative process to a date not very far from 80–90 A.D. And on the positive side the data seem to converge nearly upon the same point. Dr. Lipsius, the latest authority upon the history of Gnosticism, in speaking of the Pauline Epistles to the Ephesians and Colossians, describes them as standing in much the same relation to Gnosticism as the fourth Gospel[2]. He does this indeed leaving it an open question whether they were really written by St. Paul. But I do not imagine that an English critic will have any doubt upon this head. The Epistle to the Colossians is vouched for, not only by its language and style, but chiefly by its connection with the Epistle to Philemon, which cannot by any possibility be a forgery. And the only real difficulty in regard to the Epistle to the Ephesians is removed by the amended reading of i. 1, and the hypothesis which regards it as a circular letter. M. Renan, although he raises the question, has evidently no doubt of the genuineness of these Epistles[3]: it is maintained by all the moderate German schools, e. g. those which are

---

[1] Cf. Baur, pp. 192–195; Lipsius, *Gnosticismus*, pp. 126–133.

[2] Cf. art. 'Gnosis' in *S. B. L.* ii. 504.

[3] Cf. *St. Paul*, pp. xi, xx–xxiii. M. Renan thinks that the Epistle to the Ephesians was not written actually by St. Paul, but under his eyes and in his name by Tychicus or Timothy. This would leave its date unaltered.

represented by Bleek, Reuss, Meyer, and even Schenkel[1]; and the denial of it forms a part of the Tübingen system that is rapidly falling into discredit. The literary data, including under these the general improbability of forgery, are decisive in favour of the Epistles to the Philippians and Philemon. And from these two fixed points we argue backwards to the other Epistles of the imprisonment. It may be set down as to all intents certain that they were written by St. Paul; and to this conclusion the history of dogma clearly must conform.

But if the Johannean theology is to be grouped with that of the Epistles to the Ephesians and Colossians, and if we allow for a certain advance which it exhibits upon them, it cannot be dated much later than 80 A.D., which agrees with the results of our previous investigation.

The history of the Church at this period is exceedingly obscure. The Epistle of Clement to the Corinthians, and perhaps that of Barnabas, are the only extra-canonical books that fall within the first century[2]; while the external authorities, Irenaeus and the Philosophumena, cease to be trustworthy guides when we pass beyond the Ophites. Any theory, therefore, that we may form as to the growth and development either of orthodox or of heterodox doctrine must be based upon conjecture, derived chiefly from data contained within the canonical

---

[1] Cf. Bleek, *Einl.* pp. 444–446, 449–451; Reuss, *Gesch. der Heil. Schrift. N. T.* §§ 118, 119, 121, 123; Schenkel on Eph. in *S. B. L.*

[2] The Epistle of Clement was written about the year 95 A.D.

(Lightfoot, Ritschl, &c.). The Epistle of Barnabas falls either in the reign of Hadrian, c. 133 A.D., or in that of Nerva, c. 97 A.D.— probably the latter.

books themselves.   But there is nothing to hinder the composition of the Gospel at a date not far from that upon which we have fixed ; rather, so far as we can see, everything to favour it.   All the elements both of orthodox and heterodox development had now been for some time in existence.   Philo was an old man in 39 A.D.   The foundation of Christianity was, as we shall have occasion to show, complete in the year 30.   The dates assigned to the death of St. Paul are from 64 to 68.   Jerusalem was in ruins.   The Gentile congregations had a fixed and recognised existence in the Church.   And alongside of the conditions which these facts would represent, were the Oriental religions with their mythologies always ready to draw upon, and to give birth to heretical opinions.   On the whole, it would seem as if the decad 80–90 A.D. stood upon the line of development between the simple facts of Christianity and the final coalescence of Alexandrinism and the Oriental religions under Christian forms, very much in' the place that we should assign to the Gospel and Epistle that go under the name of St. John.

St. John.

Relation to previous developments, Judaean or Alexandrine.

There is, however, a further question that has some bearing upon the authorship of these writings.   We have seen that the theology of the prologue cannot be referred to the period of full-grown Gnosticism.   Are we then to look for its antecedents in Alexandria or Palestine?   Until recently the first of these two views has prevailed ; but the second has of late found energetic defenders!.   It is not difficult to show, both that the Logos of St. John differs from that of Philo,

---

[1] e.g. Luthardt, whose view is discussed by Alford, *Comm.* p 6;8; Weiss, *Theologie des N. T.* § 202; Wittichen, *Ev. Joh.* pp. 10–15.

and that there are apparent antecedents for it in the St. John i. Old Testament and in the Apocrypha. But we must 1–18. remember, first, that between Philo and the Evangelist there lay the historical fact of the life of Christ; this life is, according to the Evangelist, the Incarnation of the Logos; and the philosophic idea could not but undergo transformation, as soon as it came to be identified with a historical Person. And secondly, it should be remembered that Philo bases, nominally at least, his whole philosophy on the Old Testament; so that it is not strange if theories derived from him should bear a certain Old Testament colour. At the same time the books of the Apocrypha in which the nearest approximations to the doctrine of the Logos are to be found, belong to the same general stream as Philo himself. One of them, the Book of Wisdom, was actually attributed to him by a tradition older than Jerome[1]. This class of writings, therefore, cannot be alleged as showing that a doctrine of the Logos was formed independently of Alexandria.

On the other hand, it is only contended that Philo To the is the medium through which the Word of the Old Logos of Testament passed into the Logos of St. John: and I Philo. cannot think that this proposition has been satisfactorily disproved. The personification of Wisdom in the Old Testament is poetical: that of the Word in St. John is metaphysical: and this is precisely the character that had been given to it by Philo. One of the writers who assigns the doctrine of the Logos to Jewish sources, speaks of it as a creation of 'religious

---

[1] Jerome says in his preface, 'nonnulli scriptorum veterum hunc (libr. Sap.) esse Philonis Judaei affirmant.' The dates assigned to the book by modern critics range between 217 B.C. and 40 A.D. It was probably written after 145 B.C.

poetry' (religiös-dichterischer) ; but this description is, I think we must say, certainly misplaced—and it seems to be an equal error to call the Logos of Philo 'nothing but the *caput mortuum* of philosophical abstraction[1].' On the contrary, it is through the Logos that Philo saves his idea of the Deity from becoming a mere abstraction. The Logos is the agency through which the Absolute Being operates upon finite matter. It is the divine Organ, by which the worlds were made. It is 'the Captain of the host of ideas,' 'the Vice-regent of the Great King,' 'the High Priest,' in whom God and the world are reconciled, 'a second God,' 'the eldest Son of God[2].' Instead of being a pure philosophical abstraction, this conception of the Logos is rather the very point at which the Platonic Idealism begins to be intermingled with the more concrete forms of the East.

And yet there is still a wide difference from the Gospel. The Philonian Logos is a kind of fluid medium : at one moment it seems to have a separate and almost hypostatical existence ; at the next it is reabsorbed in the centre from which it issues. We find the phrase 'Logoi' as well as 'Logos,' as if Logos were a collective term. There is none of the definiteness and fixity of a person. But we have only to read in between the lines the single sentence ὁ λόγος σὰρξ ἐγένετο, and this difference is removed. Once think of the Philonian Logos as incarnate, as dwelling or having dwelt upon the earth in the likeness of a man, and the resulting conception will be found to be very similar

---

[1] Cf. Wittichen, pp. 13, 14.
[2] Cf. Lipsius in *S. B. L.* i. 95–97; Meyer, Lücke, and Alford on the prologue to the Gospel.

to that which is laid down in the prologue to the
fourth Gospel.

St. John i.
1–18.

We conclude, then, that the prologue must be taken
to show a certain acquaintance with Philo's, or at
least with Alexandrine theology. Without assuming
this I do not see what account we are to give of the
transition from that which had been hitherto a poetic
figure of speech to a metaphysical reality. For the
prologue clearly presupposes the step to have been
taken. The author is conscious that he is not now
taking it for the first time : his manner is that of one
who is introducing a new content into a current recognised and generally intelligible idea. If this had not
been the case he must have begun by sketching a
system of abstract metaphysics, before he came to
apply them specially to theology. It is not the doctrine
of the Logos which is novel, but only the identification
of the Logos with the Founder of Christianity.

But the fact that the theology of the prologue has
its origin in Alexandria, still does not give us any exact
information as to the author. Alexandrine ideas were
widely diffused, and their geographical boundary line
is too indistinct to admit of a precise conclusion.
There seems indeed to be some doubt as to how far
they had penetrated into Palestine—the peculiar culture that we find in St. Paul appears to be due rather
to an independent Rabbinical branch of the same
movement [1]. But in the centres of Greek civilisation,
and especially in Asia Minor, which was as much a
meeting-point of East and West as Alexandria itself,
Alexandrine theories were at home.

Geogra-
phical
relations
of the
doctrine.

---

[1] Cf. Lipsius, *Gnosticismus*, pp. 41, 42. Yet the later Epistles (Eph.
and Col.) surely show signs of Alexandrine influence.

All we can say then is, that so far as the prologue is concerned there is a certain probability—somewhat vague and slight in respect of place, stronger in respect of time—in favour of the tradition that the Gospel was composed at Ephesus, and between 80–90 A.D.

But before we quit the prologue, we ought to consider it in its bearing upon the other subject of our enquiry—the historical value of the facts related in the Gospel. There has been a tendency to argue immediately from the philosophical and dogmatic character of the prologue to the conclusion that the Gospel is from first to last an ideal composition [1]. In any case the conclusion would be a hasty one; because it is quite as likely *à priori* that an author would invent metaphysics to suit his facts, as that he would invent facts to suit his metaphysics. We do not suspect Comte or Hegel of inventing history because they have endeavoured to explain it philosophically.

But when the objection is especially urged to the disadvantage of the fourth Gospel, it is too often forgotten that the Synoptists also are not exempt from it. Of the three Synoptic writers, St. Luke is the only one who comes forward as a professed historian. St. Matthew and St. Mark, or the Evangelists who now bear their names, proclaim their dogmatic intention in a manner that is really little less pronounced than St. John. When the fourth Evangelist avows at the end of ch. xx, i. e. in the verse with which the first draught of the Gospel concluded, 'These things are written that ye might believe that Jesus is the Christ

---

[1] Cf. Keim, pp. 124, 125. Scholten states this point fairly, p. 182.

the Son of God,' he is using almost exactly the same words as those with which the second Gospel opens, 'The beginning of the Gospel of Jesus Christ, the Son of God;' and the modification which this receives in the first Gospel only corresponds to its Jewish object and character, 'The book of the generation of Jesus Christ, the son of David, the son of Abraham.' None of the Evangelists write otherwise than with a distinct dogmatic conclusion before their minds. But we cannot argue from this at once that the facts which they relate are fictitious, or even that they have been distorted. In the case of the Synoptists we are able to control their procedure with considerable accuracy. The groundwork of their narrative has been supplied to all three by a single document, which they have used independently of each other. We can therefore tell by comparing the parallel columns of the synopsis to what extent changes have been introduced into that document on dogmatic grounds. It cannot be said that such changes do not exist. For instance, 'the Son' is left out in Matt. xxiv. 36 as compared with Mark xiii. 32, 'But of that day and that hour knoweth no man, no, not the angels which are in heaven, neither the Son, but the Father;' and conversely Matt. xv. 24, 'I am not sent but unto the lost sheep of the house of Israel,' has been omitted in Mark vii. 26, 27; so in Mark vi. 3, 'the carpenter, the son of Mary,' seems to have been substituted for 'the carpenter's son' of Matt. xiii. 55. These are perhaps the principal instances of alterations made from dogmatic motives; and there are some others[1]. But altogether they do

[1] Cf. Wittichen, *Über den historischen Charakter der Synopt. Evangelien*, in *Jahrbücher für Deutsche Theologie*, 1866, iii. pp. 427–482.

not make up an important total. Before the fact, then, there is no greater reason for suspecting the fourth Evangelist than the Synoptists. The question must remain open for detailed investigation, and is not foreclosed either way by the prologue.

In one respect, indeed, a favourable conclusion is suggested. It has been frequently noticed that the doctrine of the Logos is confined strictly to the Evangelist's own reflections, and is nowhere introduced into the body of the history. The word λόγος occurs repeatedly, but always in the Jewish sense of the message or command, single acts and utterances of God, but not in the Alexandrine sense of a hypostatized Divine Being[1]. If the discourses in the Gospel had been really, as Baur and his followers think, free compositions, this distinction would scarcely have been observed. It is to be noticed generally, that the Hellenistic colouring is nowhere so strong as in the prologue; as though it served to indicate the standpoint of the writer, but did not materially affect his treatment of his subject.

[1] Cf. x. 35, xvii. 14, xvii. 6, viii. 47, viii. 55, &c. Also Westcott, *Introd.* p. 272; Keim, p. 124; and Wittichen, p. 11.

CHAPTER II.

THE TESTIMONY OF JOHN.

St. John i. 19–51.

Possible hypotheses as to the author of the Gospel.

B EFORE we enter upon the narrative proper, it will be well to set before ourselves distinctly the different hypotheses with which we shall have to deal.

It is sufficiently evident that the author of the Gospel intended his work to be attributed to St. John. This would seem to follow from xxi. 24, taken along with the context in which 'the beloved disciple' is elsewhere mentioned[1]. He is never named; but by the prominence accorded to him, and especially from his intimate relation with Peter, it is clear that he belonged to the first of the Apostolic groups; and as Peter and Andrew are both excluded and James fell a victim to one of the earliest persecutions,

---

[1] Lützelberger suggested that 'the beloved disciple' might be Andrew, and Holtzmann (seriously?), following Spath, that he might be Nathanael. The argument against the identification with John drawn from the silence of the fourth Gospel as to scenes, like the Transfiguration, where according to the Synoptists John was present, cannot count for very much. It is certain on other grounds that the author of the fourth Gospel had seen the other three; and it would therefore be a sufficient reason for omitting these scenes that they had been already adequately narrated. On the other hand, Dr. Holtzmann rightly calls attention to the fact that, while the two Judases are carefully distinguished, and Peter in all but a single passage (i. 42) bears his double name Simon Peter, the Baptist is designated simply by the name of ' John,' as if there was only one John external to the author. Cf. *S. B. L.* iii. pp. 329–332.

there seems no choice but to identify this disciple with the Apostle St. John. In all ages up to the present the same inference has been drawn ; and may be accepted, so far at least as the intention of the author goes, without much hesitation.

But if this is the case, then either the work must be genuine and apostolic, or else it must be a deliberate forgery. In using this term I do not wish to attach to it modern associations, but merely to imply that the presumed author and the real author are different persons. Apart from any question as to the ethics of forgery, our view of the probabilities of the case will be affected by the condition of mind in which we suppose the Gospel to have been written. There is, however, yet a third hypothesis, that the Gospel was not written immediately by St. John, but by a disciple of his, and from traditions left by him. This also is a tenable view ; but it may save confusion if we leave the discussion of it to the end of our enquiry, when we have only one other alternative with which to compare it.

Self-indication of the author.

The way in which the author alludes to himself is remarkable, and it would seem as if it ought to lead to some conclusion. But the arguments flowing from it are too much matter of subjective appreciation, and they are too variously estimated to be alleged as proof on either side.

There are some to whom the author's mode of self-indication seems a mark of genuineness. They think it too peculiar to be the work of a forger. They see in it a natural and spontaneous compromise between dignity and modesty. The author had really played a prominent part in the events he is describing ; and he wishes to insist upon this gently, not obtrusively, but yet firmly.

But there are other critics who take an opposite view. The personality of the author, they think, is too little suppressed. They characterise his expedient as 'egotism,' 'vanity,' 'self-assertion' (Eitelkeit, Selbst-überhebung [1]). And it seems to them to be more like the device of a forger.

The third hypothesis, it must be remembered, is in any case exempt from this objection. But then it is not easy to determine the exact relation of the writer to the Apostle. It is expressly stated in the supplemental chapter that 'he who testified these things' and 'he who wrote them' were the same; and it is difficult to find room for a second person, unless his functions were merely mechanical, and he wrote directly from the Apostle's dictation.

Without professing to decide between the two conflicting opinions, we yet cannot but notice, that the expedient is very far-fetched to be that of a forger. Here at least we have some objective data. In an age that was prolific in spurious works, there is none in which the pretended author has been indicated so circuitously. To go back a little before the Christian era, the apocryphal book of Baruch claims to have been written by the companion of Jeremiah, in the face of gross and palpable anachronisms. The Psalms of Solomon are each of them headed Ψαλμὸς τῷ Σολομῶν, though their date appears to be fixed at 48 B.C. [2] The author of IV. Esdras begins, 'I Salathiel

---

[1] Cf. Keim, i. 157; Scholten, p. 377; compare Meyer, *Comm.* pp. 30, 630.

[2] Cf. Hilgenfeld, *Messias Judaeorum*, pp. xv, xvi.

who am also called Ezra,' and then goes on to date his book by a vision which refers either to the latest days of the Roman Republic, or the first century of the Roman Empire[1]. On the other side of the boundary, and within the canon itself, the highly doubtful II. Peter is ascribed directly to 'Simon Peter, a servant and apostle of Jesus Christ.' The 'Acts of Pilate' are quoted by Justin Martyr as early as 150 A.D. About the same time appeared the Gospel of Thomas, which opens in an unblushing manner, 'I Thomas the Israelite.' In the Protevangelium of James, the author tells us that 'he James, who wrote this history in Jerusalem, retired into the wilderness during the tumult which arose upon the death of Herod.' We might go through a number of other books, all of which bear out their assumption with a high hand. Much allowance it is true may be made for individual idiosyncrasy; but it seems peculiarly incredible that a writer who wished to carry in a number of novel views under the shelter of an apostolic name, should have done so in such a timid and equivocal way. If the Johannean authorship was questioned, what was to be the reply? The more novel, the more dogmatic, the more esoteric his teaching was, the more the writer would be likely to enforce it by asseverations, which involved little danger of detection, and little disgrace if the 'pious fraud' were exposed[2].

---

[1] Cf. Hilgenfeld, *Messias Judae-orum*, pp. liv–lxi.

[2] Some disgrace it would involve, as appears from the history of the 'Acta Pauli et Theclae.' Cf. Tertullian, *De Baptismo*, 17: 'Quod si, qui Pauli perperam scripta legunt, exemplum Theclae ad licentiam mulierum docendi tingendique defendunt, sciant, in Asia presbyterum, qui eam scripturam construxit, quasi titulo Pauli de suo cumulans,

This seems to me to be a real and appreciable argument; and there is another somewhat of the same sort, which arises from the relation that the author maintains towards the Synoptists. It is surely improbable that a forger burdened with a quantity of doubtful matter, for which he was desirous to gain an entrance, should have gone out of his way to discredit himself by contradicting the Synoptic Gospels, on points which for his own peculiar dogmas were indifferent. He would naturally try to fortify himself by his agreement with them upon neutral ground, against those occasions when they would cease to support him. And yet this is not at all what the Evangelist has done. He corrects the Synoptists expressly, all but mentioning them by name. He frequently makes statements at variance with theirs; and that in a quiet unostentatious way, as if he were sure of his own authority, and knew that his bare word would be final. We could well expect a forger to be positive; but it would be upon a different set of points and in a different tone. It would not have been as to the details of his own imaginary history —what was to be gained by fighting for these? He would reserve his strength for the real object of battle, his metaphysics, his propaganda of the faith. In exact proportion to the degree in which the general method of the Gospel is supposed to be *à priori*, will be the difficulty of dealing with phenomena like these.

We have instances of the procedure in question in each of the two sections of narrative in chap. I. The

St. John i. 19-51.

Independent treatment of the Evangelical matter.

Instanced in two cases.

convictum et confessum, id se amore Pauli fecisse, loco decessisse.' (Quoted by Ritschl, *Entstehung der altkatholischen Kirche*, p. 292.)

Sort of John
the life interior
stars!

description that is given of the preaching of the
Baptist is not essentially different from that of the
Synoptists ; but it is narrated only from a single point
of view.   There is no picture of the Baptist's person,
no preliminary account of his baptism, no mention of
those different classes of men who attended it, none of
either the general or special exhortations addressed to
them.   The preaching of repentance retires into the
background.   For our Evangelist it has lost its interest ; his attention is concentrated upon one point
—the relation of the Baptist to the coming Messiah.
The Synoptists had indicated the outline that the
fourth Gospel fills in.   But here the circumstances
are recorded with much greater fulness and exactness.   The testimony of John to our Lord is given
on both its sides ; as brought out by the questions
put to him by the Jewish deputation ; and as given
independently by himself in his own prophetic character.   Thus the rough and summary statement of
the Synoptists is divided and particularized.   But
the Evangelist has gone further than this.   He has
incorporated one sentence into his narrative which is
almost a contradiction of the Synoptists in terms.
Among other questions put to elicit from the Baptist his own view of the nature of his mission, he
is asked, whether he is Elias ; and he is made to
answer with a direct negative, 'I am not.'   Now, if
we turn to Matt. xi. 14, we find there the solemn and
authoritative assertion, 'If ye will receive it, this is
that Elias which was for to come.'   We are not concerned at present to discuss the historical character of
either of these sayings, or the question how far they
may exclude each other.   All we have to do with

now is the relation of the fourth Evangelist to the
Synoptists. And I think we may fairly say, that a
forger, with unbounded liberty of choice, would not
have been likely to run, or to seem to run, so directly
into collision with them.

In the second section of the narrative, the account
of the call of the four chief Apostles, and a fifth
Nathanael, who is commonly supposed to be the same
as Bartholomew, the relation is similar. Many critics,
including even Meyer, are ready to maintain that this
account and that of the call of the same four Apostles
in the Synoptic Gospels are irreconcilable. Certainly
they are different : and if they are reconciled, it must
be by assuming that two distinct occurrences are
alluded to. But, supposing the fourth Gospel to be a
purely ideal composition, it is difficult to see why the
author should have gone out of his way to raise
suspicions against his own veracity. Dogmatic reasons can hardly have weighed with him ; for what
could be more impressive, more truly worthy to mark
the founding of the Messianic kingdom, than that brief
imperative 'Follow Me' of the Synoptists?

But it is not as if these passages stood alone.
We shall have occasion to notice many others, as we
go on. Throughout the Gospel we find the same
freedom and independence of treatment. The Evangelist seems neither to court nor to shun the support
of the Synoptists. Sometimes he agrees with them,
sometimes he does not : but in both cases the relation
is equally unsought. There is no trace of any system
of compensations or economizing, as if he had said to
himself, I will follow the Synoptists here in order that
I may differ from them with more licence there. His

*A charac-
teristic of
the Gospel.*

St. John i.
19-51.

And a mark
of Apostolic
authorship.

procedure is too irregular to have any discoverable motive. We may call it either caprice or independence. But a forger could not afford to be capricious : and of all men the one most likely to 'hold on his rank' without regard to his predecessors or to popular opinion, would be the last surviving Apostle.

Nationality
of the
author and
place in the
develop-
ment of
Christianity.

We will now direct our attention to another side of the subject. Do these two sections of the narrative tell us anything as to the nationality of the author, or as to his place in regard to the development of Christian ideas ?

The evi-
dence of
language
and style.

And here we may insert, first, a few words on the philological question, as to the nationality disclosed by the language and style in which the Gospel is written. This is a point that must be settled by the appeal to authority ; and fortunately it is one on which the later critics seem to be pretty unanimous. Representatives of such different schools as Luthardt, Ewald, Wittichen and Keim, all speak to the same effect. As far back as Grotius the true character of the language seems to have been discovered. 'Sermo Graecus quidem,' he writes, 'sed plane adumbratus ex Syriaco illius saeculi[1].' The Greek is purer than that of the Synoptists, not so pure or so characteristic as that of St. Paul. The Hebraism comes out less in the vocabulary, than in the construction of the sentences, the fondness for parallel clauses, the frequent repetition of the same thought, with some slight modification of sense or form, the simple modes of conjunction, the absence of complicated periods. ' The language of the book,' says Keim, ' is a reconciliation of

[1] Quoted by Lücke, i. 172.

St. John i. 19-51.

the parties (Jew and Greek) in itself, so marvellously does it combine the facility and address of genuine Greek with the childlike simplicity, the figurativeness, yes and the "gaucherie" (Unbeholfenheit) of Hebrew[1].' Ewald expresses himself similarly. It is Hebrew in a Greek dress—easily worn. The Greek has been learnt somewhat late in life, and has been fitted on to a framework of Hebrew[2]. Luthardt describes this by a different metaphor: he says, that 'a soul of Hebrew lives in it.' 'The imagery and modes of thought in the fourth Gospel are rooted in the Old Testament, and have grown up out of the prophecy of the Old Testament[3].' M. Wittichen, one of the latest writers on the fourth Gospel, has gone carefully into this part of the subject; and gives a list of expressions which betray a specifically Hebrew origin. Speaking of the number of conceptions peculiar to Hebrew theology, he adds; 'the certainty and precision with which the author employs these conceptions, makes the supposition that he was a Gentile Christian, acquainted with Jewish literature, impossible: in order to convince ourselves of this it is only necessary to compare the misuse of Hebrew conceptions in the Apostolic Fathers[4].'

St. John i. 19-51.

Philology thus seems to point to a Jew, who somewhat late in life had mixed much with Greeks, and was familiar with their language. How far is this conclusion borne out by the narrative?

vv. 19-28.

It must have been difficult for any one but a born Jew to write the account of the dialogue with the

---

[1] *Jesu von Nazara*, i. 116, 117.
[2] *Johann. Schriften*, pp. 44-47.
[3] Luthardt, pp. 61, 65.

[4] *Ev. Joh.* 5-7. The sentence quoted is endorsed by Holtzmann, *S. B. L.* iii. 336.

deputation from Jerusalem. In order to do so he must have employed an amount of careful research and self-projection which was foreign to the literary habits and spirit of the age. The character of the Jewish Messianic expectations is accurately rendered. Both the questions and their sequence—first, ' Art thou the Christ ? ' then, ' Art thou Elias or that (the) prophet ? '—correspond to the Rabbinical theories in vogue, as we see them depicted as well in Jewish literature as in other parts of the New Testament. By ' the prophet ' is meant the second Moses. Sometimes this second Moses is identified with Elias,—as also with the Messiah himself,—but more frequently both are to reappear. Allusions to the expected return of Elias are scattered throughout the Mishnah [1]. In IV. Esdras the coming of the Messiah is heralded by 'those who have not seen death,' i.e. Henoch, Moses, and Elias [2]. So in the Apocalypse we have the two witnesses, again representing Moses and Elias, whose martyrdom is to be the beginning of the end [3]. In the Synoptic Gospels the idea is embodied in the Transfiguration, and is found repeatedly [4]. We are told expressly in Matt. xvii. 10, that the return of Elias was a current belief. And in the Acts the verse Deut. xviii. 15 is twice cited in proof that a Messianic advent was to be expected [5].

The prophet is an expression which clearly betrays its Jewish origin. The Evangelist never thinks to define *what* prophet. It is a familiar phrase to him ; and he forgets that it may not be equally so to his readers.

---

[1] Cf. Hitzig *on Mal.* iv. 5.   [2] vi. 26, Lat.   [3] Rev. xi. 2–12.
[4] Cf. Matt. xi. 14 ; xvii. 10–13.   [5] Cf. Acts iii. 22 ; vii. 37.

A like conclusion is required by ver. 25, 'Why baptizest thou then, if thou be not that (the) Christ, nor Elias, neither that (the) prophet?' There do not seem to be any parallels forthcoming for the limitation of the right to baptize; which is the less surprising when we consider how scanty are the materials that throw any light upon the subject of pre-Christian baptism at all. But the precision with which the question is stated is evidence of its truth; and it will hardly be maintained that the Pharisees' scruple has been invented to suit the occasion. It does however seem to be clear, in spite of the obscurity in which the origin of baptism is involved, that it must have had a specifically Messianic application. It appears to have been founded upon Messianic prophecies, such as Ezekiel xxxvi. 25–30, 'Then will I sprinkle clean water upon you, and ye shall be clean: from all your filthiness, and from all your idols, will I cleanse you. A new heart also will I give you, and a new spirit will I put within you: and I will take away the stony heart out of your flesh, and I will give you a heart of flesh,' &c.[1] And Zech. xiii. 1, 'In that day there shall be a fountain opened to the house of David, and to the inhabitants of Jerusalem for sin and for uncleanness.' In any case the baptism of John was an act of bold and searching reformation, for which the Pharisees would naturally demand an authority; and the distinction between the baptism with water and that higher baptism which was reserved for the Messiah, is fully

St. John i. 19–51.

---

[1] This passage was applied to the Messianic time. So also Zech. ix. 6. Cf. Lightfoot, *Hor. Heb.* p. 522.

confirmed by the Synoptists. A Gentile, dealing with these ideas, would soon have been at fault.

Another point to be noticed is the composition of the deputation. 'The Jews sent priests and Levites,' 'and they that were sent were of the Pharisees.' Suspicion has indeed attached to the mention of 'priests and Levites,' instead of 'scribes[1]:' but the facts when examined explain and so verify themselves. We can hardly suppose that this was a formal deputation sent officially by the Sanhedrim, because it is confined to a single party. But that party was so large and influential that its emissaries would carry with them an almost representative importance. As coming from the metropolis the deputation would be opposed to those self-constituted bodies, made up of provincial partisans, readers in the synagogue, with here and there a wandering priest or Pharisee from Jerusalem, who appear so frequently among the Galilean scenery of the Synoptists. What the scribes were in the provinces the priests were at Jerusalem; and it was only natural that the enquiry should fall into their hands.

In passing to the next paragraph, we are struck at once by the Baptist's exclamation, 'Behold the Lamb of God, which taketh away the sin of the world.' We must not stay at present to discuss its authenticity, but content ourselves with observing that, whatever its historical character, it belongs entirely to the sphere of Jewish conceptions. It is evidently based on Isaiah liii. In ver. 30 the idea of pre-existence in the phrase, 'For He was before me,' may be bor-

---

[1] Cf. Lücke, i. 381 n.

St. John i.
19-51.

rowed from the theology of the prologue. But we are carried back on to Jewish ground immediately in the verse following, 'But that He should be manifested to Israel, therefore am I come baptizing with water.' We compare with the first clause the words which close the Judaistic document at the beginning of St. Luke[1]; the second refers to the Messianic significance of baptism.

He that *sent me* to baptize is the old Hebrew conception of the prophet. The descent of the Spirit in the form of a dove presents a combination of metaphors, that of alighting as if from flight and that of brooding, which is familiar to Hebrew poetry, and especially in relation to the gift or operation of Spirit[2]. The full symbolism of the 'dove' is not found in the Old Testament, but had been introduced in the interval between the Old and the New, and appears in the Talmud and Targums. We may suppose that there was some visible, and perhaps miraculous appearance, which through the train of associations excited in the minds of the bystanders, embodied itself to them as the 'descent of a dove.'

---

[1] Luke i. 80, ἕως ἡμέρας ἀναδείξεως αὐτοῦ πρὸς τὸν Ἰσραήλ—ἵνα φανερωθῇ τῷ Ἰσραήλ (John). We might imagine that the two phrases were translations of the same Aramaic original.

[2] Cf. Gen. i. 2, Is. xl. 2, xlii. 1, and compare the quotations given by Lücke (i. 426), from Talmudical and Rabbinical writers. 'The Spirit of God hovered over the waters, as a dove hovereth over her young, and toucheth them not.' *Tract. Chagig.* c. 2, etc.; cf. also Keim, i. 539. To suppose a real descent of a real dove, which is asserted by Ellicott and Alford somewhat vehemently, appears to me to reduce the sacred narrative to the level of legend: and though nothing should be rejected on purely *à priori* grounds, still it is fair to make a certain allowance for beliefs which the Evangelists shared with their countrymen. Before the σωματικῷ εἴδει of St. Luke is allowed to decide the question, we must know from what source it is derived. St. Luke is here using the same document as the other Synoptists, but seems to have reproduced it in somewhat loose and in this case amplified paraphrase.

D

The mode of address attributed to the two disciples of John is such as Jewish scholars would use to a Jewish teacher. We cannot insist upon the note of time in the next verse, because there is a suggestion that St. John used not the Jewish but the Roman mode of reckoning[1]. The weight of critical authority seems to be against this suggestion : but if it were true, it would not militate against the Jewish origin of the author. It would only determine the kind of readers for whom the gospel was intended, and show that the author was sufficiently familiar with their customs to adapt his narrative readily to them. In fact, it would go to confirm the conclusion that has been indicated for us hitherto, that the Gospel was written in Asia Minor by a Jew who had been for some time resident there.

We notice that the names of persons and places are handled with ease and precision : Philip, Andrew, and Peter come from Bethsaida : Nathanael knows the ill-repute in which Nazareth is held. He himself is saluted as a 'true Israelite.' Returning a few verses,

---

[1] On carefully reconsidering this question, especially with reference to the arguments of Wieseler (*Beiträge*, p. 252 foll.), I am inclined to think it at least possible that the Evangelist has followed throughout the Gospel, not the Jewish, but the Roman civil day, which began from midnight like ours. Among other evidence to show that the use was widely diffused, Dr. Wieseler quotes especially Strabo ii. 34 foll., a native of Asia Minor and the younger Pliny writing from that province, Ep. vii. 9. The supposition that St. John has adopted this mode of reckoning certainly makes the harmony of the Gospels easier in regard to the events of the Passion—a fact which ought not to tell against it where two such statements as John xix. 14, and Mark xv. 25, both bear the character of authenticity. It also removes a very slight difficulty in regard to John iv. 52. The counter argument of Meyer, drawn from xi. 9, ('Are there not twelve hours in the day?') proves nothing, because such an expression might be used as well by us as by the Jews, speaking of the average length of the working day. Still a 'non liquet,' must, I think, be the verdict.

we find that Andrew greets his brother Peter with the announcement that he has found the Messiah. In like manner Philip tells Nathanael that he has found 'Him of whom Moses in the law, and the prophets, did write, Jesus of Nazareth, the son of Joseph[1]'—a most correct representation of the current phraseology, both in regard to the divisions of the Old Testament, and the application of the Messianic idea. Again Nathanael, convinced that it is really the Messiah to whom he is speaking, answers, 'Rabbi, thou art the Son of God ; thou art the King of Israel ;' and the promise with which his faith is rewarded, takes a strictly Jewish form ; 'Hereafter ye shall see heaven opened, and the angels of God ascending and descending upon the Son of Man,' i.e. in accordance with the apocalyptic vision of Dan. vii. 13, 14.

But there is something more in these passages than the single inference that has been drawn from them. They not only give us information respecting the Evangelist's nationality ; they also help to fix his date. The Messianic idea is throughout regarded from the stand-point of the contemporaries as well as of the countrymen of Jesus Himself. 'The King of Israel,' 'He of whom Moses in the law and the prophets did write,' the speculations as to the place where the Messiah was to be born, as to the forerunner and the rite of baptism, are reproduced with far too much freshness and vigour to be a product of the second century. The phrase 'King of Israel' is especially important, because it breathes those politico-

---

[1] We may notice by the way that the 'Son of Joseph' was a phrase of which orthodox writers early began to be afraid. We saw how it had been altered in Mark vi. 3.

St. John i.
19–51.

theocratic hopes, which since the taking of Jerusalem, Christians at least, if not Jews, must have entirely laid aside. It belongs to the lowest stratification of Christian ideas, before Christianity was separated from Judaism; and there was but one generation of Christians to whom it would have any meaning.

vv. 14, 16, 17.

We have seen in the historical part of the chapter the contemporary of Jesus; by glancing back for a moment to the end of the prologue, we shall see the Evangelist at another stage as the contemporary of St. Paul. 'And of His fulness have we all received, and grace for grace (i.e. grace succeeding grace, constant streams or successions of grace). For the law was given by Moses, but grace and truth came by Jesus Christ.' Compare the first part of this with two of St. Paul's later epistles, Col. i. 19, 'For it pleased the Father that in Him should all fulness ($\pi\hat{\alpha}\nu$ $\tau\grave{o}$ $\pi\lambda\acute{\eta}\rho\omega\mu\alpha$) dwell,' and Eph. i. 6, 7, 'To the praise of the glory of His grace, wherein He hath made us accepted in the Beloved. In whom we have redemption through His blood, the forgiveness of sins, according to the riches of His grace;' and the second part with one of the earlier epistles, Rom, v. 20, 21, 'Moreover the law entered, that the offence might abound. But where sin abounded, grace did much more abound: That as sin has reigned unto death, even so might grace reign through righteousness unto eternal life by Jesus Christ our Lord.' In these three passages we have each of the three ideas, (i.) participation in the Divine Pleroma, (ii.) the outpouring of grace, (iii.) the contrast between the two dispensations, founded especially upon this outpouring.

Relation of the Evangelist to the Law.

On a superficial view we might suppose that the

Evangelist had copied or imitated St. Paul; but there is much more reason to regard his doctrine as an independent and parallel development. The characteristic of the Johannean theology generally is isolation—isolation in the midst of manifold contact and affinity. It seems to touch all systems, but to be affiliated upon none. And so here, the conception, though parallel to, is yet not the same as that of St. Paul. There are two chief points of difference. St. Paul looks upon the gift of grace especially as dependent upon the act of Atonement, of Redemption. St. John rather regards it as radiated from the Person of Christ, as the Centre of light or Revelation. And St. John's (i.e. the Evangelist's) relation to the Law is much less negative, much more neutral. He does not speak of its condemnatory character. It had not been a burden to him, as it had to St. Paul; and consequently he has not known the struggle to free himself from it. He has slipped his chains, and not burst them. He looks upon the Law simply as a part of the great preparation for the coming of Christ. The Johannean conception seems to lie midway between that of St. Paul and that of the Epistle to the Hebrews. If we may say that St. Paul insists chiefly on the *paedagogic* function of the Law, and the Epistle to the Hebrews chiefly on its *typical* function, then we shall say that that which is most prominent with St. John is rather its *prophetic* function[1].

But the interest that the Evangelist still takes in the relation of Christianity to the Mosaic Law, his broad view of the course of human history in which these are interwoven, and his profound insight into

St. John i. 19–51.

Compared with that of St. Paul.

And the Apostolic Fathers.

[1] Compare e.g. Gal. iii. 24, Heb. x. 1, John xii. 41.

the nature and purpose of Christianity as a revelation,
are all marks of the apostolic, as opposed to the sub-
and post-apostolic ages, which we find taken up rather
with homilies on minor morals, ecclesiastical discipline, and Chiliastic or semi-Gnostic dreams[1].

Incidental
use of the
first person.

We return once more to the text of the narrative in
order to enquire into its historical character. I think
it will be a favourable impression that is conveyed at
the outset, by the use of the first person plural in the
prologue. It comes in naturally and unobtrusively in
ver. 14, 'The Word was made flesh, and dwelt among
us (and we beheld His glory . . .), full of grace and truth
. . . and of His fulness have all *we* received,' &c. It
would be possible, though not probable, that the
author was speaking, not for himself and his countrymen and contemporaries, but for the whole human
race. This explanation, however, seems to be excluded by the parallel afforded in the opening to the
First Epistle, 'That which was from the beginning,
which we have heard, which we have seen with our
eyes, which we have looked upon, and our hands have
handled, of the Word of life ; (For the life was mani-

---

[1] This would seem to be a fair
description of the contents of the
writings of the (so called) Apostolic Fathers, the Epistle of Clement to the Corinthians, the Shepherd of Hermas, the Epistles of
Ignatius and Polycarp, and that of
Barnabas. This last takes an
almost Gnostic view of the Law.
'The covenant with Israel was
never concluded. It was broken
off, when Moses broke the tables
of stone. Instead of the moral
law, the ceremonial law was given

them, and that they misunderstood
by interpreting it carnally. They
erred because an evil spirit de-
ceived them' (παρέβησαν ὅτι ἄγγε-
λος πονηρὸς ἐσόφισεν αὐτούς, Barn.
ix.) Cf. Wittichen, pp. 25–29, who
insists strongly upon this argument, as proving that the Fourth
Gospel cannot belong to the period
of the Apostolic Fathers. He takes
his stand upon the very able discussion of Ritschl, *Entstehung der
altkatholischen Kirche*, pp. 274–
311.

fested, and we have seen it, and bear witness, and shew unto you that eternal life, which was with the Father, and was manifested unto us ;) That which we have seen and heard declare we unto you.' It is difficult to think that this is not *bonâ fide*. The boldness of the emphatic iteration in the one passage, and the subtle half-unconscious slipping-in of the first person in the other, are equally beyond the reach of a forger, and do not at all bear the character of fiction.

St. John i. 19–51.

We have already touched upon the curious contradiction of the Synoptists contained in the answer of the Baptist, that he is not Elias. The two passages do not really exclude each other, any more than the Baptist's disclaimer in the one case is inconsistent with his avowal in the other, when he says, 'I am the voice of one crying in the wilderness ... as said the prophet Esaias.' Probably the Jews themselves had no very definite idea of what they meant, when they said that Elias would come again before the advent of the Messiah. The evidence of his own consciousness would prevent the Baptist from claiming pre-existence ; and he was not perhaps prepared to apply the name to himself metaphorically. Both statements, that in St. John and that in the Synoptic Gospels, seem to come in naturally in their places ; and the second rather confirms the first, for the reason already noticed, as proving the independence of the testimony. It is not likely that a later writer would incur the charge of contradicting a recognised authority, unless he were led to do so by his knowledge of the actual fact.

The Baptist as Elias.

There is more difficulty in the other saying attributed to the Baptist, 'Behold the Lamb of God, that

'The Lamb of God.'

taketh away the sin of the world.' It is evidently based upon Isaiah liii. But if we are to suppose that it contains a matured doctrine of the Atonement, it would be highly improbable that the words had been actually spoken as they are recorded. Inspiration, so far as we can judge of it historically, is not found to act so violently, overleaping all conditions of time and circumstance. The conception of a suffering Messiah, if it had ever existed, was dormant in the popular mind; and though the Baptist may have had glimmerings of it, seen through the prophecies of the second Isaiah and some of the Psalms, still these must have been in any case vague and indistinct.

On the other hand, however, we remark, that the form and mould of the salutation is entirely prophetic, and entirely in keeping with the other utterances of the Baptist. This single pregnant ejaculatory sentence is precisely what we should expect from him. And it is not necessary to read into it a greater amount of meaning than it contains. We might conceive the process by which it came to be formed thus. The Baptist has been meditating in the solitude of the desert on those passages of the ancient Scriptures which seemed and were then thought to have reference to the Messiah. Among these, this one in particular, Isaiah liii, would present difficulties to him; it would seem to connect with the 'servant of Jehovah' ideas of debasement and suffering that had no place in the popular conception. He has pondered over it long and deeply, and not yet been able to find a solution. Suddenly he sees in the crowd the face of One, whom he had known perhaps in his youth, and whom he had recently under marvellous circumstances baptized; but never before had he been impressed in such an indescribable manner as now.   There is something in the face and figure; something perhaps in its singular meekness and lowliness of mien; something also, it may be, in lines that seem to foretell of suffering, that fills him with strange presentiment.   A thousand different currents of association, the product of a life of retirement and reflection, strike into one.   The thought rushes in upon him, and before he knows what he is saying, he has given it expression: 'Behold the Lamb of God, which taketh away the sin of the world!'   It is a touch of the true prophetic inspiration.   The prophet himself knows not whence it came nor whither it tends.   He cannot wholly analyse his own words.   In a calmer moment, when despondency has taken the place of hope, and the Messiah, to whom he had testified, has seemed to disappoint his expectations by a career different from that which he had anticipated, they do not prevent him from feeling a certain misgiving, and from yielding so far to his doubts as to send two of his disciples to put the question directly, 'Art thou He that should come, or do we look for another?'

All this is true to human nature.   No man remains constantly at the level of his highest instincts and intuitions.   They do not indeed leave him unchanged; and yet they cannot always retain their illuminating power.   Such may well have been that which inspired the exclamation of the Baptist.   It would be a mistake to attempt to give it too precise a signification.   All we can say of it is, that it is an application of the prophecy in Isaiah, that has been

St. John i. 19-51.

The Johan-
nean version
of the call
of the chief
Apostles.

fulfilled by the event in a way surpassing all that its
author could consciously intend or foresee.

The call of the four Apostles is the second subject
on which we found a discrepancy between the Synoptic Gospels and the Fourth. But here again there is
no sufficient reason to suppose that the discrepancy
extends below the surface. Obviously the events are
different ; but the two accounts are not such as to
exclude, though they may perhaps somewhat modify,
each other. If we are to believe the express statement of the Fourth Gospel, the Synoptists have
missed out a whole section of the life of our Lord
from His baptism by John, until after the Baptist was
cast into prison. This section would cover not much
less than three quarters of a year. During that time
the disciples have accompanied Jesus into Judaea, and
returned through Samaria into Galilee. The little
company has been for a time perhaps broken up ; and
the disciples have gone to their homes. The account
in the Synoptists is that of a second summons, to an
attachment of a closer and more permanent character,
which is before very long defined by the formal selection and separation of the Twelve. When we consider the extreme fragmentariness and incompleteness
of the Synoptic Gospels, based as they are upon a
document which was itself a collection of fragments [1],

---

[1] This is seen, e.g. from the fact
that, according to the chronology
of Wieseler and Ellicott, Mark vi.
31-vii. 23, represents the events of
two days, while vii. 23-ix. represents those of six months, and
x. 1-45 an equal period. No system of chronology can make the
proportion very different. A simple
inspection of the notes of place
and time generally, and of the
phrases which connect the several
sections of the narrative, will show
how fragmentary the record is.
According to the ecclesiastical tradition the Gospel of St. Mark was
made up of notes taken down by
the Evangelist at various times
from the preaching of St. Peter.
Cf. Papias in *Euseb.* iii. 39.

there will be nothing improbable in this. The notes St. John i. 19-51. of time at the beginning of their narrative are wholly vague: 'Now after that John was put in prison, Jesus came into Galilee.' The very phrase, 'came into Galilee,' confirms the account in St. John, according to which our Lord had been previously in Judaea. And the Fourth Evangelist warns his readers against supposing a contradiction, by saying in so many words, 'John was not at this time cast into prison.'

But if the documents admit of this explanation, historical probability supports it. It is certainly an impressive picture that we extract from the Synoptic Gospels,—that single sudden call, and the instantaneous devotion with which it is obeyed. But it is hard to suppress a doubt whether this would have happened in real life. However commanding the personality of Jesus might be, whatever rumours and expectations might be in the air, it still is not probable that four independent men would join themselves to a stranger merely upon his word, and that word a bare imperative, unaccompanied by any explanation. In St. John all this is softened down, and appropriately 'mediated' (vermittelt). In the first place there is the testimony of the Baptist; then the disciples come up by ones and twos; their stay is purely voluntary, and the cohesion of their company loose. The previous acquaintance thus formed naturally leads up to, and prepares us for the narrative of the Synoptists.

Other collateral reasons point the same way. M. Renan has very rightly called attention to the probability that the first disciples of Jesus would be taken from those who had been originally disciples of the Baptist. The later relations of the Christian church to the Baptist, the respect in which his memory was held, and the frequency with which his authority was quoted, M. Renan thinks, show that this was the case [1]. The inference that forces itself upon us, that the Evangelist himself had been at first a disciple of the Baptist, is a kind of 'undesigned coincidence.' And it helps to explain the intimate knowledge that he seems to possess both of persons and places—Peter, Andrew, Philip, Nathanael, Bethany, Cana, Bethsaida, as well as of even minute details in regard to the events as he relates them. The whole narrative, from ver. 35 to 51, is lifelike and circumstantial. The Evangelist knows the order in which the disciples were brought to Jesus; he knows the time of day at which the first two went to Him; and he knows exactly what their movements were after they had found Him. I cannot think that these are merely fictitious details, thrown in to keep up an illusion. They are not conceived the least in the manner of the Apocryphal Gospels. Topography is especially a testing matter. A forger would be sure to betray his ignorance sooner or later. And the Johannean topography as a whole is excellently authenticated [2].

'Bethany beyond Jordan.'

There is indeed a difficulty in regard to 'Bethany beyond Jordan.' Origen, who had made enquiries on the spot, could find no traces of it, and consequently substituted the reading which he found in some MSS., 'Bethabara.' Some of the earlier critics, assuming that Bethany, near Jerusalem, was meant, quoted this as an argument against the Gospel [3]. But

---

[1] Cf. *Vie de Jésus, Appendice*, p. 482.   [2] Cf. Keim, i. 133.
[3] e.g. Bolten and Paulus. Cf. Meyer, p. 104, Lücke, i 394.

the assumption was the more gratuitous, as the Evangelist has defined the position of the cis-Jordanian Bethany with much precision, 'Now Bethany was nigh unto Jerusalem, about fifteen furlongs off,' (xi. 18). An obscure local name might easily be lost in the course of two centuries. And we may either suppose that this was the case; or else we may perhaps accept Dr. Caspari's identification of 'Bethany beyond Jordan,' with Tell-anihje, on the *upper* Jordan[1]. In any case, the distinction between two places having the same name, is a mark of local knowledge, and is unlike fiction.

Another difficulty has arisen from the readiness with which the disciples accept and act upon the testimony of the Baptist[2]. The same objection applies, as we have seen, with still more force to the Synoptists. But clearly this first adhesion is something very different from the deliberate confession that St. Peter made nearly two years later. No doubt the disciples joined our Lord, much as they might have joined a false Messiah, like Judas the Gaulonite

---

[1] Cf. Caspari, pp. 77-81. Dr. Caspari urges in favour of this identification that the Arabs frequently substitute 'Tell' ('hill') for 'Beth' ('house'), and also that the site of Tell-anihje would be within one day's journey from Cana. But it seems difficult to overcome the natural presumption against fixing upon a point so far to the north—*above* the lake of Gennesaret. Besides the statement of the Synoptists (Matt. iii. 1, 13), the presence of a deputation from Jerusalem seems inconsistent with this. One of Dr. Caspari's arguments is that extensive ruins are still found at Tell-anihje—a fact which, we should have thought, told rather the other way. In the Fourth Gospel, as well as the Synoptics, John describes himself as 'a voice crying in the wilderness,' i.e. *not* in a populous region. We do not know *how much* of the course of the Jordan Origen examined. His words are merely γενομένοι ἐν τοῖς τόποις ἐπὶ ἱστορίαν τῶν ἰχνῶν Ἰησοῦ καὶ τῶν μαθητῶν αὐτοῦ καὶ τῶν προφητῶν; Bethabara itself he only knows from hearsay.

[2] Cf. Keim, i. 553, *The Jesus of History*, p. 86.

or Theudas, under the impression that He was about
to raise a revolt against the Romans. And it took
a long education, before they could enter into the
true spirit of Him, whom they thus impulsively followed. Roman, as well as Jewish, literature shows
how rife Messianic expectations at this time were[1].
And we learn from Josephus how easily Jews and
Galileans rallied round the cry. In the neighbourhood of the Baptist it would be especially potent,
and the material on which it was to act especially
susceptible.

Putting the accounts of the several adhesions together, the natural fortuitous connection between them,
the lifelike character of the narrative in detail, the
sort of background that it seems to imply—a group
of disciples in somewhat loose attendance upon the
Baptist, still keeping up their local and family connections, and not so committed to their old teacher
as to refuse to follow another;—all this seems to give
an appearance of veracity that is more intelligible, if
we suppose it to be a reflection of facts, than as an
effort of conscious imagination. If the author of the
Gospel was really the Apostle, and if he had really
been a disciple of John in his youth, then we can well
understand how the events of those few days would
cling tenaciously to his memory, because to him they
were the turning-point of his life; but that the writer
of a philosophic fiction should attain to the same
verisimilitude, is unlikely in itself, and out of all
analogy with the phenomena of the other fictitious
literature of that day.

But whether we think that the Gospel was written

[1] Cf. quotations in Keim, i. 249, compare i. 592.

by the Apostle and son of Zebedee or not, thus much, I think, we may set down, if only on the strength of this first chapter—that it was written by a Palestinian Jew, and by one who had personal knowledge of all the Messianic hopes and traditions that were current among the actual contemporaries of our Lord.

St. John i. 19–51.

CHAPTER III.

THE FIRST MIRACLE AND THE FIRST PASSOVER.

St. John ii. 1–11.

The attitude of the present enquiry towards miracles.

THE question as to the reality of miracles being a balance between the *à priori* improbability on the one hand, and the historical evidence on the other, the attitude proper to an enquiry like the present, where the exact value of the historical evidence is the point at issue, will be to assume provisionally that miracles are credible, and on that supposition to endeavour to ascertain what amount of weight results to the evidence for them, from the general character of the narrative in the course of which they occur.

The documentary evidence for miracles in the Synoptists and in St. John.

The Johannean miracles taken by themselves, and prior to the decision of the question as to their narrator, are less well attested than those related by the Synoptists. What makes the case for the latter so strong is, that they carry with them the evidence not of a single document but of several; and that all these different documents bear in the same direction. It is not as if one related miracles, and another did not, or as if one related a different kind from the rest. But all relate miracles, and miracles of the same sort. And this coincidence in regard to miracles

is checked and confirmed by a number of other
coincidences, by which the general accuracy of the
record is placed upon a high level. The fourth Gospel,
on the other hand, is an original composition, not a
compilation—and it was all made at one cast. It is
the work of a single hand, and carries with it therefore
only single authority. But it is entitled to the confirmation of the Synoptic Gospels on the general
question, and in particular instances where it agrees
with them.

The miracle recorded in John ii. 1–11 is not one
of these; and yet we may notice several points that
are in general keeping with the Synoptics. One is
the bright and festal character of the whole scene.
M. Renan and Dr. Keim agree in giving to this first
period of our Lord's public ministry the epithet
'idyllic.' It has not yet caught the gloom of those
darkening clouds of opposition and desertion that are
soon to come over it. It is the Good Shepherd
leading His flock to living waters and seeing that they
want nothing. It is the Son of Man piping to the
generation of His contemporaries, eating and drinking
with them, sharing their homely joys, exhorting them
to take no thought for the morrow, pointing to the
lilies of the field and the fowls of the air in illustration
of His lesson. The miracle at the marriage-feast in
Cana of Galilee falls in entirely with this.

Then there is something in that remarkable dialogue between our Lord and His mother, which
reminds us of the later scene with the Syro-Phoenician woman. The address 'Woman, what have I
to do with thee?' is indeed less harsh than it sounds
in our English version; as we see by comparing it

E

with 'Woman, behold thy son.' But still it is intended as something of a repulse. It is not to be supposed that Mary expected a miracle : though from seeing her Son return accompanied by disciples she may have felt that a turning-point in His life was come. She had doubtless been accustomed to depend upon Him for advice in the common accidents of domestic life ; and now, in the present emergency, caused perhaps in part by the addition which He had brought to the company, to Him she naturally turns. It appears to be not unusual for guests to make contributions of wine on such occasions, and her appeal may have had reference to this custom [1]. But the tide of miraculous power had not yet begun to flow, though it was not long to be delayed.

Difficulties.]   The difficulties of the account, apart from its miraculous nature, are three :—1. Why did our Lord repel His mother's suggestion ? 2. Why, having repelled it with the answer, 'My time is not yet come,' did He within a few moments perform a miracle by which it was more than answered ? 3. Why did the Virgin, in spite of her repulse, still give such directions to the servants as showed that she yet did not give up her point ?

Some little light, I think, will be thrown upon this by looking at it in connection with the history of the Syro-Phoenician woman. There too a petition is first refused, and then granted ; and there too the petitioner seems to divine that it will be [2].

Still there remains to be accounted for the sudden apparent change in our Lord's intention. The difficulty lies in its *suddenness ;* and that, if miracles are

---

[1] Cf. Ellicott, *Huls. Lect.*, p. 118, n.   [2] Cf. Matt. **xv.** 21-28.

true, must be beyond our ken. It is bound up with the whole question of the consciousness and nature of miraculous power, and is hidden in a depth to which psychology cannot penetrate.

We may remark, however, upon the difficulties of the narrative generally, that they lie in a certain paradoxical character which is not inconsistent with its proceeding from an eye-witness. On the contrary, they are not at all of a kind that looks like invention. At the first blush the chief features of the narrative seem strikingly human—a human impatience, a human infirmity of purpose. The last place where we should look for the origin of these would be in the doctrine of the Logos.

Again, 'the six waterpots of stone, after the manner of the purifying of the Jews, containing two or three firkins (*metretae*) apiece,' is all very circumstantial—and it is an anachronism to look for the minute invention of a Defoe at this period. We may notice too, the natural proverbial turn given to the speech of the master of the ceremonies; and generally the intimate acquaintance that is displayed with Jewish domestic customs.

The miracle may have, and probably has a typical or symbolical meaning[1]; but if so, this must not be laid to the account of the Evangelist, and in no way invalidates his testimony. The description is throughout that of an actual occurrence. The details on

St. John ii. 1-11.

Not inconsistent with authentic testimony.

Significance of the miracle.

---

[1] It seems best to refer this, with Ewald, to the 'transmutative power of the Messianic Spirit,' contact with or faith in Christ. Water represents in this case that *upon* which, not that by *means* of which, the change is operated; so that there can hardly be any allusion —unless it is a remote one, a kind of association of ideas—to the contrast between the 'baptism with water,' and 'with the Spirit.'

which stress is laid are not those which lend themselves to allegory.   And the Evangelist has indeed stated plainly in ver. 11, the only object of the miracle that he recognised.   'This beginning of miracles did Jesus in Cana of Galilee, and manifested forth His glory; and His disciples believed on Him.'

This last touch is significant.   '*His disciples* believed on Him.'   In each of the two narratives which follow, the comments of the disciples on what they witness are given.   'And *His disciples* remembered that it was written, The zeal of thy house hath eaten me up.'   'When therefore He was risen from the dead, *His disciples* remembered,' &c.   Why is this prominence given to the reflections of the *disciples?*   It is exceedingly natural if the author of the Gospel himself was one of them.   But it would be strange in a forger of the second century, wishing to exhibit the glory of the Logos.   That the disciples believed would be little better than a truism.   If they had not they would not have been disciples.   It would surely have been more to the point to tell us the effect upon the *guests*, and a forger would hardly have failed to do so.   But all is explained when we suppose that a disciple is speaking, and look at the whole chapter as written from a *disciple's point of view*.

These considerations strongly tend to make us believe that the miracle in connection with which they occur is real; though they leave some of the difficulties of that miracle unexhausted, as perhaps they are inexhaustible.

But now follows a section of which we can only say, in the words of M. Renan, 'that it constitutes a

decisive triumph for our Gospel;'—and that not only
for the reason assigned by M. Renan, but also for
others. The section begins, 'After this He went down
to Capernaum, He, and His mother, and His brethren,
and His disciples; and they continued there not
many days.' What could be more simple and un-
pretending history? If it is all an artificial composition, with a dogmatic object, why should the author
carry his readers thus to Capernaum—for nothing.
The apparent aimlessness of this statement seems to
show that it came directly from a fresh and vivid
recollection, and not from any floating tradition. It
is not the kind of fact that a tradition handed from
mouth to mouth would preserve. But from another
point of view this mention of Capernaum is important.
The fourth Gospel has not yet crossed the track of
the Synoptists, since it parted from them at the
account of St. John's baptism. Its scene has been
gradually shifting northwards from the banks of the
Jordan, through Cana to Capernaum. We have noticed that localities seem to be treated with great
ease and precision. Here then is the point to which
we are brought when the narrative again turns southwards. Capernaum is once or twice mentioned sub-
sequently, but nowhere in such a way as either to
exclude or directly to imply the fact that it was in
any peculiar sense the head-quarters of the northern
mission. Yet from the Synoptists we should certainly infer that this was the case. Their narrative
leads us at once to Capernaum, and in all the earlier
chapters seems to centre there. There is a certain
house, probably Peter's, to which our Lord and His
disciples appear to have had free access—so that it

St. John ii.
12–25.

Capernaum.

St. John ii.
12–25.

is spoken of as 'the house' simply. This all tallies with the statement in St. John that Capernaum was the last point reached before the first descent into Judaea, and that our Lord stayed there several days. But the fourth Evangelist has not got this from the Synoptists; for he mentions it in quite a different context, and at the place where it occurs in the Synoptic Gospels he does not mention it at all.

The visits
to Jeru-
salem in
the fourth
Gospel.

And now the Passover was at hand, 'and Jesus,' we are told, 'went up to Jerusalem.' This is the first of those visits to Jerusalem which have been so much debated. It would seem as if there was now a turn in the tide, but for some time they formed one of the chief arguments of those who reject the Gospel. 'The scene of the Synoptists,' it was urged, 'is laid entirely in Galilee; that of the fourth Gospel largely in Judaea and Jerusalem. Therefore the two are in opposition, and the Synoptic tradition must be followed as the most reliable.' It would perhaps be enough to answer by pointing to two things :—first, the fragmentariness

Not ex-
cluded by
the Synop-
tists.

of the Synoptists. Even the ground document is made up of a number of narratives pieced roughly together. It is clearly very far from continuous and very far from exhaustive ; and it is both possible and likely that it was formed out of some specially Galilean

Generally
probable.

tradition[1]. Combining this with the *à priori* probability that a Jew would attend the Jewish feasts, and that the Messiah would proclaim Himself at Jerusalem, and I think the objection drawn from the change of scene would be not inadequately answered.

Implied in
the Synop-
tic docu-
ments.

But it has been remarked that when the question

[1] Cf. Holtzmann, *Synopt. Evang.*, p. 102.

comes to be examined into more closely, it is found, that while the Synoptists nowhere directly mention these visits to Jerusalem, their narrative frequently seems to presuppose them[1]. Taking first the ground document of the Synoptic Gospels, the original Gospel of St. Mark, we see from this that one at least of the Apostles, Judas the traitor, was a native of Kerioth in Judaea (Mark iii. 19). Joseph of Arimathaea or Ramathaim was a disciple, though not a professed one (Mark xv. 43, 46). The account of the borrowing of the ass at Bethphage shows that our Lord must have been already known there (Mark xi. 2, 3). Similarly, the demand for the room at Jerusalem in which to eat the Passover (Mark xiv. 14). The supper given at Bethany in the house of Simon the leper, is clearly given not by strangers but by friends. And there is probability in the supposition that this epithet, 'the leper,' implies that Simon had been previously healed of leprosy. Again, quite early in the narrative, in the midst of the Galilean ministry, we read that our Lord was followed by a great multitude 'from Galilee, and from Judaea, and from Jerusalem' (Mark iii. 7, 8). He is spied upon and harassed from the first by 'scribes which came down from Jerusalem' (Mark iii. 22). He is more than once engaged in controversy with them, and denounces them face to face (cf. vii. 1).

So far we have drawn only from a single document. When we pass to the second main document, the 'collection of discourses,' there indeed the notes of place as well as of time are wanting, and the

St. John ii. 12-25.

---

[1] For what follows, compare especially Weizsäcker, pp. 308–311, and Wittichen, pp. 40–43.

St. John ii.
12-25.

various portions of it have been worked in by our present Evangelists for the most part upon other than historical principles. But there is one passage at least (Luke xvi. 34, Matt. xiii. 37), 'O Jerusalem, Jerusalem . . . how often would I have gathered thy children together,' &c., which clearly implies previous warnings and invitations. And there are others which point at least to familiarity with the capital, if we have not sufficient evidence to show that they were actually spoken there. Such are the allusion to the 'altar' in the Sermon on the Mount, and the description of the Pharisaic practices in the same discourse. On the other hand, it is not improbable that the great denunciation of the Pharisees in Matt. xxiii, though rightly localised, may be wrongly dated. There are no traces of it in this connection in the other Gospels ; and it seems to break the thread of the eschatological discourses which formed the fitting and appropriate subject of the preaching of these last days. The period of open controversy with the Pharisees appears to have been earlier[1].

The minor documents, like the collection of discourses, furnish few indications of place : but it is clear that St. Luke has had one or more that deal especially with events happening in Judaea. Thus we notice that even more frequently than St. Mark he calls attention to the presence of Scribes and Pharisees from Jerusalem. In Luke v. 17, in a passage which belongs quite to the beginning of the Synoptic narrative, we are told that at the healing of the para-

---

[1] So Weizsäcker, p. 311 ; compare Wittichen, p. 42. The data are too uncertain to lay any stress upon ; though it is sufficiently clear that many of the Matthean discourses did not originally belong to the places assigned to them.

St. John ii.
12–25.

lytic 'there were Pharisees and doctors of the law sitting by, which were come out of every town of Galilee and Judaea and Jerusalem.' It is possible however that this is merely an expansion of Mark ii. 6, 'There were certain of the scribes sitting by,' combined perhaps with the original of Matt. iv. 25. Luke iv. 44 ('He preached in the synagogues of Galilee [Judaea]') contains, if we are to accept the reading Ἰουδαίας, which has certainly strong MS. attestation, a direct notice of a Judaean ministry. But the reading Ἰουδαίας, supposing it to be correct, is very remarkable; and I cannot say that I am as yet prepared with a definite opinion about it.

A clearer point is the visit of our Lord to Martha and Mary, which has no definite localisation, but if it is authentic, and there is no reason whatever to suppose that it is not, must belong to an earlier journey to Jerusalem. Again, it is probable that some of the parables peculiar to St. Luke, such as the Good Samaritan, and the Pharisee and the Publican, were spoken originally in the neighbourhood of the scenes to which they refer—the road to Jericho and the Temple. The later events subsequent to the Resurrection are placed by St. Luke entirely in Judaea.

When we turn to the Acts of the Apostles we find that the head-quarters of the disciples and the centre of the Apostolic mission is at once established in Jerusalem, which would be highly improbable if they had arrived there for the first time only some few days before the Crucifixion.

And by the narrative of the Acts.

These are a number of points, some of them indeed based upon conjecture, but others quite clear and indisputable,—which taken together with the known

St. John ii.
12-25.

incompleteness of the Synoptic narrative, with the historical probability of earlier visits to Jerusalem, and with the absence, so far as we can see, of any adequate motive which could lead the Evangelist to challenge upon this head the received authorities, justify us in saying that the Synoptic version does not exclude the Johannean, but is rather naturally supplemented and explained by it. It must be remembered that it is not as if the fourth Evangelist had propounded an entirely new scheme of the history, or as if his disposition of the narrative made that of the Synoptists impossible. He mentions four visits to Jerusalem in all, of which one occurs before the Synoptic account has well begun, and another, the last, is recorded also by them. So that there are only two, or if we are to treat the raising of Lazarus as a separate visit, three, for which places have to be found in the course of their narrative. And in spite of these, the fourth Evangelist makes no attempt to shift the general centre of gravity. He still devotes a considerable space to the Galilean ministry; he still lays the scene of four out of seven, or five out of eight miracles there; and our Lord is with him still the 'prophet of Galilee.' In this respect as in others his Gospel is supplementary, and in this respect as in others his motive and procedure are strictly historical.

Admitted
by most
critics.

So then, with M. Renan and with most impartial critics, we set it down to the advantage of the fourth Evangelist, and not the reverse, that he mentions this early visit to Jerusalem.

The
cleansing
of the
people.

But it is not here that the difference from the Synoptists ceases. The first event recorded after the

arrival of our Lord and His disciples in Jerusalem, is   St. John ii.
12–25.
one that appears in the Synoptic Gospels, but with
them in a different context, on the occasion of the
last journey to Jerusalem, and immediately after the
triumphal entry [1]. It is not likely that two events so
exactly similar in every particular should have happened. We must therefore suppose that one of them
is misplaced. And remembering, first, that the Synoptic accounts, though apparently three are virtually
only one, all of them being evidently based upon the
same document; remembering, further, that the chronology of that document is far from perfect; and
remembering, lastly, that other events have been referred to this last visit which probably do not belong
to it,—we shall, I think, naturally be led to infer that
the advantage is once more on the side of St. John.
The objection urged against this is, that such a pronounced Messianic act is not likely to have fallen so
early. But the act is more prophetic than Messianic.
It might at least well be so regarded: and it has precisely that *reformatory* character which marked the
outset of our Lord's preaching and ministry. It
stands better in connection with the Sermon on the
Mount, than with the eschatological discourses of the
Passion week.

But on *à priori* grounds, though we may reach a
higher degree of probability, we shall find nothing
decisive one way or the other. Our decision will be
determined by the conception we are led to form of
the comparative value of the Johannean and Synoptic
testimony generally. If St. John really wrote the

---

[1] Cf. Matt. xxi. 12, 13; Mark xi. 15–17; Luke xix. 45, 46.

Gospel, then, as proceeding from an eye-witness, it must have the superiority.

Now, I cannot but think that the narrative itself gives us information on this very point. The passage is significant not only as bearing upon the relation of St. John to the Synoptists, but also upon the relation of the Synoptists to one another. The Synoptists, all of them, describe the cleansing of the Temple in somewhat general terms. St. Luke most. 'And He went into the Temple, and began to cast out them that sold' ['therein, and them that bought,' Tischendorf and Tregelles omit]. St. Mark has, in common with St. Luke, the phrase ἤρξατο ἐκβάλλειν, where St. Matthew has the simple ἐξέβαλεν. Both St. Mark and St. Matthew add in precisely the same words, 'And overthrew the tables of the money-changers, and the seats of them that sold doves.' But St. Mark alone has yet another detail. 'And would not suffer that any man should carry any vessel through the Temple.' In continental churches one may often see market-baskets placed just outside the doors, while the peasants to whom they belong go in to say an Ave. Something of this sort may be meant here, except that the baskets, instead of being left outside the Temple, were brought into it, and carried through the courts.

From the peculiar relations of these three accounts there is something to be learnt. First, that all three must have had the same source, and that source must have been in writing[1]—otherwise the verbal

[1] The argument that seems to prove almost conclusively that the original of the Synoptic Gospels must have been in writing, is less the mode in which the several incidents are narrated, than the fact

coincidences could hardly have been so exact. The accounts in St. Matthew and in St. Mark are almost word for word identical. But of these it is clear that St. Mark most nearly represents the original. For it is much easier to suppose that the additional detail in St. Mark fell out through the loose way in which documents were reproduced [1], than that it was put in by pure invention. And further, the ἤρξατο ἐκβάλλειν is confirmed by St. Luke. St. Luke's account is the farthest removed from the original of the three; for he omits all mention of the money-changers and the sellers of doves.

And now we return to St. John. Let us suppose for a moment that he enters the Temple himself as an eye-witness of what happens. His narrative begins, 'And Jesus found in the Temple those that sold oxen and sheep and doves, and the changers of money sitting.' The Synoptists had said nothing about 'oxen and sheep,'—yet oxen and sheep and doves would be exactly the objects of sale, because they were used in sacrifice. This goes to show that the author was a Jew, and knew Jewish customs. But taken with the context, I think it shows more. The epithet καθημένους is reserved specially for the money-

---

that so many of the *same* incidents are selected for narration. How is it that out of twenty-eight miracles related by the Synoptists, nineteen are common to all three of them, while three only are peculiar to St. Matthew, two to St. Mark, and four to St. Luke? It is not that these were the *only* miracles performed, for we gather that there were many others (cf. Matt. iv. 24, viii. 16, ix. 35, xi. 20, &c.), or that they were specially distinguished from the rest—but they happened to be those contained in the document that the three Evangelists took as their groundwork. The same holds good for the incidents of the narrative generally. But I hope to discuss this subject more fully at some future time.

[1] We have specimens of this in the way in which the Old Testament is quoted in the New, and by the Apostolic Fathers.

changers. The money-changers would be sitting, the sellers of the doves and animals for sacrifice, standing. This is exactly as they would appear to a person entering the Temple. 'And when He had made a scourge of small cords—perhaps some that had been used to tie up the animals—He drove them all out of the Temple, and the sheep and the oxen; and poured out the changers' money, and overthrew the tables; and said unto them that sold doves, 'Take these things hence; make not my Father's house an house of merchandise.' Observe how exactly the different *stages* of the action are reproduced, both in the order in which they occur, and the way in which the action is characterised. First, there is the making of the scourge, which is not mentioned by the Synoptists; and then, the expulsion in each of its parts. First, the men are driven out—they see what is coming, and hasten to escape. Then the dumb animals, who follow next as capable of being driven. Not till then is there time to notice the tables of the money-changers, which are overthrown and the change poured out upon the ground—a graphic touch. And at the same moment the owners of the cages of doves, which could be neither driven out nor overthrown, are recalled and bidden to take away their property with them. How lifelike and vivid is all this! What perfect propriety is there in all the different parts of the action. How the rough, dull, general statement of the Synoptists is particularised and defined, broken up into its details, and each of them depicted with minute distinctness and accuracy. On one point only have the Synoptists perhaps an advantage; that is, in the sentence with which the expulsion is accompanied. It is possible that both may really have been spoken. That in St. John seems very natural, as addressed especially to the sellers of doves. But the quotation from the Old Testament in the Synoptists is so exactly what we should expect, that it must not in any case be omitted. We shall see presently that if there is a qualification to the accuracy of the Evangelist's recollections, it will be to a point of words, such as this, that it will apply. But we cannot doubt his recollection of the impression made by the act upon himself (ver. 17).

It was only natural that the bystanders seeing such an act should ask the Author of it, by what authority it was done, and demand a sign in token of that authority. The demand for a sign is in accordance with what we read both in the Synoptic Gospels and in St. Paul[1], and may be certainly set down as a genuine trait of Jewish character. From the reply Mr. Blunt has drawn one of his 'undesigned coincidences,' which is perhaps of less doubtful value than some of the others in connection with which it occurs[2]. St. Matthew and St. Mark relate as part of the evidence that was brought against our Lord before the High Priest, this very saying. They put it into the mouth of ' false witnesses.' We are not told on what occasion the words were spoken, or that they were really spoken at all. The clue to their origin is not found until we look back to this entirely different part of the Gospel of St. John. It is all but impossible that in such a different context and form, the author of the fourth Gospel should have derived his

St. John ii. 12–25.

The sign of the Temple destroyed.

---

[1] Cf. Matt. xii. 38, xvi. 1; 1 Cor. i. 22. (' The Jews require a sign.')
[2] *Scriptural Coincidences*, pp. 269, 270.

statement from the Synoptists. Yet the Synoptists confirm its historical truth. But if this passage itself is historical, it creates a presumption in favour of the rest of the Gospel, which is evenly composed, and in which it presents nothing singular.

We are not concerned for our present purpose with the question whether the interpretation put upon the words by the Evangelist, as a prophecy of the Resurrection, is the right one. Already in the Apostolic age another interpretation seems to have been current, as we find in St. Mark[1] the epithets added τὸν ναὸν τοῦτον τὸν χειροποίητον—ἄλλον ἀχειροποίητον, making the saying practically equivalent to John iv. 21, 23.

But it is more pertinent to notice that the Evangelist gives the history of his interpretation. 'When therefore He was risen from the dead, His disciples remembered that He had said this unto them; and they believed the Scripture, and the word which Jesus had said.' Does not this look extremely like a page from his own autobiography? Putting altogether aside the common *ad captandum* argument about the immorality of forgery, is it likely that any other than an Apostle should have written these words? Dr. Keim speaks of the 'tact' which the Evangelist has exercised in his composition, but I doubt whether he has formed any exact estimate of the amount and kind of tact required, and of its relation to the rest of contemporary literary phenomena.

There is one more point in the chapter which must not escape our observation—and that is, the chronology of ver. 20. 'Forty and six years was this

---

[1] Cf. Mark xiv. 58.

Temple in building.' The building of the Temple, we are told by Josephus[1], was begun in the eighteenth year of Herod the Great, i. e. Nisan 1, 734—Nisan 1, 735 A. U. C. Reckoning forty-six years from this point, we are brought to the year 781 or 782 A. U. C. = 28 or 29 A. D. Comparing this with the data given in Luke iii. 1, the much-debated question arises, whether we are to reckon the fifteenth year of Tiberius Caesar from his joint reign along with Augustus, which began in 765 A. U. C. = 12 A. D.; or from his sole reign after the death of Augustus, which took place on Aug. 19, 767 = 14 A. D. This would give us 27 A. D. or 29 A. D. for the first public appearance of the Baptist, and at the earliest 28 A. D. or 30 A. D. for the passover mentioned in this second Chapter of St. John. We can define perhaps somewhat more nearly the date at which the work of rebuilding the Temple commenced, by means of the festival mentioned by Josephus in Ant. xiv. 16, 4, as the month Kisleu, 734; forty-six years from that gives Kisleu (December), 780. So that this passover would be that of the year 781 or 28 A. D.; which agrees exactly with the earlier of the two dates extracted from St. Luke. Whether that earlier date can be accepted, all turns upon the admissibility of the assumption that St. Luke has reckoned from the joint, and not from the sole, sovereignty of Tiberius. Without saying that this is indisputably established, it seems to me to have been brought quite within the range of possibilities by the recent arguments of Wieseler[2]. It is significant that this admirably

---

[1] *Ant.* xv. 11. 1.
[2] Cf. *Beiträge*, pp. 177 foll. Wieseler's arguments are :—(i.) A general one; the breach between republican and imperial institutions was at first glossed over as much as possible; accordingly the emperors reckoned rather the num-

St. John ii.
12–25.

conscientious and accurate chronologist has seen cause
to abandon the view maintained in his earlier work,
the Chronological Synopsis, and now accepts unreservedly that which is based upon the earliest date of
Tiberius' accession.   And to the evidence and reasons
adduced by him, I think we must allow a considerable
degree of cogency.   We should thus have an exact
coincidence between the two Evangelists.   And the
mutual support that they would afford to each other
would be of the very strongest.   In any case, the
discrepancy would not be great; and, allowing for
rough calculations on both sides, would almost dis-
appear.   Dr. Keim objects to the Johannean statement that we have no evidence that the Roman procurators of Judaea took part in the building of the
Temple, which would thus have been for some time
intermitted [1].   But we have positive evidence that the
building of the Temple was not completed until the
reign of Herod Agrippa II. in 64 A. D.   And the Greek
does not at all compel us to suppose that the building
had been continuous.   We might almost paraphrase
it, 'Forty-six years is it since the building of this
Temple began, [and is not yet finished.]'   It is notice-

Chrono-
logical
importance
of this
date.

ber of times that they had held
consular and tribunician power
than the years of their reign in the
strict sense. (ii.) This general proposition is proved from coins, &c.
(iii.) But Dr. Wieseler also produces
direct evidence from coins in proof
of the particular proposition that
the reign of Tiberius was thus
reckoned; one, a coin of the
Syrian Antioch, bears the head of
Tiberius with the inscription
Καισαρ . Σεβαστος . Σεβαστου, and
the date 12 A.D.; two others, respectively in gold and silver, have
the head of Tiberius uncrowned,
and the inscription TI. CAESAR AUG.
TR. POT. XV. on one side, and the
head of Augustus crowned with
laurel and inscribed CAESAR AU-
GUSTUS DIVI F. PATER PATRIAE on the
other. If these coins are accurately
described (and Dr. Wieseler is
obliged to take the description at
second hand) there would seem to
be little doubt that the Evangelist
may have reckoned from the joint
rule of Tiberius. Cf. also *Herzog*,
xxi. 546, 7.

[1] *Jesu von Nazara*, i. 615, n. 2.

able that the tense used is the aor. ᾠκοδομήθη, and not the pres. οἰκοδομεῖται.

Dr. Keim seems to have a very imperfect idea of the logical force of a coincidence so evidently unde-signed. Compared with it the data on which his own chronological system is constructed are the most broken reeds. Not only does the accuracy of this particular date go far to determine the historical cha-racter of the whole Gospel, but even if it had been less accurate than it is, it would have left a strong presumption that the Gospel was really written by St. John. By what conceivable process could a Greek in the second century have come to hit upon this roundabout expedient for giving a fictitious date to the subject of his invention? When we think of the lengthened calculations, the consultation of documents, the elaborate adjustment of the date propounded to the other events of the Gospel history, that would have been necessary before a result could be arrived at that should at all approximately suit the situation, it becomes quite incredible that the result thus ob-tained should have been thrown in so easily and incidentally, so entirely as a side-touch on which there is no emphasis whatever. Besides the utter improb-ability that a forger at that date would have taken the trouble to work out such a problem, it is equally improbable that he should make no more parade of his labours when he had done. The only *possible* hypothesis, as it appears to me, to account for the way in which this verse came to be written, is to sup-pose that it is the spontaneous reproduction of words that were actually spoken by a person who actually heard them.

St. John ii.
12–25.

Reflection
of the
Evangelist.

The chapter ends with a comment of the Evangelist, which, like the rest, carries us back to the time when he was himself a disciple of Jesus, looking up with reverence to his Master, and pondering silently over the wisdom by which His conduct seemed to be guided. Here, too, we have a reminiscence of that early restraint and delayed and guarded assumption of the full Messianic prerogative of which we also find traces in the Synoptic Gospels.

CHAPTER IV.

THE DISCOURSE WITH NICODEMUS.

WE have hitherto had several fragmentary discourses or dialogues, but we now meet with
the first of those long connected didactic addresses
which are so peculiarly characteristic of the fourth
Gospel. It becomes time, therefore, that we should
make some remarks on the question of the Johannean
discourses in general.

Can we regard these discourses as strictly authentic? Are they the veritable records delivered by an
Apostle of the actual sayings of our Lord Himself?
Here there are two questions which ought to be kept
separate. It is possible that the discourses in the
fourth Gospel may not represent the actual words
spoken by our Lord, and yet that they may have
been committed to writing by an Apostle. This
second possibility we shall consider presently. But
it is necessary first to determine the relation in which
the discourses stand to their original. It is well
known that the style and subjects of the Johannean
discourses have from the first supplied one of the
gravest arguments against the Gospel. It is urged
against them doubly; that they are unlike the

St. John iii.

The dis-
courses in
the fourth
Gospel.

St. John iii.

discourses contained in the Synoptic Gospels [1], which on the other hand correspond exactly to the description given of our Lord's discourses by tradition ; and that, while they differ from the discourses in the Synoptists, they present a close and suspicious similarity, both in style and matter, to the Epistle which goes under the name of St. John and was certainly written by the author of the Gospel.

Compared with those in the Synoptists.

We will begin by granting that both the difference and the likeness exist, though both may be exaggerated on the question of degree. The only way to determine the amount of difference satisfactorily, will be to deal with the separate discourses in detail, as we come to them. But in the meantime we may say, that the difference is considerable. Justin Martyr describes the 'discourses of the Lord' as 'short and concise, not like those of a sophist [2].' This is very much as we find them in the Synoptic Gospels. They are made up of a number of brief aphoristic sayings, each compact and clear cut in itself, like a well-set and polished diamond. When they assume longer proportions, it is either by accumulating details of description or illustration, as in the several discourses contained in the Sermon on the Mount, the denunciation of the Pharisees, and the discourses on the 'last things' which occur in the week before the Passion. A still more common mode of amplification is that by casting the subject into the form of a short but pointed narrative, or parable. The subject-matter in these varied kinds of discourse is also varied. It is

---

[1] 'Si Jésus parlait comme le comme le veut Jean.' Rénan, *Vie veut Matthieu, il n'a pu parler de Jésus*, p. lxix. (13th edition.)

[2] Cf. Keim, i. 128, n. 4.

St. John iii.

frequently ethical, sometimes didactic or theological; sometimes it concentrates itself upon the Person of the Speaker: but at any rate it cannot be said that the last class of discourse preponderates.

In the fourth Gospel many of these characteristics are changed. Strictly speaking, it contains no parable. The expanded metaphors of the tenth and fifteenth Chapters must rather fall under the more general name of 'allegory.' The action is stationary and not moving or dramatised; and the thing figured is not cut loose from the figure as in the parable. Then the discourses are as a rule longer, and not progressive or self-evolving as with the Synoptists, but frequently returning to the same point, appearing to revolve round a fixed centre; and that centre is, not indeed exclusively, but very largely, the Speaker Himself, His works, His Person, faith in Him, that Divine Paraclete, who was to take His place when He was gone.

Assuming, what we may assume, that the Synoptic discourses accurately represent the original, is it credible, or rather is it probable, that the Johannean discourses are equally authentic? Can two such different types at one and the same time be true? To a certain extent I think we shall say they can. Professor Westcott[1], who maintains the complete authenticity of the Johannean discourses, argues thus. The difference in style answers to the difference of localisation. It is not to be expected that the same style of discourse would be used to the simple, hardy, 'warlike' peasants of Galilee, and to the subtle and

How far authentic.

---

[1] *Introduction*, pp. 263–265, 267. Compare the elaborate discussion of Luthardt, pp. 167–191, especially 190.

learned doctors of the law at Jerusalem. We find here and there in the Synoptists traces of the same high personal claims and self-assertion. Undoubtedly there were other sayings like them; and supposing the fourth Evangelist to start with the idea of bringing this side of our Lord's teaching into relief, it is only natural that he should select that portion of it which bore specially upon his purpose. On the other hand, the resemblance to the First Epistle is accounted for by inverting the supposed relationship. It is urged that an Apostle who stood in such close and intimate relation to his Master, the disciple 'whom Jesus loved,' who leant on His breast at supper, and had been at His side in all the most important scenes of His ministry, drinking in and meditating for a whole lifetime upon those precious words, would consciously or unconsciously model his own utterances upon them.

Every one will feel that there is truth in these observations, and that they will carry us a certain way. But will they carry us so far as to cover the whole of the phenomena in question? An absolutely impartial judge would, I think, say No. It must be remembered that there is a long discourse in ch. vi. which is addressed, not to the doctors of the law at Jerusalem, but to a mixed audience in the synagogue at Capernaum. Yet this does not differ substantially from the others: it has all the same peculiarities of structure and style; it is rather more than less exalted and mystical. On the other hand, not all the Synoptic discourses are laid in Galilee. The last discourses especially, and we have seen reason to think some also of the others, were delivered in Jerusalem. Yet they too present the same terse aphoristic parabolic character. Just as the Johannean discourses are not addressed exclusively to doctors of the law, so also those in the Synoptists are not addressed exclusively to the populace. From both versions we should gather that the audiences were for the most part collected casually, and that they were composed in the main of the same mixture of classes. Again, it is noticeable that this peculiar style and language is not only attributed to Jesus, but also to the Baptist. The passage iii. 31–36 bears precisely the same resemblance to the Epistle as the other discourses in the Gospel. Yet no one would maintain that the Baptist also conformed to the same type[1].

St. John iii.

We conclude then that, if the Evangelist is also the Apostle, the discourses must have undergone a sensible modification in his mind, before they came to be written down. But it will be asked, is it not simpler and more natural to suppose that the Evangelist and the Apostle are different persons, and that the discourses are ideal compositions, ' like the speeches in Livy or Thucydides?' The results of our investigation, so far as we have at present gone, make it difficult to accept this alternative. But really

A certain amount of subjectivity need not imply un-Apostolic or ideal composition.

---

[1] Cf. Scholten, p. 229. Dr. Scholten has drawn up tables (pp. 224-8) of a number of expressions which are found equally in the discourses of our Lord, reflections of the Evangelist, and in the Epistle. It appears from Luthardt (p. 173) that one critic, Ebrard, has actually suggested that the Evangelist acquired his style *from the Baptist* as well as from our Lord—as if an intercourse of a few days (it cannot at most have been more than three-fourths of a year) would suffice to form a style for life, or as if this would account for the further resemblance between the sayings attributed to the Baptist, and those attributed to our Lord. (Cf. especially vv. 34–36). Such are the lengths to which apologetics can be carried. Luthardt, who sees the absurdity of Ebrard's reasoning, allows that the subjectivity of the Evangelist has been at work ' in a slight degree' (p. 174).

all depends upon the nature and extent of the modifications introduced—and that, as we said, is a question of detail. There is a certain kind of modification which would be quite compatible with Apostolic origin ; that is, such as might naturally result from a strong intellect and personality operating unconsciously upon the facts stored up in the memory, and gradually giving to them a different form, though without altering their essential nature and substance. St. Paul had compared his Gospel with that taught in the mother church at Jerusalem. He had evidently satisfied himself that it was substantially the same : and so in its ground lines it was. But the difference was probably considerably greater than St. Paul himself imagined. Without supposing fundamental differences of doctrine,—which St. Paul's own words are sufficient to prove did not exist[1],—still would there not be room for considerable divergence of form ? Are we to suppose that all that keen dialectic, those allegorizing interpretations, that peculiar mysticism vanished from the Apostle's direct exposition of the facts of Christianity ? If St. Paul had written a Gospel, would it have shown less divergence from the Synoptists than this of St. John ? That it would have diverged from them, I think we may consider almost certain, unless the ordinary laws of psychology were suspended in a way that we have no valid reason to anticipate they would be. However, the extent of St. John's divergence has still to be determined.

The discourse in this third Chapter is said to have been held with a certain Nicodemus, a member of the Sanhedrim, who came to Jesus by night. Nicodemus

[1] Cf. Gal. ii. 2.

is an entirely new personage, who is not mentioned by the Synoptists. This, however, does not tell against, but rather for, the historical character of the part attributed to him : because, if it had been fictitious it would have been more likely to be left vague. The circumstances under which he is described as coming to our Lord are exceedingly natural ; and it shows how defective the Synoptic Gospels are, that they relate nothing like them.

We gather from the answer that he receives what was Nicodemus' opening question,—the introduction and apology for which only is recorded. It is that which occurs so frequently in the Synoptists, 'What shall I do to inherit eternal life,' or ' to enter into the kingdom of heaven [1] ?'

On two occasions when this question was put to Him, our Lord is said to have answered by appealing to the law [2]. But these were both at a comparatively late period of His ministry ; and the questioners were in neither case persons who were capable of entering fully into the spirit of the demands made upon them. Therefore the answer does not go beyond the immediate condition requisite : this was, under the circumstances, enough. But the further question might be asked—But *how* is the law to be kept satisfactorily ? How is this condition of entrance into the kingdom of heaven to be complied with ? The answer to this is given in another place where our Lord is speaking to His own disciples, and is sounding with them the deep things of the kingdom of heaven. 'Except ye

---

[1] It may be that our Lord Himself anticipates the question, which is withheld through modesty (cf. Meyer, *Comm.*, p. 153); but I incline to the supposition in the text.

[2] Cf. Matt. xix. 16–22 ; Luke x. 25–28.

be converted,' He says, 'and become as little children, ye shall not enter into the kingdom of heaven'
(Matt. xviii. 3). It is noticeable that this doctrine of
conversion or repentance is that with which His
public ministry was first opened — 'Repent, for the
kingdom of heaven is at hand.'

So far the Synoptic Gospels take us. Now let us
return to St. John. There our Lord is made to
reply, 'Except a man be born from above, he cannot
see the kingdom of God.' And in further explanation
He adds, 'Except a man be born of water and of the
Spirit, he cannot enter into the kingdom of God.'
Here three conditions are described as necessary.
First, a birth—which, as distinguished from the physical birth, might be called a 'new' or 'second birth;'
secondly, baptism; thirdly, the Spirit. But all these
three are really different sides or elements in the
same act. Perhaps in describing this we should naturally invert the order. In order of time, that which
comes first is the gift of the Spirit, by virtue of which
the need of repentance and reformation is felt, and the
power to carry it through communicated. Then
comes the emphatic symbolical act of baptism, in
which the convert signifies by the washing of his
body that he at the same time puts away once and
for ever the blots and stains upon his soul. In this
the Spirit still sustains him, and in reward for his
resolution is given to him in fuller measure. And
so the Spirit of God co-operating with the will of
man, that new birth is completed—the man becomes
a new being, a new creature; 'old things are passed
away; behold, all things are become new.'

This is the conception that we find embodied in

our Lord's answer to Nicodemus as recorded in St. John iii. St. John. What does it contain in addition to the Synoptists? Taking the first term, 'the new birth,' there is really very little in excess of the Synoptists. The metaphor from 'childhood' is only pressed a degree further. The second term, baptism, is not mentioned by the Synoptists until quite the end of their narrative. Neither is the third, the gift of the Spirit in connection with it.

But this is one of those points on which the incompleteness of the Synoptic record comes out. If we are to believe the fourth Evangelist, the rite of baptism was already practised during the lifetime of Jesus Himself, and at the very beginning of His ministry. If so, there can be little doubt that it was associated with the preaching of Repentance, just as the two were associated by John the Baptist. At any rate the Johannean conception in its triple form is Apostolic, and belongs to the earliest cycle of Apostolic teaching. Among the speeches attributed to St. Peter in the Acts the conclusion of the first is this—'Repent, and be baptized every one of you in the name of Jesus Christ for the remission of sins, and ye shall receive the gift of the Holy Ghost[1].' The document in which this speech is contained bears the marks of early composition; and here we find fully developed every element of the Johannean conception, with the one exception of the pre- as well

---

[1] Acts ii. 38. Sufficient reasons for assigning to this document an early date, seem to be (1) the Christology, cf. ii. 22, 32, 36; iii. 13–15, &c.; (2) the appearance of the politico-theocratic idea in i. 6. But the composition of the Acts is an important subject of enquiry, on which much still remains to be done. Another starting-point ought, I think, to be the singular vividness of the narrative in ch. xii.

as post-baptismal gift of the Holy Ghost—the 'birth *from above.*' According to St. John it is the divine grace and inspiration which lead the convert to be baptized, as well as dwell in him after baptism.

In the Epistle of St. Peter[1] this element also appears. 'Blessed be the God and Father of our Lord Jesus Christ, which hath begotten us again to a lively hope,' &c. (I Pet. i. 3). 'Being born again, not of corruptible seed, but of incorruptible' (I Pet. i. 23). 'The like figure whereunto even baptism doth also now save us (not the putting away of the filth of the flesh, but the answer of a good conscience towards God,) by the resurrection of Jesus Christ' (I Pet. iii. 21). In St. Paul the triple combination is well known. The difference between the Pauline and Petrine conceptions turns chiefly upon the relation of baptism to the death and resurrection of Christ, into which it would be beside our purpose to enter.

The result that we obtain is:—first, that there is a chronological coincidence as to the place assigned especially to the preaching of repentance in St. John and in the Synoptists. In both it marks the outset of our Lord's ministry, and is indeed the point at which it attaches itself to the preaching of the Baptist. Secondly, if the full conception drawn out in these verses belongs in part to the Evangelist, it belongs to him not alone, but in concert with the

---

[1] The genuineness of this Epistle may, I think, safely be assumed. It is doubted by De Wette and denied by Schwegler, but has been consistently maintained by the best critics of the more moderate school, Ritschl, Bleek, Weiss, &c. The only real argument against it. is the relation of the theology of the Epistle to that of St. Paul; but this, —however it is to be accounted for, and several ways are open,—is insufficient to outweigh the many reasons that confirm the traditional view. Cf. Reuss, *Gesch. d. H. S.*, §§ 147-150; Bleek, *Einl.*, pp. 568–572; Ritschl, *Entstehung d. a. K.*, 116 foll.

earliest leader of the Christian community, and that as well in the earliest as in the later portion of his teaching. This would lead us to suspect that the two Apostles (accepting for a moment the hypothesis which seems to be suggested, that the author of the Gospel was the Apostle) did not develope their ideas independently, but that they had some common ground or foundation in the actual teaching of Jesus more than has been handed down to us by the Synoptists.

Though we should grant then that there is something in the form of this discourse with Nicodemus which is not perfectly original, we yet shall hesitate to allow that there has been any serious transformation of the matter.

These remarks are intended to cover especially the verses from 1–5. From verse 6 onwards, the nature and effects of the Spirit's operation is enlarged upon. We should be tempted at first sight to attribute this entirely to the Evangelist. Little is said about the operation of the Spirit in the Synoptic Gospels. And so far as it is mentioned there it is rather as a special gift conferred upon the Apostles, with a view to their ministry after their Master was taken away from them. The idea of the Spirit as determining the hearts of men to conversion, or as an agency sustaining the ordinary Christian life, does not seem to be brought out directly in the Synoptic Gospels[1]. And yet indications at least of something parallel are to be found. When it is pointed out that riches are an almost insuperable hindrance to conversion,

---

[1] Cf. especially Matt. x. 20. Luke xi. 13 *appears* to be a later version of Matt. vii. 11.

the qualification is added, that the disposition which makes the heart accessible to transforming influences, is not merely dependent upon circumstances or upon the free will of man—'And with God all things are possible' (Matt. xix. 26). Then in the expression 'children of the kingdom' (Matt. xiii. 38) there is contained the idea of a heavenly parentage, a divine element in the work of regeneration. Even for the opposition between the flesh and the Spirit, there is something of a parallel in 'the Spirit indeed is willing, but the flesh is weak' (Matt. xxvi. 41).

It is true that we have here only the hints or germs of which the Johannean conception is the full development : but it is a development logically in a direct line ; and when we come to think (1) of the manner in which the Synoptic Gospels were composed ; (2) of the comparatively small proportion which the didactic elements in them cannot but have borne to the sum of these elements in our Lord's teaching ; (3) and lastly, of the popular character of the great majority of the discourses and sayings contained in them,—we can hardly refuse to acknowledge that considerable room is left for a nearer approximation to the doctrine of St. John than the written records would lead us to suppose. Again, our conclusion is confirmed by a comparison of the Johannean theology with that of St. Paul. The parallels which are scanty in the Synoptic Gospels become abundant in the Pauline Epistles. The antithesis of flesh and Spirit, the divine predestination and election, and the permanent indwelling and inspiration of the Spirit, as well as the concentration of these ideas round the public confession and inner change denoted by baptism—all these

are standing themes with St. Paul. And yet the St. John ii.
difference in the mode of presentation is so marked,
and the independence of the Johannean theology as a
whole is so striking, as to make it altogether more
likely that the elements which are apparently common
are rather a bifurcation from a common stock than in
any way directly descended the one from the other.
The interval which separates the Gospels from the
Apostolic teaching becomes at once easier to fill,
when we take into account the materials supplied
by the fourth Gospel.

There is something very remarkable in the way in
which the Evangelist seems to pass without announcement and almost unconsciously from reflections put
into the mouth of the *dramatis personae* to his own.
Here in ver. 11 he is already wavering between the
original preaching of the Gospel and the missionary
experiences of the Apostles. And he very soon glides
into the exposition of his own theoretical view of the
scheme of salvation. 'God so loved the world that
He gave His only-begotten Son that whosoever believeth in Him should not perish but have everlasting
life:' on which theorem the verses to the end of the
21st are a comment.

A still clearer and more decisive instance of a vv. 27–36.
similar transition is supplied by the end of the
chapter. The objective element in the discourse
attributed to the Baptist gradually diminishes till
it reaches the vanishing point about ver. 31. There
is probably a kernel of objective fact in that beautiful
figure of the friend of the bridegroom who hears the
bridegroom's voice, and when he hears it is glad,
though his own functions should cease. But the

beauty, the tenderness, and the pathos with which it is clothed, belong less to the stern prophet of the wilderness, than to the 'Apostle of Love.' The remainder of the chapter we may say with confidence is purely Johannean. There is indeed nothing to indicate a change of speaker in the text. Still, I can hardly imagine a critic seriously maintaining that the words were spoken, as they stand, by the Baptist[1].

We notice as one mark of the perfect *naïveté* with which the Evangelist permits himself this procedure, that the historical notices usually occur before and not after these Johannean climaxes[2]. The introduction is the purest history; and to this the first few sentences of the discourse keep more or less closely. It is only gradually that it, as it were, drifts from its moorings and is carried out into the open sea of Johannean theology. But the historical substantiation does not occur at the end as it does at the beginning. If the Evangelist gives the reins somewhat to his imagination, he nowhere endeavours to claim for it more than a subjective authority. How different from the proceeding of a forger! How natural if the writer is really St. John — one who felt that his own words were clothed with authority, and who was conscious that he

---

[1] 'Yet on a careful reading of these passages (iii. 10–21 and 27–36) it seems impossible not to feel that the Evangelist is in part commenting on and explaining the testimony which he records. The comments seem to begin respectively at verses 16 and 31.' Westcott, *Introd.* p. 272 n. I would only ask on what principle it is possible to draw a sharp line at these two passages, iii. 16–21 and 31–36, and still to maintain the rigid authenticity of the rest of the discourses in the Gospel? When once the subjective freedom of the Evangelist is admitted, there seems to be no stopping except at the point which is fixed by critical analysis and comparison.

[2] Cf. i. 15, iii. 1 foll., 25 foll., v. 17 foll., xii. 44 foll.

had himself so put on 'the mind of Christ,' that St. John iii.
he did not care to distinguish, and probably could
not distinguish if he had tried, the constituent elements in the thoughts and memories that thronged
in upon him.   Even now, with all our modern notions
of literary morality, and with all our western precision
of thought, such phenomena are not infrequent[1].
How much less then should we be surprised to meet
with them not only under circumstances so peculiar,
but in an age when it was almost as common a
thing for an author to write in another person's name
as in his own.

We will now glance rapidly over the chapter, pick- Marks of
ing up such marks as present themselves of its Johan- genuineness
nean authorship and historical character. and authen-
ticity.

Mr. Blunt[2] has drawn an 'undesigned coincidence' The
Ascension.
from the allusion to the Ascension in ver. 13.   'No
man hath ascended up into heaven,' &c.   The Ascension is nowhere directly related in the fourth Gospel.
Indeed the narrative terminates before it is reached.
But there are several incidental allusions to it in connection with previous events.   It is prophesied, though
the fulfilment of the prophecy is not recorded.

The observation is doubtless correct, but it does
not prove very much.   Whether the Ascension actually took place or not, it was certainly believed to
have taken place at the very earliest date.   The
Epistles of St. Paul, and the documents which compose the early part of the Acts, afford proof that the
belief was from the first currently received.   So that
the author of the fourth Gospel, whoever he might

---

[1] E. g. notoriously in the case of S. T. Coleridge.
[2] *Scriptural Coincidences*, p. 308.

have been, would necessarily presuppose it as part of that common groundwork of tradition which was the property of every Christian. It was a fact so notorious, that we should not be surprised to find it alluded to incidentally even in a writing which was not genuine. It is rather a proof of the subjective character of this part of the discourse, that the language should be so evidently coloured by an event which had not yet happened, and which we gather from the Synoptists (Matt. xvi. 21) was not even predicted until a considerably later period.

When we look into the allusion a little more nearly, we perceive that it is an Apostolic gloss upon the preceding verse,—'How shall ye believe if I tell you of heavenly things?' He only could tell of the things of heaven, who had proved by His Ascension that He came down from heaven.

The rite of baptism.

A sounder instance of 'undesigned coincidence' might be drawn from ver. 21. 'After these things came Jesus and His disciples into the land of Judaea; and there He tarried with them and baptized.' It is afterwards explained that our Lord did not Himself baptize, but His disciples. Now it is in the first place antecedently probable, that as our Lord took up the preaching of the Baptist precisely where he left it, 'Repent, for the kingdom of heaven is at hand;'— and as further baptism was essentially a Messianic rite, associated with these ideas of repentance and admission to the kingdom, the rite would be continued along with the invitation and announcement to which it was conjoined. That it was so we are led to infer from the fact that it is included in the last instructions to the disciples, and also that it formed part of their practice from the very beginning of their independent ministry. Yet this is the one passage in which it is positively stated that our Lord authorised baptism during His lifetime.

The other notices in the midst of which this occurs are evidently of high historical value. 'John also was baptizing in Aenon near to Salim, because there was much water there : and they came and were baptized. For John was not yet cast into prison. Then there arose a question between some of John's disciples and the Jews about purifying.' This is minute and circumstantial on a number of points of absolutely no dogmatic importance, and that would only have interest for one who had been himself an actor in the scenes he describes.

Several identifications have been proposed for Aenon and Salim [1]—quite sufficient to show that these places had a real existence. Aenon represents the general name for 'Spring.'

We have before alluded to the correction of the Synoptic Gospels contained in ver. 24. 'For John was not yet cast into prison.' The Synoptic account of the public appearance of Jesus does not begin until after the imprisonment of John. Therefore the whole of these first three and indeed part of the fourth Chapter of St. John must be inserted before it. This

---

[1] Such are (1) Tell Ridghah, (Sheikh Sâlim), Ellicott, Van de Velde, G. in S. D., following Jerome and Eusebius. Pressel, in *Herzog*, adheres to the same authorities. (2) = 'Shilhim and Ain,' Joshua xv. 32, in the wilderness of Judaea, Ewald, Wieseler and Alf. (3) Salim, a village near Nablûs (Sichem), Robinson. (4) Wady Seleim, five miles N.E. of Jerusalem; Dr. Barclay, quoted in *S. D.* Of these on the evidence I should be inclined decidedly to prefer (1). It is hardly necessary for Aenon and Salim to be in Judaea, as Meyer seems to think, for though at no great distance from the place where our Lord was, they were also not very near it (cf. ver. 25).

is to me much more the work of an independent historian handling his facts with the mastery of knowledge, than of a forger separated by a considerable interval both of time and space from the events, and consciously manipulating the tradition so as to adapt it to a novel system of theology. All the ingenuity of the Tübingen school has failed to establish any adequate dogmatic motive for this remarkable redistribution of the history. Every dogmatic purpose could have been equally served by keeping to the existing lines. But there are certain portions of this added material (ii. 12, iii. 22, 23) that it is impossible to regard as embodiments of dogma. It is equally impossible to regard them as fragments detached from the mass of tradition. The only conclusion then remains, that they are facts lodged in the memory of a living witness of the events described. And the same hypothesis is found to give a simple and complete account of a historical procedure, which upon any other must be to all appearance inexplicable.

CHAPTER V.

SAMARIA AND GALILEE.

FEW portions of the Johannean narrative have been more called in question than the Samaritan episode, which fills a great portion of the fourth Chapter. I will notice briefly the chief objections brought against it; and then state some of the opposite arguments, that may be urged in its favour.

St. John iv.

And here I am brought into collision with a writer [1] whom I should wish to mention with honour, because of the admirable ability that he has brought to the treatment of his subject. It is only to be regretted —though at the same time in a writer so situated, it could not have been expected—that this ability is not joined with an equally adequate knowledge. In spite of the remarks which somewhat deprecate this criticism, I feel compelled to express my belief that a little more extended knowledge might have been found to give quite a different turn to the author's conclusions. On a subject where the facts and data are so complicated, it is impossible to come to a satisfactory conclusion from imperfect premises [2].

Sir Richard Hanson on the Samaritan episode.

---

[1] The author of *The Jesus of History*, which was published in 1869 anonymously, but has been since acknowledged by Sir Richard Hanson, Chief Justice of South Australia.

[2] Sir Richard Hanson has been unfortunate in his authorities. The chief of these is D'Eichthal, *Les Evangiles*, Paris, 1863. I am not acquainted with this work, but in those with which I am acquainted

A conspicuous instance of this is afforded by the author's treatment of this particular subject, the interview with the woman of Samaria[1]. It is one of the principal charges that he has to bring against the fourth Gospel.

The argument urged as conclusive is to some extent *à priori*. Starting from the notorious hostility of the Samaritans towards the Jews, and from their supposed rejection of the rest of the Old Testament, besides the Pentateuch, it is inferred that they cannot have shared the Jewish expectation of the Messiah. Consequently it is contended that the whole of the discourse with the Samaritan woman turns upon a false assumption; that to a genuine Samaritan the Messianic claim put forward in it would have excited not eager curiosity, but repulsion; and that the alleged conversion of the Samaritans cannot be other than a fiction.

Thus a neat theoretical argument is constructed, which bears upon the face of it a considerable degree of plausibility. But it shatters against the single fact that the Samaritans did at that time actually

it is not spoken of with respect. Meyer (*Pref. to Mark and Luke*, p. vii) characterizes it as a specimen of 'Französischer Leichtfertigkeit,' a verdict which seems to be justified, if we may judge by Sir Richard Hanson's note on p. 294. Of all the instances that Sir Richard Hanson cites against the Gospel (pp. 79-91) there is only one, the raising of Lazarus, that will bear the least examination —and that is only the general objection against miracles.—The argument drawn from the history of the Samaritan woman I have discussed above.—V. 4. is almost certainly spurious.—Why should not Peter have been a disciple of the Baptist?—The difference in the position assigned to that Apostle in the fourth Gospel and in the Synoptists corresponds exactly to the difference between a narration at first and at second or third hand. He is still 'primus inter pares,' cf. vi. 68, 69, xviii. 10, xx. 2, 3, 6, xxi. 3, 7, 15 foll. ($\pi\lambda\acute{\epsilon}o\nu$ $\tauο\acute{\nu}\tau\omega\nu$): but St. John does not forget that there were other Apostles besides. Hearsay always elevates the great and suppresses the small.

[1] Cf. *The Jesus of History*, pp. 82-85.

expect a Messiah, and that they continue to do so to this day[1]. It is true that they reject the prophetic books; but there was a single prediction in their own cherished Pentateuch, which served to keep alive in them the hope of a Messiah—that, namely, which relates to that second Prophet like unto Moses, to whom all the world was to hearken. This prediction sufficed to gather round it a legend, as defined if less copious than that of the Jews. The hopes of the Samaritans were centered especially on the restoration of the sacred vessels, the manna and the tables of the Law, which had been lost at the destruction of Solomon's temple. These, it was thought, had been hidden by the prophet Jeremiah in a place which when He came the Messiah should reveal. The rediscovery of the law was to be followed by its universal acceptance. All the world was to be converted, and the Messiah was to reign for 110 years. It appears from Josephus[2], that in the later years of the procuratorship of Pilate, there was an actual rising of the Samaritans, who assembled on Mount Garizim, under the influence of these Messianic expectations. Who can say that they may not have been originally set in motion by the event recorded in the fourth Gospel?

Another objection to the historical character of that event is derived from the history of the evangelisation of Samaria[3]. In Acts viii. 5, Philip the

---

[1] Cf. Keim, i. 518. Petermann in *Herzog.* xiii. 373.

[2] *Ant.* xviii. 4. 1.

[3] This objection is noticed by Meyer, *Comm.* p. 208. I have not been able to trace it to its source, but imagine that I have seen it somewhere on English ground. With regard to that which is founded on Matt. x. 5, there are some good remarks in Alford, p. 732. It is a mistake to square down the Gospel history by rule and line; just as it would be to

deacon is represented as going down 'to a city of Samaria,' where his preaching is attended with much success. It is assumed with perhaps some probability that Sichem is meant. And it is argued that no room is left for Philip's missionary visit if the Gospel had already been preached in that same district. But, waiving the question as to the identity of the two places, which is however far from being certain, there is still really nothing inconsistent. We are apt to forget—and this has been a source of especial confusion and difficulty in regard to the fourth Gospel—that the acceptance of Christianity involved not only the admission that Jesus was the Messiah, but also a total recasting of the Messianic idea itself. No doubt the first stage was much more often reached than the second. We have seen that it was at this first stage that the Baptist stood, when he declared that He upon whom the Holy Ghost descended was the Christ. He was cut off by death, before his shaken conviction could receive its due enlargement. And doubtless there were many who never got beyond the simple verbal confession, which remained a dead letter in their minds, incapable of growth and devoid of practical consequences. Thus it is quite possible that in those two days, our Lord may have found willing and attentive hearers; but a settled, permanent, and intelligent belief, could scarcely have been formed in so short a time. When the crowd dispersed, and the Teacher was gone, and no tidings came of Messianic triumphs, while the sacred vessels

---

treat any other history in the same way. This incident, like that of the Syro-Phoenician woman, is pre- cisely one of those 'exceptions which prove the rule.'

and the tables of stone were still undiscovered, we can easily understand how the seed sown would soon wither away.

The last objection that need be noticed, is that of Dr. Keim—according to whom the whole story is allegorical [1]. He finds the central part of the allegory in the allusion to the woman's five husbands, 'and he whom thou now hast, is not thy husband.' Dr. Keim sees in this an allegorical representation of the Samaritan history. The five husbands are the five religions which the heathen immigrants into Samaria brought with them out of Asia ; the sixth is the mutilated worship of Jehovah. But if this is the centre of the allegory, surely it ought to be also the centre of the story. On the contrary, it is thrown in quite by the way, and the rest of the story has apparently nothing to do with it. The fourth Gospel certainly does contain allegorical representations ; but the Evangelist is always careful to call attention to them. Where he indicates the allegorical interpretation himself, we may well follow him ; but we ought no less to accept his silence as final. Beyond the mere accident of numbers, there is no appropriateness in the allegory, and there is nothing to bear it out in the details.

We cannot then regard any of these objections as resting upon a solid foundation. On the other hand, apart from that general conclusion as to the character of the Gospel, which is for us, I venture to think, by this time sufficiently established, there are many little touches in the narrative that favour its authenticity.

St. John iv.

The allegorical theory.

---

[1] Cf Keim, i. 116, n. 3 ; also Scholten, p. 156; and on the other side, Wittichen, p. 58, n. 1.

The introduction has all the value that attaches to
the historical notice in the last chapter, of which it is
a continuation.   It shows an accurate sense of the
relation of metropolitan Pharisaism to the milder
religious spirit of the provinces, and affords a natural
motive for the retirement into Galilee, which, if we
had only had the Synoptic Gospels, would have been
unexplained.

Ver. 2. 'Jesus Himself baptized not, but His disciples,' serves the double purpose of correcting the
report which had just been described as coming to
the Pharisees' ears, and also of defining more closely
the Evangelist's own language. No doubt it has also a
dogmatic motive. The special prerogative of the Messiah was to baptize, not with water, but with the Spirit.
But this is recognised equally by the Synoptists.

The direct road from Judaea to Galilee of course lay
through Samaria.   And there is the less contradiction
to the narrative in Luke ix. 51–56, because in that
case the opposition of the Samaritans is expressly
grounded upon the fact that the faces of our Lord
and of His company were as though they would go
to Jerusalem. Here the party was moving northward,
away from Jerusalem. But we gather from Josephus [1],
that it was not at all an uncommon thing for the
Galilean caravans to brave the hostility of the Samaritans, and to pass directly through their country
on their way to the Jewish feasts.

The topography of Sychar and of Jacob's well corresponds to the description of modern travellers. The
name Sychar is not the common one, Sichem, but is
a mock title (='liar,' or 'drunkard,') that was given to

[1] *Ant.* xx. 6. 1.

the town by the Jews[1]. This is a clear reminiscence St. John iv.
of the vernacular that the Apostle spoke in his youth,
and is a strong touch of nature. It is not quite certain that the name Sychar has this force, but the
hypothesis is in itself more likely than that a forger
should have by accident got hold of the wrong name.
And that alternative becomes impossible when we
take into account the abundant instances where the
Evangelist's topography and local knowledge is beyond suspicion. It is not, however, by any means
improbable that Sychar may represent, not Sichem,
but the modern village Askar, which is somewhat
nearer to Jacob's well.

The incident is told with the Evangelist's usual
circumstantiality. 'Then cometh He to a city of Samaria, which is called Sychar, near to the parcel of
ground that Jacob gave to his son Joseph. Now
Jacob's well was there. Jesus therefore, being wearied
with His journey, sat thus' (as He was) 'on the well:
and it was about the sixth hour.' 'Thou hast nothing
to draw with, and the well is deep' (100 feet)[2]. 'His
disciples had gone away into the city to buy meat.'
'The woman then left her waterpot, and went her way

---

[1] This may perhaps be called
the current explanation of the
name. It is accepted as well by
those who deny the genuineness
of the Gospel as by those who
maintain it. Cf. Keim, i. 133. But
there is much to be said for the
identification with El Askar, cf.
Caspari. p. 107 and G. in *S.D.*
[2] Cf. Keim, iii. 15, 16. Dr. Keim,
in his new volume, though still
holding to his allegorical theory,
fully acknowledges the truth and
accuracy of the description, which
is called by Furrer (the geographer)

'eine Perle der Anschaulichkeit'—
immediately in the front of the
picture the well 100 feet deep,
Mount Garizim rising to a sheer
height of 800 feet above it, with
the ruins of the temple destroyed
by Hyrcanus visible upon its sum-
mit, and a little to the east the
smiling corn-lands of Mokhnah.
Dr. Keim has come round to the
identification with El Askar, though
he tries to combine this with the
old view—as though the town had
been chosen on account of its con-
temptuous name.

into the city.' 'Then they went out of the city, and came unto Him.' (Nablûs, or Sichem, is about a mile from the traditional site of Jacob's well; Askar, apparently about half that distance). Can Dr. Keim find dogmatic symbolism, or symbolism of any sort in these details?

The local colouring, like the topography, is well preserved. 'The Jews have no dealings with the Samaritans.' 'Art Thou greater than our father Jacob,' &c. 'Our fathers worshipped in this mountain' (Garizim, which rises immediately above Jacob's well). 'Ye say that in Jerusalem is the place where men ought to worship.' 'I know that Messias cometh: when He is come, He will tell us all things.' We might suppose, though I do not know that there is direct evidence for it, that the function of the Messiah as a *teacher* would be especially prominent in the Samaritan belief. The description of the Great Prophet of the future in Deuteronomy, points chiefly to this. 'Him shall ye *hear*!' 'I will put My *words* in his mouth; and he shall speak unto them, all that I shall command him.'

It is impossible to say exactly how much of the dialogue was spoken in the terms in which it is recorded. It is generally assumed that it must have been related to the disciples by Jesus Himself; but seeing that the whole company remained two days in the neighbourhood, it is as possible, and perhaps more probable, that much of it came from the woman.

Of the symbolical language of the first part of the discourse, and the apparent unintelligence of the woman, we shall have occasion to speak later [1].

[1] In the mean time we may quote a good note of Schöttgen's

The gradual development of the woman's belief is psychologically true; especially its first stage, 'Sir, I perceive that Thou art a prophet.' Her next question is grounded upon this[1]. It is the vexed question of the time which she puts to this prophet, thinking that He can solve it for her. · Confused and dazzled, as it were, at the answer she receives, and as if confessing her inability to understand it, she appeals to the Christ ⸱who should come, and should then make all things clear.

We shall surely be justified in attributing the wonderful words of verses 21, 23, 24, to One greater even than St. John. They seem to breathe the spirit of other worlds than ours—'of worlds whose course is equable and pure;' where all that is local and temporary is done away; where media and vehicles of grace are unneeded, and the soul knows even as also it is known. There is nothing so like them in their sublime infinitude of comprehension, and intense penetration to the deepest roots of things, as some of the sayings in the Sermon on the Mount: 'He maketh His sun to rise on the evil and on the good,' (Matt. v. 45); and, 'Thou, when thou prayest, enter into thy closet, and shut thy door,' (Matt. vi. 6). It is words like these that strike home to the hearts of men, as in the most literal sense Divine.

The incidental glimpse of the theology of the Gospel afforded by ver. 22, 'Ye worship ye know not

in regard to the parallel case of the unintelligence of Nicodemus, 'Tempora tunc erant obscura et perturbata, quibus plerique in luto traditionum πατροπαραδότων volvebantur, ita ut veritates solidae ac divinae negligerentur, et a pauci-oribus vestigia quaedam retinerentur. Si exemplo simili rem illustratam cupis, propone tibi Scholasticorum tempora, quibus eadem prorsus rerum facies erat.' (*Hor. Heb.* p. 328.

[1] Cf. Meyer, *ad loc.*

St. John iv.

what : we know what we worship : for salvation is of the Jews'—destroys at once the hypothesis that it was written by a Gnosticizing Greek. Accordingly those who assume this hypothesis are obliged to suppose that the verse is an interpolation, without a shadow of reason beyond what is supplied by their own faulty *à priori* system [1].

Ver. 27. 'Upon this came His disciples, and marvelled that He talked with the woman : yet no man said, What seekest Thou ? or, Why talkest Thou with her ?'—has all the appearance of a personal reminiscence on the part of the Apostle. It was against the Rabbinical code to hold intercourse with a woman [2].

A dialogue such as that in verses 31–34, may very well have happened ; ver. 34, especially, ' My meat is to do the will of Him that sent me, and to finish His work,' recalls the Synoptic ; ' Thou shalt not live by bread alone,' if not also, ' Wist ye not that I must be about My Father's business,' (*al.* ' in My Father's house').

The note of time [3] in the verse following is given precisely in the manner of the Synoptic Gospels. ' Say ye not, There are yet four months, and then cometh the harvest ? Behold, I say unto you, Lift up your eyes, and look on the fields ; for they are white already to harvest.' The sight of the springing corn suggests the thought of the harvest of souls. To our Lord the future is visible in the present. The corn is barely appearing above the ground, and yet He sees

---

[1] Cf. *The Jesus of History*, p. 85, n. 1.

[2] Cf. Meyer, p. 202. Lightfoot, *Hor. Heb.* p. 543.

[3] Alford contests the chronological application of this verse; but I do not see how τετραμηνύς ἐστιν, κ.τ.λ. can be made into a proverb ; and οὐκ ὑμεῖς λέγετε merely expresses the different range of vision in the Speaker and those He is addressing.

it already in ear and white for the sickle. What fol-   St. John iv,
lows is a prophecy of the success which should attend
the labours of the Apostles' building upon His foundation. It is possible that there may be mingled with
it something of the experience of the aged missionary
Apostle himself, feeling that he has but reaped where
he had not sown.

Objection has been taken to the expression, 'Saviour of the world,' in verse 42 [1]. It probably belongs
not to the Samaritans, but to the Evangelist. At the
same time it is possible that such an epithet might
be applied by them merely as synonymous with
'Messiah.'

The next section of the chapter opens with a well-   vv. 43-45.
known difficulty [2]. We read that 'Jesus went from
Samaria, and came into Galilee. For Jesus Himself
testified that a prophet hath no honour in his own
country.' But how could this be? Galilee was the
ἰδία πατρίς. Surely then the reason assigned would be
one for avoiding it, rather than for going thither.
There is an apparent contradiction ; and it is at all
events clear that the *primâ facie* explanation is not
the right one.

It hardly seems admissible to suppose that Galilee
was sought for the sake of privacy and retirement ;
or, with Ellicott, that Samaria was left for the same
reason ; or, with Lücke and Tischendorf, that γὰρ is
simply introductory, and that the verse defines the
character of the ensuing Galilean ministry. One is
perhaps reluctant to give up the old explanation of

---

[1] Cf. *The Jesus of History*, p. 85.
[2] Cf. *Huls. Lect.* p. 133, n. 1.; Lücke, i. 617 ; Tischendorf, *Synopsis.*
p. xxvi ; Meyer, p. 209.

H

Origen, that by ἰδία πατρὶs is meant Judaea, as the 'home of the prophets;' but it seems to be necessary, as Judaea has not been mentioned since the beginning of the chapter, and the only two districts in question are Samaria and Galilee. We seem therefore to be driven to accept some such view as that of Meyer. ' A prophet has no honour in his own country.' Therefore our Lord had left Galilee, in order to announce and substantiate His prophetic character in Jerusalem; and now, the obstacle being removed and the credentials secured, He returned. This agrees well with what follows; 'Then when (when therefore) He was come into Galilee, the Galileans received Him, having seen all the things that He did in Jerusalem at the feast:' and in English, the idiom by which the removal of an objection is regarded as a positive cause, is not uncommon. There is, indeed, some room to question whether the same idiom would be equally natural in Greek. But it should be remembered that we are not dealing with classical Greek, and that much would depend upon the individual writer. The causal connections in the fourth Gospel are often perplexing.

But the difficulty, whatever may be its true solution, is strictly one of exegesis. To infer, as some members of the Tübingen school have done [1], that the saying is taken directly from the Synoptic Gospels, and that the Evangelist has not known where to place it, is not warranted either by the relation which he usually bears to the Synoptists, or by his own character. Whatever we may think of the author of the fourth Gospel in other respects, he is one who tho-

[1] So Schwegler and Hilgenfeld, as quoted in Meyer's note (p. 210).

roughly knows his own mind, and is thoroughly capable of fitting his facts into the framework that he has
chosen for them. It is rash to argue an historical error
from a mere obscurity of style. | St. John iv.

At last we touch the ground that is occupied by
the Synoptists ; and the Evangelist hardly sets foot
upon it before he leaves it again. It is really little
or no objection that the part of the fourth Gospel
that we have just traversed, has to be inserted in the
interval between the Synoptic account of the Baptism
and the imprisonment of the Baptist. Any one who
has studied the Synoptic Gospels at all, must be prepared to find great gaps in their narrative. And precisely at this very point a gap seems to be indicated [1].
Indeed it seems to be almost necessary to assume the
truth of the Johannean narrative, in order to make
that of the Synoptists intelligible. For we find that
not only do the disciples obey a mere command, but
the crowds evince an eagerness, and 'the scribes' an
amount of jealousy, that can hardly be accounted for,
except by supposing that the public ministry had
been for some time in progress. The chief difficulty
is the Synoptic account of the calling of the Apostles.
But I still think it would be a hasty judgment to say
that it excludes the Johannean. If we knew all the
circumstances, the difference would probably be less
than it seems. The Synoptic account would perhaps
receive some modification, which should make it

vv. 46–54.
The ad-
ditional
matter in
St. John.

---

[1] Cf. Mark i. 14. After giving
an account of the Temptation, the
Evangelist continues, ' Now after
that John was cast into prison
Jesus came into Galilee.' It is
natural to suppose that an interval,
and a considerable one, is implied
here ; and the expression ' came
into Galilee' involves a change of
place such as that described in the
fourth Gospel.

appear that this was not the first calling, but a *re-calling*. My own surmise would be, that the little company, probably of some five or six, but not twelve disciples, who had voluntarily attended our Lord into Judaea, parted for a time after His return. But this is but conjecture. Taken exactly as they stand, the two accounts are not easy to fit into one another[1]; but they would doubtless be much more so, if we had them in a fuller form. At any rate, to assert a sweeping negative, as if their reconciliation was impossible, is to ignore daily experience, and to narrow the latitude of possibilities quite unjustifiably.

The one fact out of this prolonged sojourn in Galilee selected for narration in the fourth Gospel, is the healing of the 'nobleman's son.' Are we to regard this as the same with the miracle recorded in Matt. viii. 1 foll.; Luke vii. 2 foll.? In spite of considerable difficulties, I cannot help thinking that we are. The two Synoptists have here derived their account from different sources[2]; and they help to reconcile each other in turn with St. John. St. Matthew, by writing παῖς, shows how St. Luke misunderstood the document from which he is quoting, by writing δοῦλος. On the other hand, St. Luke's mention of the elders of the Jews is valuable; and explains much that would otherwise be obscure. It explains, first, the consent of our

---

[1] Cf. *The Jesus of History*, p. 173, note 1. 'Irreconcilable; that is, if we regard the spirit and intention of the writers, though no doubt capable of being reconciled if we look to the mere facts they relate.' This difference in spirit and intention may well have proceeded from imperfect knowledge on the part of the Synoptists.

[2] Or rather, they are both drawing from the same source, which in St. Luke's case is enlarged by a special tradition. This may be connected with the fact that the third Evangelist displays generally a peculiar acquaintance with the court of Herod.

Lord to perform the miracle at all,—otherwise, supposing the centurion to be a heathen, it would be
unprecedented and almost in contradiction with Matt.
xv. 21–28, (the Syro-Phoenician woman). But we
gather that he came within that somewhat vague
term, a 'proselyte of the gate.' He was at least a
benefactor of the Jewish community, and had built
them a synagogue. In the second place, the mention
of the elders explains the different tone assumed by
our Lord in the two Synoptists and in St. John. We
are to suppose that the centurion comes attended
by these elders who support him in preferring his
petition. St. John will then give the address *to the
elders* ('Except *ye* see signs and wonders *ye* will not
believe[1]); while the Synoptists record the reply to
the centurion himself. Both versions thus remain
intact, and the chief obstacle in the way of har-
monizing them seems to be removed. The hypothesis,
too, by which this is done, is simple and easy in
itself ; it is suggested, if not necessitated, by the
relation of the two Synoptic accounts to each other;
and it agrees with an incidental expression in St.
John. I incline, therefore, to think that the two
miracles are to be identified.

On this supposition we shall give the advantage
in one respect alone (the centurion's prayer) to the
Synoptists. This is characteristically a matter of
words. But in all other respects, as to the time, place
and circumstances of the miracle, the advantage in
definiteness and precision is on the side of St. John.

It appears to agree with the context here *slightly*

---

[1] Those who insist upon the plural οἴδαμεν in xx. 2, can hardly refuse
to admit a special force in the plural here.

better to suppose that the Roman civil mode of reckoning time has been followed; and that therefore the interview of the centurion with our Lord was at seven o'clock in the evening. Otherwise it is not quite obvious, why he should not have returned to Capernaum until the next day, the distance being only about twenty-five miles. But there are many causes that might have detained him; we do not know that he had not come out from Capernaum that same day. Or is it wholly impossible that the Jewish day beginning with sunset, 'yesterday' might not apply strictly to the afternoon just elapsed?

CHAPTER VI.

THE MIRACLE AT BETHESDA.

NOW occurs a gap in the Johannean narrative nearly as large as that which we have already discovered in the Synoptists. The fifth chapter contains an isolated fragment of history, the date of which is fixed, according to the chronology that we are following, at the Feast of Purim, in March A.D. 29; but which may bear almost any relation to the Synoptic history from the healing of the centurion's son to the feeding of the five thousand[1].

[1] I do not know what may be the 'insurmountable chronological difficulties' (Luke iv. 16, vi. 1?) which according to Bishop Ellicott stand in the way of 'Lange's attempt to interpolate a considerable portion of the events of the earlier Galilean ministry between the return through Samaria and the Feast of Purim.' (Cf. *Huls. Lect.* p. 149 n.) If these events (from Mark i. 14 to Mark vi. 45) can be fitted into less than one month, surely they can be fitted into four. To crowd them into three weeks is to exaggerate the want of proportion in the Synoptic narrative. And it must be very forced to suspend that narrative again for as much as three months just as it seems to be upon the point of beginning (i. e. in the space between Mark i. 15, 16). It might perhaps be suggested that the visit to Jerusalem was made during the absence of the Apostles upon their mission, which the harmonistic theory reduces to *two days!* But without pressing this, I do not see that there need be any difficulty, unless we assume for the Synoptic chronology a fixity that does not belong to it, and that leads to a reconstruction of the narrative which is artificial and mechanical in the extreme. According to the harmonists the Gospel of St. Mark is distributed thus. *a.* Mark i. 15, 16, blank, period of three months; *β.* Mark i. 16—vii. 23, twenty-one sections, *twenty-three days exactly;* *γ.* Mark vii. 24—ix. 50, eleven sections,

Spurious-
ness of
verse 4.

Our Lord pays a short and rapid visit to Jerusalem, and there performs the miracle recorded in the first nine verses of the chapter. Before we examine this miracle more closely, it is well to clear the text of an insertion, which would otherwise be a strange exception to the general sobriety of the canonical Gospels, and might tend to prejudice the credit of the Evangelist. The whole passage from ἐκδεχομένων in ver. 3 down to the end of ver. 4, containing the legend of the moving of the waters, is on documentary grounds, we may say, certainly spurious. The Alexandrine is the only one among the best MSS. that contains it, and that in a different and abridged form. It is wanting in some of the most ancient versions; and is expunged by the best editors[1]. We may therefore ignore it without any fear of having been led to do so by other extrinsic considerations.

When we leave out this passage, and read through the rest of the narrative as it stands in St. John, it is impossible not to feel a strong sense of its vividness and reality. The author of the Gospel was evidently well acquainted with the topography of Jerusalem.

Bethesda.

What could be more precise than his description of 'the pool by the sheep(-gate),' with its five porches or colonnades, and its Hebrew name Bethesda, 'the house of mercy.' The 'sheepgate' occurs in Nehemiah xii. 39, 'And from above the gate of Ephraim, and

---

scattered promiscuously over six months; δ. Mark x. 1—45, scattered over six months; ε. x. 46—xvi. 9, about eight days. Surely it is better to break down the barrier between α and β and distribute Mark i. 16—vii. 23 promiscuously over the whole four months like

the rest, thus giving three periods of four, six, and six months respectively. Compare Ellicott, *Lect.* iii, iv, v. Wieseler, *Chron. Syn.* pp. 239-285.

[1] Tischendorf, Tregelles, Meyer, Lücke, Ewald, Alford.

above the old gate, and above the fish gate, and | St. John v.
the tower of Hananeel, and the tower of Meah, even
unto the sheep gate : and they stood still in the prison
gate :' it appears to have been situated on the north-
east circuit of the city wall, near the tower of Antonia.
The name Bethesda is not found elsewhere ; but
tradition identifies the locality with a ruined reservoir
now called Birket Israin[1], and the word itself, Bethesda,
is one of legitimate and natural formation[2]. The pool
appears to have possessed mineral qualities, and to
have been subject to intermittent disturbance, doubtless from the nature of the spring that supplied it.
Round it there appears to have grown up a sort of
charitable institution, by which these five colonnades
had been provided for the protection of the sick
persons who were kept waiting for the moment when
the spring should become active. It would seem that
the space covered by its activity was only large enough
to contain one person at a time. Hence the very
natural complaint of the poor cripple, that having no
one to carry him to the pool he was always forestalled.
We are not told how long he had been there, but he
had been ill thirty-eight years. The simple words,
' Rise, take up thy bed and walk,' are sufficient ; and
the man at once obeys the command.

The cure had been performed on the sabbath-day.
Accordingly the Jews, seeing the man walk, remonstrate with him, and afterwards finding it was Jesus
by whom the cure had been performed, they seek to
kill Him. The whole narrative is in keeping with

---

[1] Cf. Caspari, p. 114; Ellicott,   n. 1.   According to Ewald, p. 202,
p. 139, n. 2 ; G. in *S. D.*, &c.   the name is not pure Hebrew but
[2] Renan, p. 495 ; Ellicott, p. 140,   Aramaic.

St. John v.

parallel cases in the Synoptists[1]. At the same time the localisation is so distinct and minute, that there can hardly have been any confusion. It is exceedingly probable that several miracles of this sort would take place, and it would be only likely that they would reproduce somewhat similar features.

vv. 17–47.

The discourse which follows, while it arises out of the accusation based on the supposed breach of the sabbath, has otherwise no fixed historical framework. There is no notice of the effect made by it upon the hearers, except, perhaps, incidentally in verse 31. It ends, as it were, in the air: and the sequel is not told. We are therefore not surprised to find that it bears a Johannean colouring. But the question is, how deep does that colouring extend?

vv. 17, 18.

Let us, first, map out the discourse briefly in its several sections. A. *a.* It begins with a defence of the healing upon the Sabbath day, based upon the relation of the Son to the Father. Just as the activity of the Father is continuous, notwithstanding the rest on the seventh day—the work of Creation only giving place to the work of Redemption—so does the Son exercise His proper work in spite of the obligation of the Sabbath, to which it is indeed no contradiction.

vv. 19, 20.

β. Then the closeness and intimacy of the relation between the Son and the Father is further asserted;

---

[1] ' Arise and walk,' cf. Mark ii. 9; miracle on the sabbath-day, followed by hostile attempts, Mark iii. 2–6. These very passages show that the Johannean narrative is not consciously constructed out of material furnished by the Synoptists. For the mechanical combination of two such passages would be in the highest degree far-fetched and improbable, especially when the same purpose might have been equally well served by reproducing either or both separately as they stood. Such elaborate and gratuitous art would be not less contrary to the practice of that age than of all ages.

and proved by a twofold power that the Son has
committed to Him.   γ. This is, (i.) the power of com-
municating spiritual life, by virtue of the life which
He Himself possesses.   Parenthetically the honour of
the Son is asserted as grounded upon this. (ii.) That of
causing the bodily resurrection of all the dead, both
good and bad ; when the Son shall also sit in judgment, and dispense both the consummated life in the
perfected heavenly kingdom, and the final condemnation.   ε. That by which the Son is qualified for the
exercise of these high prerogatives is the perfect
identity of His will with that of the Father.

B. ζ. Such are His rightful claims.   If they rested
merely upon His own word, there might be reason to
doubt and dispute them ; but they rest on that of One
whose witness cannot but be true.   John, indeed, bare
witness ; but that witness our Lord will not urge.   He
only mentions it in order to call to the mind of the
Jews their neglect of it and of him who gave it.   His
was a secondary light kindled at another flame
(καιόμενος, pass.)[1].   The Son of Man can appeal to no
less a witness than that of the Father : η. as borne
(i.) through the works, i.e. the sum of those Messianic
powers, that He has given Him, θ. (ii.) through that
revelation which the Jews would not receive.   Neither
the written Word, in which they professed to look for
salvation, nor yet his own Visible Presence had led
them to Him.   Thus they belied their pretended
knowledge of the Father.   ι. Not that the Son of God
need seek for honour from men ; but that He saw in
those who rejected Him a spirit and a state of mind,

St. John v.
———
vv. 21–24.

vv. 25–29.

v. 30.

vv. 31–35.

v. 36.

vv. 37–40.

vv. 41–44.

[1] Cf. Lightfoot *on Revision*, p. 117.   The phrase is a Hebraism, cf. *Hor. Heb.* p. 550.

St. John v.

that must necessarily close their eyes against the truth. They were too full of worldliness and selfish ambition to recognise that which was true and divine. If one had come appealing to these motives, him they would have acknowledged. But it is to the single-hearted love of God alone, that God and Christ are

vv. 45–47.

revealed. κ. It is vain to fall back upon Moses. His writings themselves condemn this unbelief: for they had prophesied of Him against whom it was directed.

Summarily we may say that the first half of this discourse (A. vv. 17–30) relates to the powers and prerogatives of the Son of God; the second part (B. vv. 31–47) is an exposure of the unbelief of the Jews, its nature, and causes, and the guilty obstinacy with which it was persisted in, in the face of clear and convincing evidence.

a. It is remarkable that in the Synoptic Gospels as well as in the fourth, our Lord vindicates His claim to suspend the obligation of the Sabbath: but with this difference, that there it is by virtue of His relation to *man;* 'The Sabbath was made for man, and not man for the Sabbath: therefore the Son of Man is Lord also of the Sabbath' (Mark ii. 27, 28). Here it is by virtue of His relation to God. But in the passages from the Synoptists, as indeed wherever the title of Son of Man is mentioned, it is not merely a common humanity that is meant. The argument is *à fortiori,* If the Sabbath is subject to man, much more to the Son of Man. The exalted Messianic dignity implied in the term is not left out of sight. In St. John this side is put forward alone: and it forms the complement to the other. It is highly probable that words similar to those recorded were actually spoken.

β. The argument in the next clause has many
parallels in St. John and but one in the Synoptists.
That, however, seems to be decisive in favour of its
substantial authenticity. The relation of the Son to
the Father is seldom alluded to in the Synoptic
Gospels. But a single verse in which it is, seems to
contain the essence of the Johannean theology, Matt.
xi. 27 : 'All things are delivered unto Me of My
Father; and no man knoweth the Son but the Father;
neither knoweth any man the Father, save the Son,
and he to whomsoever the Son will reveal Him.' This
passage is one of the best authenticated in the Synoptic
Gospels. It is found in exact parallelism both in
St. Matthew and St. Luke ; and is therefore known to
have been part of that 'collection of discourses[1],' in
all probability the composition of the Apostle St.
Matthew, which many critics believe to be the oldest
of all the Evangelical documents. And yet once grant
the authenticity of this passage, and there is nothing
in the Johannean Christology that it does not cover.
Even the doctrine of pre-existence seems to be im-
plicitly contained in it. For how and when is this
unique and mutual knowledge to be regarded as
obtained ? Clearly it is no empirical guessing ; it does
not appear possible that it should be grounded on
anything short of an essential unity.

On the other hand, if the Synoptic saying is
authentic[2], no stress can be laid upon the fact that

---

[1] There is a strong consensus on
this point. Cf. Holtzmann, *Synopt.
Evangelien*, p. 184. Ewald, *Evangelien*, pp. 20, 255. Weizsäcker,
pp 166-169.

[2] Dr. Keim contests (ii. 379 foll.)
the reading of the passage, but not
its originality. 'To deny this, he
thinks, is an act of violence than
which none can be greater' (388).
He interprets the sense as a claim
to the possession of 'the highest

it stands alone. The isolation is in language rather than in idea. We may quite safely assume that there were other sayings of similar purport. The point really proved is the fragmentariness of the Synoptic tradition. With all its richness it is after all only 'the crumbs from the rich man's table.' And we must be prepared to find that there is a great deal of equally authentic matter that has no place in it.

In section γ, ver. 22, 'For the Father judgeth no man, but hath committed all judgment unto the Son,' corresponds almost exactly to the first clause in the verse just quoted from St. Matthew, 'All things are delivered unto Me of My Father;' and to Matt. xxviii. 18, 'All power is given unto Me in heaven and in earth [1].' Ver. 23 = Matt. x. 40, 'He that receiveth you, receiveth Me ; and he that receiveth Me receiveth Him that sent Me.' The *form* of a great part of this section is Johannean. This appears to be proved by the intricacy of the thought ; the parenthetic character of verses 22 and 23 ; and the want of a clear line of demarcation between the spiritual resuscitation of the spiritually dead, the miraculous raising of the physically dead, and the general resurrection at the last day. But the conception of 'eternal life,' 'everlasting life,' is a common one with the Synoptists : and with them

knowledge of God and of perfect beatific life in God' (384)—resting upon 'likeness of spiritual activity, upon likeness of natures, of being' (auf der Gleichheit geistiger Thätigkeit, auf der Gleichheit des Wesens, der Naturen, p. 382). Yet he seems to think that this language is tenable along with a strictly humanitarian view of the Person of Christ. It is much to be desired that Dr. Keim and writers who hold the same standpoint, would abjure metaphor, and express their meaning in precise terms. Dr. Schenkel is a great offender in this respect.

[1] This verse is referred by Holtzmann to the other great document A. the 'Ur-Marcus,' p. 99. Cf. also Ewald, pp. 59, 364, 365.

too the mean by which it is to be obtained, is by contracting a personal relation to Jesus. 'Come unto Me all ye that labour and are heavy laden, and I will give you rest,' is the simpler and more metaphorical expression for that which is expounded in these verses; but its meaning is really not less profound.

The command addressed to the too lukewarm disciple, 'Follow Me, and let the dead bury their dead,' shows that this imagery of life and death in especial connection with the relation to His own Person, was not foreign to the original sayings of Jesus (Matt. viii. 22).

Though the life-giving power of the Son is meant chiefly in an ethical or spiritual sense, there is an undercurrent of allusion, even in these earlier verses, to the miraculous acts like the raising of Jairus' daughter, or the widow's son at Nain. This, too, is in accordance with the intention of our Lord, whose miracles have all of them a typical value [1].

δ. The description of the final resurrection, and the Last Judgment, is entirely in the manner of the Synoptists, and shows that the theology of St. John was essentially at one with theirs, on a point where some critics, overlooking this passage, have asserted the contrary. The two doctrines of everlasting life spiritually revealed in the present, and of everlasting life conferred at the resurrection of the just in the future, exist side by side, not only in St. John and in St. Paul, but also in the Synoptic Gospels, without coming into conflict with each other. This is seen, for the Synoptists, by comparing Matt. xix. 16 foll. and Luke

---

[1] See p. 130 below.

x. 25 foll. (esp. ver. 28, 'thou shalt live'='inherit eternal life') with Matt. xxv. 46.

ε. Ver. 30. 'I seek not Mine own will, but the will of the Father which sent Me'= Matt. xxvi. 39, 'Nevertheless, not as I will, but as Thou wilt.' The doctrine of the divine submission of the Son to the Father as the ground of His exaltation, is thoroughly Apostolic [1]. Its wide diffusion would tend to make us suppose that it is pre-Apostolic in its origin; at least, that it is based on intimations that had been given by our Lord during His lifetime.

In the second half of the discourse the form is again in a great degree peculiar to St. John. But, when we come to look beneath the form, there are numerous points of affinity with the Synoptists, or rather, a broad substratum of unity. The one point on which this would seem to be most wanting is in ζ, the claim to a higher witness than that of John, by comparison with and to some extent in depreciation of it. If we suppose the author of the Gospel to be the Apostle, it is only natural that he should insist upon the transcendent authority by which his Gospel was sealed. But it would seem that here, as elsewhere, he has penetrated a degree beyond the fact. The Father bore witness to the Son through the miracles, which He wrought in the Divine Spirit and with the Divine co-operation. In the Synoptic Gospels our Lord appeals to these miracles. In St. John He is made to appeal immediately to that of which the miracles were the outward sign and manifestation.

---

[1] Cf. Phil. ii. 9; Heb. v. 8, 9; x. 7 foll.; Acts ii. 33.

Then again, in η, ἔργα has a wider signification than
the δυνάμεις of Matt. xi. 20, 21 (Luke x. 13, foll.) It
includes not only the visible miracles, but also that
which is inferred through those miracles, all Messianic powers and functions.

θ. The appeal to the Scriptures is essentially in the
spirit of the Synoptists (cf. Luke xxiv. 26, 27, 44–46 ;
Matt. xxvi. 54, ver. 17, &c.)   And so is the contrast
drawn between the advantages and opportunities
which the Jews really possessed, and the blindness
which prevented them from making use of them,
which may be compared with the adaptation of the
prophecy of Isaiah in Matt. xiii. 14–17.

ι. The ethical cause assigned for the Jews' unbelief
has a parallel in the same passage : 'This people's
heart is waxed gross, and their ears are dull of hearing, and their eyes they have closed, lest at any time
they should see with their eyes, and hear with their
ears, and should understand with their heart, and
should be converted, and I should heal them' (Matt.
xiii. 15).   A like ethical disqualification is implied in
the phrase which occurs so often, 'A wicked and
adulterous generation seeketh after a sign,' &c.   We
have an exact parallel to the particular impediment
alleged in ver. 44 : 'How can ye believe, which
receive honour one of another,' &c.   In Matt. xviii.
1–4, where, in answer to the question, 'Who should
be greatest in the kingdom of heaven ?' the disciples are told that no man should enter there at
all, who did not first humble himself, and become as
a little child.

κ. The declaration of the sufficiency of Moses and
his writings, reminds us at once of Luke xvi. 29, 31,

I

'If they will not believe Moses and the prophets, neither will they be persuaded, though one rose from the dead.'

It is not impossible that in some of these cases, the saying quoted from the Synoptists may have been actually the original which appears thus metamorphosed in St. John. What is here presented as a single discourse is probably made up of the fragments of several fused together and transmuted in the mind and memory of the Apostle. But with all this outward individuality of form, we have seen how closely the substance is allied with that of the Synoptists, and what a large proportion of the constituent elements can claim an authentic and objective reality. At the same time, it becomes clear how erroneous is that view, which detaches the Johannean theology from its true Apostolic surroundings, and correlates it with a system of thought, to which it has only a superficial resemblance, and its differences from which are profound. What Gnostic in the second century would have cared to discuss a breach of the Sabbath, and to discuss it upon these grounds, as overborne by a higher relation and a higher obligation? What Gnostic would have stayed to contrast the evidence of miracles with the oral testimony of John? What Gnostic would so have probed to the quick the moral hindrances to the reception of truth? How many clear parallels to Johannean dicta can be quoted from Gnostics or Gnosticising writers? Set these by the side of those which present themselves in the Synoptic Gospels and the real affinities of the Johannean theology will soon become evident. The doctrine of the Logos has not only, as we have seen, led to mistaken conclusions in itself, but it has also, from its mere position at the beginning of the Gospel, given a bias to the critical verdict that has led to the neglect of indications far more numerous and certain.

St. John v.
——

CHAPTER VII.

THE MULTIPLICATION OF THE LOAVES, AND THE DISCOURSE AT CAPERNAUM.

St. John vi.

The Chronology.

IF we take the feast of chap. v. to be the feast of Purim, the events of chap. vi. will then happen within a month of it. But the Purim hypothesis, though perhaps on the whole probable, is not without difficulties. We must beware of laying too much stress on the chronology. I fear Dr. Wieseler's labours, valuable and admirable as they are, have hardly given us so certain a result as he seems to think. One point I believe he has made out to a very high degree of probability; that is, the substantial accuracy of the single date for which we have positive data in the Gospels—that of the public appearance of the Baptist, and along with it the first Passover of our Lord, after His baptism. This, I think, we may safely fix at the year 28 A.D. But with this exception, I doubt whether we can rise above the region of more or less probable conjecture. I firmly believe that the Johannean chronology is to be trusted, so far as it goes; but there are several points in it that cannot be precisely determined; of which this is one. With regard to the closing scene, too, I cannot think that Dr. Wieseler's system is satisfactory. His view as to the date of the Last Supper is based upon harmonistic interpretations, with which I cannot agree; and is really less consistent with the astronomical data than that to which it is opposed [1].

St. John vi.

With the beginning of chap. vi. the scene shifts suddenly from Judaea to Galilee. The time is fixed by ver. 4. as near the Passover (i. e. probably that of the year 29). But nothing whatever is said about the circumstances of the journey northwards, or of the rest of the series of events which connect the two portions of the narrative together. The whole of the interval from ver. 18, where we were left in Judaea, at the feast of Purim, to chap. vi. 1, where the narrative takes us across the sea of Galilee, just before the Passover, is left entirely blank. Ewald thinks that something must have fallen out [2]; but there is not the slightest documentary evidence for such a supposition; and really the abrupt transition is only in accordance with the practice of the Evangelist. It brings out clearly the eclecticism of his narrative,—which does not profess to be continuous, but, while it treats the particular sections selected with great minuteness of

The change of scene.

The subjects of the narrative selected, not continuous.

---

[1] Nisan 1, or the first day of the Jewish year, coincided with the (appearance of the disc of the) first new moon after the spring equinox. This can be determined astronomically; and two astronomers, Wurm and Oudemans, working out the calculation independently, have arrived at results which only vary by a few minutes. In accordance with these, tables have been drawn up for the years on each side of 30 A.D.; from which it appears that the year 30 itself is the very one in which Nisan 14th fell upon a Friday, so satisfying the conditions of the problem. Wieseler, who holds that the Last Supper took place on Nisan 14th and the Crucifixion on Nisan 15th, supported his view by an appeal to these astronomical data: but he apparently forgot, in fixing Nisan 1, to allow for the fact of the Jewish day beginning in the evening. It seems that the exact date of the Crucifixion may be set down with some confidence as the afternoon of April 7th in the year 30 A.D. Cf. Caspari, pp. 7–17; Ellicott, p. 323 n. Dr. Wieseler, however, still maintains his position. (*Beiträge,* p. 162.)

[2] *Johann. Schriften,* p. 221.

detail, leaves the links of connection between them wholly vague and indefinite. We had an instance of this at the beginning of chap. v ; again in chap. vii. 1 ; so too in x. 22 and xii. 1. It would be a mistake to look for any far-fetched motives for this. Probably the simple reason was, that the Evangelist found it necessary in order to keep his book within a reasonable compass, either to abridge the whole narrative, or to give only parts of it ; and of these alternatives he chose the latter. The principle of selection pursued we can hardly determine. The motives of literary procedure, like those of all action, are highly complex, and often beyond the power even of the writer himself wholly to analyse. Much of the matter contained in the fourth Gospel may have been selected unconsciously, merely because it happened to come uppermost in the author's mind. Doubtless there would be at the bottom of this some subtle train or trains of association ; but we are not in a position completely to unravel them. The main element probably was the desire to choose out those passages which tended most to exalt the subject of the history, and to show Him in His supernatural power and glory. Another may have been the intention to furnish a historical supplement to the Synoptic Gospels, bringing out especially those parts of the narrative, like the Judaean ministry, where they were most deficient. Some polemical motives may have entered in ; but these at all events lie very much in the background. Unconsciously such motives would operate to a greater or less degree ; but consciously the Evangelist seems to have felt that both himself and his subject were above polemics. He may have had besides some such minor objects as those suggested by Ewald ; (i.) to bring out the *universalism* of our Lord's teaching ; (ii.) to meet the charge of obscurity brought against the new faith, by laying stress upon the rank and estimation of the first converts, e. g. Nicodemus, and by showing that Christianity did not originate in a corner of Galilee ; (iii.) to confront the disciples of the Baptist, &c. All these, as well as other motives and objects, may have been present to the writer in different degrees. But we must beware of thinking that we can exhaust them. In order even to guess at the whole of such motives, we should have to know much more of the circumstances under which the Gospel was written, than we do. And then we should be very liable to be mistaken; so rich is human nature ; so active, so sensitive, so mobile is the human mind.

The section before us does certainly tend to bring out the Divine Majesty of our Lord in a remarkable way, and the discourse which follows in the synagogue at Capernaum turns upon a special subject with our Evangelist, the mystical relation of the Redeemer to His people. From a critical point of view the history of the feeding of the five thousand and the storm at sea are important ; because here we have a full and undoubted synopsis of all four Gospels. The first three here depend upon a single document, which is found in its most original form in St. Mark. This document supplied the common groundwork of the whole Synoptic tradition, and competes with the ' collection of discourses,' to which we have already

St. John vi.

Critical importance of the feeding of the five thousand.

---

[1] *Johann. Schriften*, pp. 8–13.

St. John vi.

vv. 1-4.

alluded, for the place of the oldest document of Christian history [1].

There is some little difficulty about the circumstances which precede the miracle. These are clearly described by the Synoptists. According to them, the Apostles have just returned from their mission; and our Lord, who is now on the west side of the sea of Galilee, probably somewhere near Capernaum, finding that the crowds will not permit any degree of privacy, enters into a ship with His disciples, and crosses over to the other side. But the crowd, observing what was done, hastens round by land, gathering contingents as it goes from the cities along the coast, and arrives at the place where our Lord and the Apostles had landed not long after them. This is not impossible; for supposing the desert place and the hill on which Jesus sate to be, as St. Luke says, in the district of Bethsaida (that is, Bethsaida Julias on the north-east shore of the lake), the distance from Capernaum would not be above ten miles. The account in St. John is briefer and less detailed than that in the Synoptists: and to the end of ver. 3 it seems to agree with it very fairly. 'After these things Jesus went over the sea of Galilee, which is the sea of Tiberias. And a great multitude followed Him, because of His miracles which He did on them that were diseased. And Jesus went up into a mountain (τὸ ὄρος, 'qui prope erat,' Meyer) and there He sat with His disciples.' So far the accounts seem to agree well together. But in ver. 4 a new reason for the gathering of the crowd seems to be suggested: 'And the passover, a feast of the Jews,

[1] Cf. Holtzmann, p. 83, and compare Ewald, *Evang.* p. 72.

was nigh;' as if the crowd were made up, not of the inhabitants of the west shore of the lake, but of the troops of pilgrims who were already beginning to stream from the north southwards on their way to the passover at Jerusalem. If we do not suppose this, we must suppose that the Evangelist merely wished to give a chronological notice; and this appears to be the more probable view [1].

We notice that the impulse to the performance of the miracle comes in the Synoptists from the disciples; in St. John, solely from our Lord Himself. It is accordingly assumed by those who deny the Johannean authorship of the Gospel, that the miracle has no reference to the bodily needs of those satisfied by it, and that it is regarded as purposed from the first merely as a display of Divine power [2]. This may be true; but there is no very decisive ground for asserting it. The ἐπάρας τοὺς ὀφθαλμοὺς of St. John may contain the idea of human pity, which is more fully expressed in the εἶδεν καὶ ἐσπλαγχνίσθη of the Synoptists. They too certainly intimate that the miracle was purposed from the first. The answer, 'Give ye them to eat,' corresponds exactly to the question, 'Whence shall we buy bread that these may eat?' For the rest the superiority in distinctness and precision is all on the side of St. John. He knows to whom the question was put, that it was to Philip; he knows exactly what Philip answered; and again the remark of Andrew, Simon

St. John vi. 1-4.

vv. 5-13.

---

[1] Meyer, *Comm.* (pp. 250, 251), insists that ver. 4 is not a mere chronological notice, but is meant to explain the preceding narrative. He therefore sees in it a discrepancy from the Synoptists. But if there is a discrepancy it is not with the Synoptists alone, but with St. John himself; see below, p. 126.

[2] Cf. Hilgenfeld, p. 274.

Peter's brother.   The particulâr expression, 'two hundred pennyworth of bread,' (like the 'three hundred pence' of xii. 5,) is probably an unconscious reminiscence of St. Mark's Gospel, which St. John had certainly seen.   It is quite possible and probable that the expression may have been originally used ; but it is most natural to suppose that it had been recalled to the recollection of the Apostle by his having seen it in writing.   The same will apply to the use of κοφίνους for 'baskets' in ver. 13 below. Here, again, there is a verbal coincidence both with St. Mark and the other Synoptists.   In the account of the feeding of the four thousand, σπυρίδας is the word used [1].   On the other hand, the touch in ver. 10, 'Now there was much grass in the place,' compared with 'on the green grass' in Mark vi. 40, has all the force of an original, if not altogether independent, reminiscence.   At least it would hardly have been suggested by the parallel phrase, unless the fact had already been impressed upon the Apostle's memory.   If such were the case, the Synoptic tradition may have helped to revive it.   But a first or second century forger would not have had the art to choose a trait like this to develope as the Evangelist has done.   It is far more probably a genuine part of a picture actually presented to the Apostle's mind.   Some memories are essentially pictorial ; and the Apostle's appears to have been one of these.   It is wonderful with what precision every stroke is thrown

---

[1] With Mr. Blunt this becomes an 'undesigned coincidence.'   But it must be remembered that really σπυρίδας is only found in one docu-ment, and κοφίνους only in two, that which has been used by the three Synoptists and St. John. (Cf. *Scriptural Coincidences*, p. 264.)

in.   Most minds would become confused in reproducing events that had occurred so long ago; but
there is no confusion here.   The whole scene could
be transferred to canvas without any difficulty.

St. John vi.
5–13.

We notice besides the prominence that is given to
the two figures Philip and Andrew, and besides the
abundance of grass, the παιδάριον ἓν, with an emphasis
as it were upon the number, who supplies the fishes
and the loaves; the very loaves are particularised as
of barley, ἄρτους κριθίνους.

But a decisive proof that the narrative in the fourth
Gospel is not merely constructed out of that of the
Synoptists, and we might almost add a decisive proof
of the historical character of the Gospel itself, is supplied by the two concluding verses, 'Then those men,
when they had seen the miracle that Jesus did, said,
This is of a truth that prophet that should come into
the world.   When Jesus therefore perceived that they
would come by force to make Him a king, He departed again into a mountain Himself alone.'   The
Synoptists have nothing of this.   They pass immediately from the miracle to the embarcation of the
disciples.   Yet how exactly it corresponds with the
nature of the current Messianic expectations!   Our
Lord had performed a miracle, a σημεῖον of His
divine mission; and at once He is hailed as the
Messiah.   But it is as the Jewish, not the Christian,
Messiah.   The multitude would take Him by force
and make Him king.   At last they think they have
found the leader who will head them victoriously
against the Romans and 'restore the kingdom to
Israel.'   And just because He refused to do this, we
are told a few verses lower down that many of His

vv. 14, 15.

disciples 'went back, and walked no more with Him ;' and for the same cause, a year later, they crucified Him. It is this contrast between the popular Messianic belief and the sublimated form of it, as maintained and represented by Christ, that is the clue to all the fluctuations and oscillations to which the belief in Him was subject. This is why He was confessed one day and denied the next ; because men found that the hopes which had been roused in them were disappointed, and that the Son of Man, though He would preach and heal, yet would not bring them the deliverance or the glories which they desired. For a time they bore with it ; but at last, impatient of constant disappointment, and incensed against claims which did not offer the expected justification, they rejected their proper King for one more after their mind, who at least redeemed the crime of brigandage by the virtue of active sedition.

It is almost superfluous to point out how difficult, how impossible it would have been for a writer wholly *ab extra* to throw himself into the midst of these hopes and feelings, and to reproduce them, not as if they were something new that he had learned, but as part of an atmosphere that he had himself once breathed. There is no stronger proof both of the genuineness and of the authenticity of the fourth Gospel than the way in which it reflects the current Messianic idea [1]. It is only surprising how, with such phenomena before them, critics could have been found to place the composition of it in the middle of the second century, and to explain it by an impossible combi-

---

[1] The subject of the Messianic idea in the fourth Gospel is especially well worked out by Weizsäcker, pp. 260–262.

nation of orthodoxies and heterodoxies, when the true and simple solution lay so near at hand.

St. John vi. 14, 15.

The disciples embark, and Jesus retires alone to pray. Soon after dark a storm arises. The disciples had rowed about five and twenty or thirty furlongs, when they see their Master walking upon the water towards them. At first they are afraid; but He calms their fears, and they receive Him into the ship, which at once reaches land.

vv. 16–21.

This account is much abridged from the Synoptists. The episode of Peter attempting to walk upon the water is omitted altogether. But the 'five and twenty or thirty furlongs' betrays the eye-witness, and agrees sufficiently with the Synoptic 'midst of the sea,' which Josephus says was forty stadia across[1]. I hardly see the necessity, with Lücke and Meyer[2], to press ἤθελον λαβεῖν into opposition to the Synoptists, as though Jesus were not actually received into the ship. The stress is really on the willingness of the disciples. 'Before they shrank back through fear, but now they were glad to receive Him.' The sudden bringing of the ship to land we are tempted to explain psychologically. The Apostle, intent upon the marvellous occurrence and occupied with his own devout conclusions (cf. Matt. xiv. 33 ?), would not notice the motion of the ship; and, a favourable breeze arising, it might easily be at the land before he was aware. At least this may serve as a conjecture. Those who accept miracles because they are compelled to do so both by the quality and the amount of the evidence for them, will of course allow that the whole may be miraculous; but they will notice such features as can

[1] *B. J.* iii. 10. 7.   [2] *Comm., ad loc.*

be reasonably explained otherwise. Those who look upon the question of miracles as foreclosed on *à priori* grounds, cut the knot for themselves easily enough in one way; but in another they are compelled to violate all the canons of historical evidence, or else to fall back upon rationalizing expedients that are considerably more incredible than miracles[1].

The verses which follow, 22-24, describing the transit of a part at least of the crowd from the east to the west bank on the next day, betray a certain literary awkwardness, but great historical accuracy. The position described by the Evangelist is this. The people had seen on the day before that there was only one ship drawn up on the beach—that in which our Lord and His disciples had crossed over. This, we may remark in passing, confirms the statement of the Synoptists that the people themselves had come round by land, just as the fact that they

---

[1] Such for instance is the older mode of explaining the feeding of the five thousand :—The demand for food had been foreseen and secretly provided for; bread had been brought over and was kept concealed in the boat. Less coarse, but not very much less improbable, is the explanation that survives in Keim, ii. 494, 495. The multitude had brought provisions with them which they are persuaded, by example and precept, to divide. Weizsäcker (p. 449) regards the history as an embodiment of the sentences in the Sermon on the Mount; 'Take no thought for this life,' and 'Seek ye first the kingdom of God.' This writer, however, firmly holds to the 'Pragmatismus' of the rest of the Johannean narrative, especially vv. 14, 18, 30. Dr. Keim describes the miracle as 'the greatest and best attested of all those that affect external nature.' I cannot quite understand the grounds on which Dr. Weizsäcker draws the line of credibility at the point where the process of the miracle *ceases to be capable of description* (p. 445). This is surely a very accidental circumstance. It seems to me impossible to carry out this eclectic method of picking out just the difficulties—to be tortured to death in some way or other—and leaving the narrative on each side of them untouched. I feel compelled to believe in the truth of the general narrative—because of its consistency, because of its marvellous and transcendant originality, because of the utter impossibility to account for it either by conscious or unconscious invention; and the difficulties must be accepted in its train.

are now ready to cross the sea tends to show that
they were not, at least that part of them, on the way
to the passover at Jerusalem.   They see that this
single ship has disappeared, that Jesus and His disciples also are gone, and they prepare to follow them.
Presently other boats arrive from Tiberias—perhaps,
as Mr. Blunt suggests [1], driven across by the gale
which was 'contrary' to the Apostles' rowing towards
Capernaum.   They enter into these, and so cross over
to the west side.

The structure of the sentence is somewhat complicated by the parenthesis of ver. 23.   But there is
no argument in this against the truth of the statements which it contains [2].   On the contrary, if these
had been fictitious, we may be sure that they
would have been much simpler.   Indeed a forger
would never have thought of relating how the crowd
got across the sea at all.   We see the natural par-
tiality with which the Evangelist dwells upon scenes
with which he was so familiar.   He had been a fisherman on the sea of Galilee himself.   He knew the
boats of Tiberias from those of Capernaum and the
other cities, and had probably friends or relations in
that very crowd.

Our Lord is found in the synagogue at Capernaum,
and there to a mixed audience, partly composed of
those who had been present at the miracle, and partly
of the more hostile section represented by the Scribes
and Pharisees, he delivers the discourse which occupies the next thirty-three verses of the sixth

St. John vi.
22–24.

St. John vi.
25–71.

---

[1] *S. C.* p. 292.   [2] Cf. Strauss, *Neues Leben Jesu,* p. 496.

chapter.   As in so many of the Johannean discourses, the thought is rather stationary than progressive ; but yet there is a certain development, which we may indicate perhaps by marking off three main divisions : one including ver. 26–34 ; another extending from ver. 35 to ver. 50; and the third beginning with ver. 51 to the end of the discourse.   In the second of these divisions there will be two long parentheses, from ver. 37 to 40 inclusive, and from ver. 43 to 46 inclusive.   These have a separate subject, divine grace as the source of faith ; and it will be best to take them by themselves.   The subject of the rest of the discourse is the 'Bread of Life :' and following our divisions, we may say that *a.* contains the distinction between the material bread and the spiritual bread, ver. 26–34 ; *β.* the identification of the spiritual bread with the Person of Christ Himself, ver. 35–50 ; *γ.* the further definition of it as residing not merely in the Person of Christ, but specifically in His Death, in the giving of His Body and the outpouring of His Blood, which are to be appropriated by the believer, ver. 51–58.

*Marks of a
subjective
element in
the dis-
course.*

Now in the first place we must notice, that this very characteristic of the discourse, its slow progression and continual recurrence to the same point, stamps it as at least deeply tinged with the individuality of the Evangelist.   There are a number of

*Recurrent
forms.*

expressions which recur almost like a fixed refrain, such as verses 39, 40, 44, 54, 'I will raise him up at the last day.'   Verses 33, 50, 58 are almost exactly identical.   So again are verses 35, 48, &c.   Then not only do the ideas recur within the discourse, but some of them are also found almost in the same words in

other parts of the Gospel, and in the Epistle. 'He
that believeth on Me shall never thirst,' reminds us at
once of the discourse with the Samaritan woman,
iv. 14, which is again almost exactly repeated in
vii. 38. Verse 34 again has its counterpart in the case
of the Samaritan woman, just as ver. 52 in the discourse with Nicodemus. The dialogues in the Gospel
seem to be cast to a great extent in the same mould.
They turn upon the same contrast between the true
ideal sense and the false literal sense. They seem to
follow a fixed rule or scheme, and not to reflect the
variety and many-sidedness of life. From whatever
point the discussion may begin it is sure to lead up to
some of the stereotyped Johannean formulae, e. g.
verses 36, 46, 56. And in some of these cases the
logical connection with the rest of the argument is
exceedingly subtle and remote, quite unlike anything
that is found in the Synoptic discourses. This, I
think we may say, is true of the whole of the paren-
thetical matter; but it is especially striking in ver. 46.
It has just been said that no one can come to Christ
who is not drawn by the Father. This expression
'drawn by the Father' is then explained to mean
'heard and learnt of the Father.' But the Evangelist, suddenly seeing that one of his main tenets
is verbally at least endangered, throws in the saving
clause, 'Not that any man hath *seen* the Father.'
'Drawn by'='heard and learnt of,' but does not=
'seen.' That is a privilege reserved for a later stage
in the spiritual life, and is only to be attained
mediately through the Son (cf. i. 18).

We shall have little hesitation then in saying that
a certain amount of deduction must be made from

St. John vi.
25-71.

Digressions.

this discourse as representing rather the words of the Evangelist himself than those which were actually spoken. But how far is the deduction to extend? Does it touch the matter as well as the words? We can only answer this question by instituting a comparison with the Synoptic Gospels and with the Apostolic writings generally.

vv. 26-34.

a. The discourse we are discussing is based upon a miracle—which miracle is also found in the Synoptic Gospels, and is described there in a manner very similar to that in which it is described by St. John. But there is strong reason to think that all the Evangelical miracles have a typical value. It is this indeed which distinguishes them from all other miracles either before or since. When we compare a saying like that in the Sermon on the Mount, 'Every tree that bringeth not forth good fruit is hewn down and cast into the fire' (Matt. vii. 19), first with the parable and then with the miracle of the barren fig-tree, we feel that we have before us only three different grades or kinds of ethical teaching, all having the same object. So again, when the casting out of devils is put side by side with the discourse in Matt. xii. 22-30, 43-45, and the healing of the sick generally with the description of the 'acceptable year of the Lord' in Luke iv. 18, it becomes clear that the miracles reflect and embody the preaching. But if this is the case, then it is highly probable that this miracle, the feeding of the five thousand, has a meaning, and if so, it is difficult to seek it elsewhere than in the application that is given to it by St. John. If we may assume that the Gospel miracles have a typical value—and there is only one so far as I am aware

The typical value of miracles.

(the stater in the fishes mouth), in which that typical value is not more or less transparent—then it is *à priori* probable that on some occasion it would be explained. The Synoptists record no such explanation, though they hint at it more than once—but here in the fourth Gospel it is recorded. And that, I think, is antecedently what we should have expected.

St. John vi. 26-34.

Now let us look at it from a different side. We saw that in the sequel of the miracle in question, the crowd was suddenly fired with the Messianic enthusiasm. But that enthusiasm was as yet undisciplined. It was clothed in those coarse material forms which ran through the whole of Jewish thought at this time. When Papias, bishop of Hierapolis, in describing the glories of the Messiah's kingdom, said that every vine should have 10,000 stems, and every stem 10,000 branches, and every branch 10,000 shoots, and every shoot 10,000 bunches of grapes, of which every bunch would yield twenty-five metretae of wine, he was but standing upon the common level of his contemporaries, and carrying on into Christianity the superstitions of later Judaism[1]. It is frequently

Materialism of the Jewish Messianic expectations.

---

[1] Cf. Oehler, Art. 'Messias' in *Herzog*, ix. 439 : 'Es beginnt dann für das Bundesvolk die Zeit des grössten irdischen Glücks, das bekanntlich von den Rabbinen in der abenteuerlichsten Weise ausgemalt wird.'

'Many affirm that the hope of Israel is, that Messiah shall come and raise the dead ; and they shall be gathered together in the Garden of Eden, and shall eat and drink and satiate themselves all the days of the world ... and that there are houses built all of precious stones, beds of silk, and rivers flowing with wine and spicy oil.' Rambam in *Sanhedr*. c. 10. 'He made manna to descend for them, in which were all manner of tastes, and every Israelite found in it what his palate was chiefly pleased with. If he desired fat in it, he had it. In it the young men tasted bread, the old honey, and the children oil.... So it shall be in the world to come [the days of the Messiah] he shall give Israel peace, and they shall sit down and eat in the Garden of Eden, and all nations shall behold their condition, as it is said, behold my servants shall eat, but ye shall be brought as an objection against the fourth Gospel that it presupposes an incredible amount of unintelligence both on the part of Jews and Samaritans, and on that of the disciples. But those who bring this objection forget the depths of degraded literalism to which the Rabbinical system of interpretation had descended[1]. With this the exalted spiritualism of Christianity could not but be in constant conflict and collision. A miracle such as the multiplication of the loaves and fishes could not fail to be grossly misunderstood. It would be taken at once as the beginning of that reign of earthly abundance, which the prophets were thought to have foretold. It was but a natural consequence that the crowd should seize upon the Author of it and wish to make Him king; and again, that in the synagogue at Capernaum they should press for a repetition and continuation of these Messianic signs. The Messianic theocracy, it was thought, would reflect and reproduce that of Moses, not only in general outline, but also in its details[2]. To this the Jews point; 'Our fathers did

---

hungry.' Is. lxv. 13. *Shemoth Rabba*, sect. 3, quoted by Lightfoot, *Hor. Heb.* p. 552.

[1] It is quite true that amongst a great deal of chaff the Talmud contains many grains especially of practical wisdom. But the instances quoted by Mr. Deutsch in his famous article (*Quarterly Review*, Oct. 1867) do not, and can hardly be intended to, disprove the statement in the text, any more than the scepticism of individual Rabbis like Hillel disproves the existence of a Messianic expectation. The intellectual and religious condition of the Jews at this time is well, and, it would

seem, impartially described by Keim, i. 208-306. Cf. esp. the section on the Pharisees pp. 251-272.

[2] 'The later redeemer [i. e. the Messiah, opposed to the 'former redeemer,' Moses] shall be revealed among them. . . . And whither shall he lead them? Some say into the wilderness of Judah. Others into the wilderness of Sihon and Og. And shall make manna descend for them.' *Midrash Schirm.* 16. 4. The former redeemer caused manna to descend for them, in like manner shall our later redeemer cause manna to come down, as it is written, There shall be an handful

eat manna in the desert; as it is written, He gave them bread from heaven to eat.' And the first step in the discourse is directed to the correction of this mistake. 'Verily, verily I say unto you, Moses gave you not that bread from heaven; but My Father giveth you the true bread from heaven.' *St. John vi. 26–34.*

It is remarkable that, while this discourse is found only in St. John, there should be another in the Synoptists which represents as it were the reverse side of the same subject. Here the bread of life is used as a metaphor in a good sense. There the disciples are warned to beware of the leaven of the Pharisees and of the leaven of Herod! And the metaphor is there too misunderstood, and that in a manner still more gross, and to our modern ideas seemingly inexplicable. But it was a long course of education that the disciples had to go through. They had almost as much to unlearn as they had to learn. It was not until their Master had left them, that they discovered really 'what spirit they were of.' All His life long He had to contend with a dulness and perversity of understanding that was not peculiar to the disciples but was shared generally by their countrymen and had been the growth of centuries. The wonder is less that the husks and shells should still here and there remain, than that such a revolution as was actually wrought should have been possible at all.

The discourse with the disciples concerning leaven is the most direct parallel to the Johannean discourse to be found in the Synoptists; but there are others also that seem to lead up to it. Leaven is used *Synoptic parallels.*

of corn in the earth.' *Midrash* p. 552. Cf. also Buxtorf in Lücke, *Cobeleth*, 86. 4, quoted in *Hor. Heb.* ii. 132.

elsewhere as a simile for the 'kingdom of heaven,' i. e. we may say, either the spread of the new Gospel in the world, or its gradual appropriation by the individual. But the appropriation of the Gospel is almost another name for faith in Jesus Christ Himself.

β. There is indeed a slight step between the two; but it is easily taken. And it depends chiefly upon the idiosyncrasy of the writer, which side is made most prominent. We have seen already that there are many expressions in the Synoptists, which imply that Christ required faith not only in His word, but also in His Person. As a rule these Evangelists give rather the popular side of His teaching, but this feature in it was too prominent for them to ignore. It is indeed part and parcel not of His teaching alone, but still more deeply and radically of His Life. That Life loses a very great part of its significance, unless it is seen that it is to be not only imitated or copied, but personally apprehended and realised by the believer. The believer must become *one* with his Lord, not by any outward conformity but by an inner change.

Such language may sound transcendental and mystical: but the greater part of the Apostolic writings are saturated with it through and through; and not the Apostolic writings alone, but those which express the highest Christian experience in all ages. The state of mind intended is too much of an emotion to be defined; and as an emotion it is too complex in its character to be expressed in a single word. It is blended together of love, gratitude, admiration, awe, devotion, in such a way as to unite them all at once. And though we sometimes use the one word and sometimes the other, still we feel that taken alone they are the part and not the whole. If this is mystical it is not therefore unreal. There is a true mysticism as well as a false. The false is only that which professes to have an intuitive insight into intellectual propositions, which do not in themselves admit of proof. No intellectual proposition is apprehended intuitively; and no proposition is worth believing which cannot in some legitimate and satisfactory way be proved. But here the facts are given by the ordinary laws of historical enquiry. And true mysticism is that emotional, spiritual, and we may truly add, inspired force, by which they are converted out of the abstract into the concrete, and become an active moving principle in daily life. It is by its very nature sober and practical. The unhealthy reveries and nervous excitement, which are sometimes thought to stimulate, really stifle it, because they divorce it from its two great supports, in reason on the one side and practice on the other. The atmosphere in which it breathes most freely is that which is most natural, the calm and tempered yet sympathetic intercourse of man with man.

We cannot call such Christian mysticism unreal; because we see too much of it around us, and in spite of the countless imperfections of humanity to which it is allied, its action is too deep and too beneficial to be numbered among mere illusions. If this is illusion, then we ask in despair, What else is not? To a strict philosophy indeed 'we are such stuff as dreams are made of,' 'the world is a stage, and men and women are but players.' Or in more scientific language, all knowledge and all truth, all rightness,

St. John vi. 35-50.

all goodness, all reality, is merely relative. It holds good only for man as man. What the absolute value of any fact or emotion may be, we can only guess or imagine, we cannot know. But judged by the sole standard that we are capable of applying, the Christian emotions are as real as anything human. So long as the facts on which they rest are not demonstrated to be in their essence false, so long as large masses of the most cultivated portion of mankind are visibly influenced by them, so long as there is no competitive force displaying equal efficacy and activity over the same ground, they will have a right not only to exist, but to govern the lives and actions of men.

γ. The third section of the discourse presents difficulties which have not as yet been raised in connection with the other two. The apparent Eucharistic references which it contains, seem to Lücke and Meyer, if they were true, to be inconsistent with the Apostolic authenticity of the Gospel[1]. That, I think we may say, is established for us by this time too firmly to be shaken. But I proceed to offer a series of considerations which may help to place the bearing of the facts in a clearer light.

(i.) In the first place these commentators seem to limit too narrowly the amount of deflection from perfect accuracy, which is still consistent with the testimony being that of an eye-witness. Words are fluid matter—much more so than visible outward fact. It is difficult to suppose that they could lie for fifty years in the memory—even a Jewish memory—

---

[1] Cf. Lücke, ii. 157, 158. Meyer, p. 271. The latter writes, with his usual decisiveness, 'Diese Erklär- ung . . . kann nur mit *Aufgebung der Authentie* des Joh. bestehen.'

and then be produced in the same shape in which they had entered. The improbability that this should be the case, increases in exact proportion to the originality and native power of the mind in which they are contained. The sharp crisp outlines of tangible facts, presented to the eye and to the senses, it will retain ; but it will mix something of itself with the impalpable substance of thought. It will digest, shape, rearrange the verbal utterances treasured up in it, and they will be coloured by its individuality and the other impressions that it has received.

(ii.) But it is rather Eucharistic *imagery* that we really find than direct references to the Sacrament. The arguments of Lücke and Meyer seem to go far enough to prove this. The substitution of σάρξ for σῶμα (which is found invariably in other parts of the New Testament, and has a different signification[1]), and especially the total absence of any such application by the Evangelist according to his usual custom, point this way. And there is sufficient motive in the miracle itself, conceived first as typifying the relation of the believer to Christ, and then especially the relation contracted through His Death, to account for the substance at least of the ideas expressed in this section without supposing any immediate reference to the Eucharist.

[1] The ‘bread which came down from heaven’ is the σάρξ or Incarnation of Christ, in which the Passion, or offering up of the σῶμα, is but a single moment. Hence while σάρξ is still reserved for the glorified Resurrection-Body, σῶμα is specifically the name for that which died upon the Cross. Thus in accordance with the ground ideas of his theology, the Evangelist, while insisting upon the necessity of Faith in our Lord's Death and Atonement, still does not lose sight of that which is the centre of his system, the perpetual apprehension of the Logos as the Eternal, Incarnate Word. Compare on the signification of σάρξ and its distinction from σῶμα, Lücke, Meyer, Alford, *ad loc.*

(iii.) It is difficult for us to realise or appreciate the extent to which symbolism reached in this age generally, and in the writings of the fourth Evangelist in particular. That in these verses we have a system, not of literal conceptions, but of profound symbolism, is proved by noticing the different expressions that are used as equivalent. 'I am the bread of life: he that *cometh to Me* shall never hunger; and he that *believeth on Me* shall never thirst' (ver. 35). 'Verily, verily, I say unto you, He that *believeth on Me* hath everlasting life. I am that bread of life' (vv. 47, 48). 'He that eateth My Flesh, and drinketh My Blood, dwelleth in Me, and I in him' (ver. 56). Compare with this, 'Whosoever shall confess that Jesus is the Son of God, God dwelleth in him, and he in God. . . . He that dwelleth in love dwelleth in God, and God in him' (1 John iv. 15, 16). By the help of these key-passages we are enabled to determine the general meaning of the discourse. Christ is the bread of life: Faith is the means whereby we partake of that bread, and receive into ourselves its nourishing and sustaining properties. But it must be above all faith in His Death—in Him who died for our sins.

By means of faith we make the virtue of His Death our own, and become partakers of that life which He has with the Father. The doctrine is throughout extremely similar to that of St. Paul. 'If we be dead with Christ we believe that we shall also live with Him' (Rom. vi. 8), nearly = 'Whoso eateth My Flesh and drinketh My Blood, dwelleth in Me, and I in him.' And in proof that the language used is symbolical, we may appeal to 1 Cor. x. 17, 'We being many are one bread, and one body: for we

are all partakers of that one bread '—where the symbolism is evident from the context. A parallel is
drawn which is assumed to be exact between the
Lord's Supper on the one hand, and the heathen
idol-feasts as well as the Jewish sacrifices on the
other. Without conceding to these last any reality,
the Apostle yet argues that they imply the same
relation between the worshipper and the object of
his worship. 'But I say, that the things which the
Gentiles sacrifice, they sacrifice to devils, and not to
God : and I would not that ye should *have fellowship
with* devils.' The words κοινωνοὺς γένεσθαι, μετέχειν,
are applied indifferently to the 'Lord's table' and to
the 'table of devils;' whence it is clear that in both
cases they are symbolical, and that the symbolical
sense is to be preferred in ver. 16, 17. The same
results from a comparison of 1 Cor. xi. 25, 26 with
27, 'As often as ye eat this bread and drink this
cup, ye do *shew* the Lord's death till He come.
Wherefore whosoever shall eat this bread and drink
this cup of the Lord, unworthily, shall be guilty of
the Body and Blood of the Lord.' The idea of
'shewing' is strictly correlative with that of incurring
guilt by appropriation. It is not in accordance with
our modern use to employ symbolism so deeply.
We draw a sharper line between the sign and the
thing signified ; the spiritual truth does not so readily
embody itself with us in material imagery. But the
neglect of this distinction between ancient and modern,
between Latin or Greek and Hebrew, between the
lofty spirit of Christian doctrine and the forms that
it has assumed in contact with particular phases of
thought and civilisation, has been a fertile source of

St. John vi.
51–58.

misunderstanding from the days of the Apostolic Fathers to our own. 'It is the spirit that quickeneth, the flesh profiteth nothing [1].'

We have seen, then, that in this discourse so far there is an important basis of objective fact, and where this is deserted it still keeps strictly within the limits of Apostolic doctrine. A like conclusion holds good for the parentheses, ver. 37–40, and ver. 43–46. 'Him that cometh to Me I will in no wise cast out,' is essentially a Synoptic saying. And the other text, 'No man can come to Me except the Father which hath sent Me draw him,' is entirely in the spirit of St. Paul, though not in his style. It is in fact the Pauline doctrine of election stated in Johannean language.

Casting back a glance over the whole discourse,

---

[1] There is a valuable comment of Lightfoot's (*Hor. Heb.* pp. 553, 554) on this passage. He looks at it from a Hebraist's point of view, and shews (i.) that 'eating and drinking' are common metaphors. 'Every eating and drinking in the book of Ecclesiastes is to be understood of the Law and good works.' *Midrash Cobeleth,* 88. 4 (ii.) That 'bread' is frequently used of 'doctrine.' Is. iii. 1, Prov. ix. 5 are thus interpreted. (iii.) That the phrase 'eating' occurs in connection with the Messiah: 'Israel shall eat the years of the Messiah' (i. e. shall enjoy the plenty and satiety that belong to the Messiah). (iv.) Putting this together with the warning in ver. 63, 'The words I speak unto you, they are spirit and they are life,' he concludes that the discourse is 'wholly parable.' 'But what sense did they take it in that did understand it?' Not in a sacramental sense surely, unless they were then instructed in the Death and Passion of our Saviour; for the Sacrament hath relation to His Death; but this sufficiently appears elsewhere that they knew or expected nothing of that. Much less did they take it in a Jewish sense. For the Jewish conceits were about the weighty advantage that should accrue to them from the Messiah, and those merely earthly and sensual. But to partake of the Messiah truly, is to partake of Himself, His pure nature, His righteousness, His spirit; and to live and grow and receive nourishment from that participation of Him. Things which the Jewish schools heard little of, did not believe, did not think; but things which our Blessed Saviour expresseth lively and comprehensively enough, by that of eating His flesh, and drinking His blood.'

we see plainly that it has nothing whatever to do with Gnosticism, and moves in an altogether different circle of ideas. Election, grace, faith in the Person of the Redeemer, faith in His death, are Apostolic, not Gnostic, themes. The words ἀναστήσω αὐτὸν τῇ ἐσχάτῃ ἡμέρᾳ so trouble Dr. Scholten [1] that he casts doubt upon their genuineness, though they occur in four separate verses, 39, 40, 44, 54. The mode of citing the Old Testament, the allusions to the 'manna,' the demand for a sign, and the Jews' question in ver. 42, 'Is not this Jesus, the son of Joseph, whose father and mother we know?' are all marks of genuineness and of the true date and character of the Gospel. The one trace of the doctrine of the Logos is in ver. 46, 'Not that any man hath seen the Father, save he which is of God, he hath seen the Father;' which however shows from the context in which it occurs [2] how thoroughly that doctrine was engrafted on a system, the roots and stock of which are not Greek but Jewish.

St. John vi. 51-58.

This is the first discourse that we have come to as yet that has a historical notice at the end. But this must not mislead us as to its true character. It had become impossible for the Apostle to separate the subjective and objective elements in his own mind; though we can now to a certain extent reconstruct them by the methods of analysis and comparison.

The Evangelist connects with this discourse the defection of many disciples. The ultimate cause is probably to be sought in our Lord's refusal to assume

vv. 60-71.

---

[1] p. 129.

[2] The preceding verse (45) begins thus, 'It is written in the prophets, And they shall be all taught of God.'

the outward insignia of the Messianic dignity, and in His persistent spiritualisation of the Messianic idea. This is intimated in ver. 63; and it accords well with the importance attached to the confession of St. Peter. This is no mere repetition of i. 41. It was one thing to confess the Messiah, attaching to the word its common meaning, on the testimony of the Baptist; and another thing to renew that confession, now that His character was fully developed, and it became daily more and more evident that to confess Him now would be to open a breach with the whole mass of cherished Jewish traditions and expectations, and to run a risk of sharing the fate which that breach must sooner or later involve. St. Peter deliberately did this, and thereby drew down upon himself the commendation, 'Blessed art thou, Simon Barjona: for flesh and blood hath not revealed it to thee, but My Father which is in heaven.'

It is possible that ver. 65 ('No man can come to Me,' &c.) may contain something of a reminiscence of these last words. Just as ver. 61, 62 seem to point to the prophecies of the Passion, which with the Synoptists begin from about this time, and were an additional cause of offence to half-hearted followers.

The confession of St. Peter is related in terms similar, so far as they go, to the Synoptists, and in part more vividly, though it is considerably abridged from them. The tendency of this passage is not intentionally anti-Petrine; because, if the commendation (Matt. xvi. 17) is omitted, so also is the rebuke (Matt. xvi. 23). St. Peter is rather spoken of throughout the Gospel in a kindly manner, that does justice to his zeal and to his prominence in the Apostolic circle. In the last chapters the Evangelist freely records the intimacy of his own relations with him [1].

Altogether this chapter shows a great superiority over the Synoptists in the sense and appreciation it reveals of the true situation, as a crisis in the development and definition of the Messianic character. The Johannean narrative 'dove-tailed into' the Synoptic makes the latter much more intelligible. And how natural are all these allusions to the inner life and belief of the Apostles, especially to the traitor, if the author of the Gospel were himself an Apostle. Doubtless he had often mused upon the strangeness of the fact that a traitor should have been chosen. Still he cannot but reconcile it with the omniscience of the Chooser. Notice the familiar knowledge implied in the addition, 'Judas Iscariot *the son of Simon*,' which is found again in xiii. 26, but not in the Synoptic Gospels. Is this the work of a forger?

The mention of the 'twelve' now for the first time without further explanation shows that the Synoptic tradition is presupposed. It is important to observe that the phrase is nowhere used throughout the early chapters i–iv, where it is probable that the 'twelve' as a definite body had not been collected.

---

[1] Cf. xiii. 23, 24; xviii. 15, 16; xx. 2 foll.; xxi. 3, 7 foll., 15 foll., 20.

CHAPTER VIII.

THE FEAST OF TABERNACLES.

St. John. vii.

CHAPTER vii, like chapter vi, is very important for the estimate of the fourth Gospel. In it the scene of the Messianic crisis shifts from Galilee to Jerusalem; and, as we should naturally expect, the crisis itself becomes hotter. The divisions, the doubts, the hopes, the jealousies, and the casuistry of the Jews are vividly portrayed. We see the mass of the populace, especially those who had come up from Galilee, swaying to and fro, hardly knowing which way to turn, inclined to believe, but held back by the more sophisticated citizens of the metropolis. These, meanwhile, apply the fragments of Rabbinical learning at their command in order to test the claims of the new prophet. In the background looms the dark shadow of the hierarchy itself, entrenched behind its prejudices and refusing to hear the cause that it has already prejudged. A single timid voice is raised against this injustice, but is at once fiercely silenced.

vv. 1-9.

The opening scene, which is still laid in Galilee, is described by M. Renan [1] as a 'gem of history' (un petit

[1] p. 499.

St. John vii.
1-9.

trésor historique). He argues justly that an apologist, writing merely *ad probandum*, would not have given so much prominence to the unbelief which Jesus met with in His own family. He insists, too, on the individualising traits which the whole section bears. The brethren of Jesus are not 'types' but living men ; their ill-natured and jealous irony is only too human.

The Johannean turn that is given to the language of verses 6 and 7 ('The world cannot hate you, but Me it hateth') might cause suspicion, but they merely express the natural answer, 'You may go up to the feast, for you can do so without danger ; for Me it is otherwise.'

The commentators call attention to an apparent change of purpose. 'I go not up to this feast ;' 'Then went He also up unto the feast.' Before we assume that the change is real, we must be sure that we have before us the exact expression used. But it would seem as if the Evangelist himself intended the meaning of οὐκ ἀναβαίνω to be exhausted by verse 9, 'When He had said these words unto them, He abode still in Galilee.' Οὐκ would therefore be practically equivalent to οὔπω. Still the fact that room has been left for the suggestion of a change of purpose, does not seem to be consistent with the statement that the doctrine of the Logos 'has been carried out through the Gospel with mathematical accuracy.'

vv. 10-15.

An equal degree of authenticity belongs to the verses which follow 10–15. The whispered enquiries and debatings among the people, the secret journey, the sudden appearance in the temple in the midst of the feast, and in particular, the question that alludes to the Rabbinical schools and the custom of professed

St. John vii.
10–15.

teachers to frequent them, compose a varied, clear, and graphic picture that has every circumstance of probability in its favour.

St. John vii.
16–36.

In the dialogue we shall expect to find a larger subjective element; but this does not seem to extend quite so far as in some others. The part of it which is borne by the Jews serves to accredit the rest. The question and comments in ver. 25–27 ('when Christ cometh, no man knoweth where He is'), ver. 31, ('will He do more miracles?'), ver. 35 ('will He go unto the dispersed among the Gentiles?'), vv. 40–43 ('shall Christ come out of Galilee?') are all exactly what we should expect from the popular mode of interpreting and applying the Messianic prophecies. If we do not possess full historical verification on every point, e. g. in ver. 27, the obscurity of the Messiah's origin [1], this does not go far to invalidate it. For our knowledge of the Messianic expectations is too imperfect to warrant us in affirming positively that any particular feature was not included in them. If a similar feature had been found in a less disputed book, e. g. one of the Synoptists, it would doubtless at once have been accepted. And it is difficult, if

---

[1] It is true that the passages usually quoted, Justin *c. Tryph.* p. 226, Χριστὸς δὲ εἰ καὶ γεγένηται καὶ ἔστι που, ἀγνωστός ἐστι κ.τ λ., and p. 336, εἰ δὲ καὶ ἐληλυθέναι λέγουσιν, οὐ γινώσκεται, ὅς ἐστιν κ.τ.λ. are not exactly to the point. For they assert, not that the *origin* of the Messiah will be unknown, but that the world in general and the Messiah Himself will be ignorant *of His Messiahship*, until He is anointed by Elias. And yet the two conceptions are clearly cognate; we could conceive them to be derived from the same prophecy, e. g. Is. liii. 8, or Is. lviii. 10. Another cognate idea is found in Lightfoot, *Hor. Heb. ad loc.* 'A Roe appears and is hid, appears and is hid again. So our first Redeemer (Moses) appeared and was hid, and at length appeared again. . . . So our latter Redeemer (Messiah) shall be revealed to them, and shall be hid again from them; and how long shall he be hid from them,' etc. Compare Meyer *ad loc.* Hilgenfeld, p. 282; Lücke, ii. 212.

not impossible, to conceive any train of thought that could have suggested such a point as an invention. When a statement of this kind is made incidentally and with precision, it may generally be taken as authentic ; at all events the burden of proof must rest with those who deny its authenticity.

The ironical question of the Jews, when our Lord announces His approaching departure, 'Will He go to the Gentiles and teach the Gentiles?' is pointed and natural. And the way in which they insist that the Messiah must come of the seed of David and from David's city, Bethlehem, is confirmed by the first Evangelist's application of the prophecy of Micah (Matt. ii. 5, 6).

We may notice, as equally in character, the telling *argumentum ad hominem* of vv. 22, 23, and especially the correction of ver. 22 ; 'Circumcision is a rite older than Moses, and dating back even to the time of the patriarchs. You allow it therefore to override the obligations of the Sabbath. How much more then should that obligation yield to a work of mercy by which a sick man was made entirely whole?' For the form of the argument, which is altogether cast in a Synoptic mould, we may compare Matt. xxii. 41–45 ('the Son of David'). The concluding verse, 'Judge not according to the appearance, but judge righteous judgment,' may be readily authenticated out of the Synoptists. The proposition is general : but we see that it has especial reference to what precedes, the observance of the Sabbath. 'Aim at observing it in the spirit and not in the letter, and judge others on the same principle [1].' Very similar

[1] We may compare with this the remarkable fragment of tradi-

L 2

St. John vii.
16-36.

to this are the instructions upon prayer and fasting in the Sermon on the Mount, 'Thou, when thou fastest, anoint thine head and wash thy face, that thou appear not unto men to fast, but unto thy Father which is in secret.' Compare Matt. xv. 18–20 ('the things which defile a man').

Ver. 30 is a natural comment of the Evangelist after the event, interpreting the abstention of the Jews from immediate violence, as providentially ordered. How much of such passages as vv. 17, 18 ('he that speaketh of himself seeketh his own glory'); 18, 29 ('I am not come of Myself'); and again 33, 34 ('yet a little while am I with you'), may be due to the Evangelist we cannot say, but probably in each of these cases the basis is original. Something like vv. 33 and 34 is implied by ver. 35, though we should perhaps be right in excluding, with Meyer, the words πρὸς τὸν πέμψαντά με, as apparently too definite to allow of the question which follows. Similarly ver. 28 has both its accurate localisation in its favour, and succeeds naturally to ver. 27. Ver. 17, which asserts the moral qualification for a right belief ('if any man will do His will'), has implied though not direct parallels in the Synoptists; e. g. the converse thought lies at the bottom of Matt. xiii. 14, 15 ('their heart is waxed gross'), also Matt. xi. 21, 22 ('Chorazin and Bethsaida').

St. John vii.
37-39.

Mr. Blunt [1] draws an undesigned coincidence from vv. 37, 38 ('if any man thirst'), on the ground that

tion quoted by Westcott (*Intr.* p. 428), 'On the same day, having seen one working on the Sabbath, He said to him, "O man, if indeed thou knowest what thou doest, thou art blessed, but if thou knowest not, thou art cursed and art a transgressor of the law."'

[1] *Scriptural Coincidences*, p. 288.

on the eighth day of the feast of Tabernacles 'it was
the custom to offer to God a pot of water drawn
from the pool of Siloam.' This act, Mr. Blunt thinks,
was taken as the text for a deep spiritual lesson.
There appears indeed to be some question as to the
matter of fact. Libations took place upon the seven
other days of the feast, but it is somewhat doubtful
whether they also took place on the eighth and last [1].
Perhaps the exclamation in vv. 37, 38 may have
been suggested by the custom. But the coincidence
is hardly sufficiently clear to be used as an argument.

'He that believeth in Me, as the Scripture hath
said, out of his belly shall flow rivers of living water.'
The exact words of this quotation are not to be
found in the Old Testament. The idea may be made
up out of passages like Is. xii. 3, xliv. 3, lv. 1, &c.
but the expression ἐκ τῆς κοιλίας αὐτοῦ seems, in particular, to have no equivalent [2]. The Apostolic
quotations from the Old Testament are, however,
notoriously inexact; and this is, at least in form,
probably Apostolic. That the Evangelist remembered
something similar to it appears from his comment, ver.
39, which has also a strong ring of genuineness. Once
more the Apostle is speaking from his own experience. To him the gift of the Spirit had been the
work of a definite moment; and to that he now
looks back. The chronology is that of his own life,

[1] Cf. Meyer, *Comm.* pp. 310, 311,
also Caspari, pp. 144, 145. It is
objected further against the supposed reference to the libations,
that these would not suggest the
idea of *drinking*. ('If any man
thirst, let him come unto Me and
drink'); but the parallel to this
would be in the drawing of the
water from the pool of Siloam,
and the outpouring of the libation
would symbolise the resulting ef-
fluence of spiritual life.

[2] Cf. Meyer, pp. 311, 312.

which a writer in the second century would not have cared or been able to reproduce. We have here too another instance of the Evangelist's profound use of symbolism.

The concluding section of the chapter contains a graphic description of the meeting of the Sanhedrim. The relation of the Pharisees to the chief priests (who belonged mostly to the Sadducees), to their officers, to the multitude, whose ignorance of the law they despise, to wavering members of their own order, is well preserved. It is not of much consequence that they overlook the fact that the prophet Jonah was by birth a Galilean[1]. Galilee was in any case the part of the two kingdoms least honoured by the prophetic activity; the Messiah was expected to arise out of Judaea; and it is only natural that a point should be strained in the heat of argument. The account of this meeting, like that of the interview in chap. iii, was perhaps communicated to the Evangelist by Nicodemus himself. We shall see later that he seems to have had acquaintances in high place at Jerusalem; and if Nicodemus was not among them at the first, he may have become so during the long period that the Apostles remained at Jerusalem. It is noticeable that most of the early Christian documents—the Acts as well as the Synoptic Gospels—contain more or less detailed accounts of transactions in the Sanhedrim.

In reviewing the chapter we cannot but see that it

---

[1] Gath-hepher, the birthplace of Jonah, was situated in the territory of Zebulun. This is the only clear exception. It is possible that Nahum the Elkoshite may have been also a native of Galilee. One tradition places Elkosh there, but another in Assyria. Thisbe, the birth-place of Elijah, was in Gilead, across the Jordan. With respect to Hosea, we do not know more than that he was a prophet of the northern kingdom.

has added largely to the already abundant proof that the standpoint of the Evangelist is strictly that of a Jew of Palestine and of a contemporary. The doctrine of the Logos has receded far into the background ; and though it may, perhaps, have helped to determine the selection of the subject, as part of the great conflict between light and darkness, still in the execution it has given way to an entirely different circle, both of language and of ideas. The fact that these are so marked *in spite of* the theology of the prologue, is a proof at once of the tenacious nationality of the author, and of his strictly historical motive in writing.

St. John vii. 37–39.

Few results of textual criticism are more generally accepted than that which removes the twelve verses from vii. 52 viii. 11, from their present context and from the fourth Gospel[1]. There is much acuteness and plausibility in the suggestion of Dr. Holtzmann, which has some countenance from the cursive Mss. of St. Luke, that they originally formed part of the ground document of the three Synoptists (the 'Urmarcus'), and that their proper place is among the events of the last week before the Passion. But this is a question that we need not go into. The chronological question, too, as to the number of days covered by the events of chapters vii. viii. and ix. is one that cannot receive any decisive answer; vii. 14–31, we know, falls about the middle of the feast of Tabernacles ;

St. John viii. The woman taken in adultery.

The chronology of these chapters.

---

[1] Lachmann, Tischendorf, Tregelles, Alford, Meyer, omit or bracket them. Compare also Ellicott, p. 253, text and note. Dr. Holtzmann's theory is worked out in his *Synopt. Ev.* pp. 92, 93.

vii. 37 falling on the last day of the feast: but where we are to draw the line, as marking the conclusion of that day, is not clear. The next definite date that we possess is in x. 22, the feast of Dedication, which is separated from the feast of Tabernacles by an interval of two months. It is hard to say how far the intermediate discourses are to be regarded as continuous, or even to which extremity of the period they are to be attached. On the whole it appears best to place the chief break at x. 21; there is a slighter one at the end of chapter vii; and the discourses in chapter viii. are probably to be placed in close proximity to the cure on the Sabbath-day in chapter ix.

Taking up the narrative at viii. 12, we find much to which it is difficult to assign the highest objective value. The opening verse, 'I am the light of the world: he that followeth Me shall not walk in darkness, but shall have the light of life,' is remarkable as illustrating the Evangelist's peculiar syncretism. The conception of 'light' belongs as much to the Old Testament as to the Philonian philosophy. It is found in Messianic passages like Is. ix. 1 ('the people that sat in darkness'), xiii. 6, 7 ('a light of the Gentiles'), Mal. iv. 2, 3 ('the Sun of Righteousness')[1]. These seemed to blend and be assimilated very completely with the doctrine of the prologue. Indeed the starting-point of the Evangelist appears to be everywhere the Old Testament: and it was only because it had so many points of affinity and contact with this that the philosophy of Philo had such

---

[1] So the Talmud, 'Light is the name of the Messiah' (Lightfoot, *Hor. Heb.* p. 564).

attractions for him.   The dialect of the two systems
was nearly the same ; and in passing from the one to
the other, it was only necessary to give to the same
terms a somewhat different and more abstract meaning, and to co-ordinate them somewhat differently
with one another.   However, in the case before us, it
is probable that the groundwork of the saying is
not Johannean, but authentic and original.   In the
Sermon on the Mount, it is true, we find, not 'I am
the light of the world,' but 'Ye are the light of the
world.'   But the two sayings do not at all exclude each
other.   Both St. Matthew (iv. 15, 16, 'The people
that sat in darkness'), and St. Luke (ii. 32) adopt
the prophecies of the Messianic light, and St. Luke
gives it the same universalizing turn that it has here
in St. John—'A light to lighten the Gentiles and the
glory of Thy people Israel.'   That which is peculiar
to St. John, is the close individual relation which he
assumes on the part of the believer with the Person
of Jesus.   But this, as we have seen, is in accordance as
well with the Evangelic as the Apostolic tradition, and
has been from the first an essential part of Christianity.

The Pharisees dispute this exalted self-assertion :
'Thou bearest record of thyself ; thy record is not
true.'   The answer is double.

(1) If My witness stood alone it would still hold
good ; for it is based upon a consciousness that
reaches far beyond yours.   I know whence I came
and whither I go, what lies beyond the sphere of
this My earthly existence : you judge merely as men,
'after the flesh,' or by the senses [1].

vv. 14-16.

---

[1] Ye judge after the flesh, [I
judge no man].   This is another
instance of the way in which the
Johannean discourses suddenly start

(2) But My witness is not Mine alone ; it is also that of My Father. And your own Law says that the witness of two men is true [1] ; how much more such witness ?

In the argument thus nakedly stated there are traces of extreme condensation. At first sight it seems more like a Rabbinical sophism than one of the 'words of life'; but by referring to the parallels in v. 36–38 and xiv. 10, 11, we perceive that it is really a highly condensed expression of what is there given more fully. Of the 'two witnesses,' one is the self-evident force of truth—or of the personal embodiment of truth—apprehended by ethical sympathy ('If any man will do His will, he shall know of the doctrine whether it is of God') : the second is that of which the outward manifestation is in the miracles and miraculous signs of the Divine approbation (xii. 28, &c.).

Still it is difficult to regard this condensation as otherwise than forced ; the dialogue leaves little room for it ; and the recurrence of the argument tends to make us hesitate in accepting any one form of it as completely authentic. That there is at least an authentic basis, is guaranteed by the exact note of place in ver. 20, 'These things spake Jesus in the treasury, as He taught in the temple.' The reminiscence of the actual discourse may have been somewhat obscured in the Apostle's mind.

away upon some merely verbal association. None of the many attempts to bring the words in brackets into the strict line of the argument can be called successful. Certainly not, 'I judge no man *now*' (Augustine, Chrysostom, and others)—the 'now' is quite arbitrarily introduced ; nor 'I judge not after the flesh, as you do' (Lücke), 'no man's person' (Ewald), which cannot be got out of the Greek ; nor 'I come not to judge but to bless' or 'save' (Luthardt and Meyer). This is the true sense ; but the idea of 'saving' is quite foreign to the argument—it is a sudden digression.

[1] The phase of the moon had to be attested by two persons ; cf. Lightfoot, *Hor. Heb.* p. 565.

Again, the Evangelist sees the hand of Providence
restraining the keen irritation of the Pharisees.

The interview is continued; and our Lord repeats
the announcement of His approaching departure. 'A
time will come when you will repent of these lost
opportunities. Then you will seek and will not find
Me; then too you will know who it is that you have
lost.' The connection appears to be confused by that
reiterated self-assertion, which was indeed there, but
which the Evangelist regards somewhat too exclusively. We can well believe that there was more in
the original of the winning pathos of the lament over
Jerusalem (Luke xix. 42–44); in which case we could
perhaps better understand the concluding statement,
'As He spake these words, many believed on Him.'

The new converts, who come forward with a profession of faith, receive a word of encouragement as
well as of warning. They were not to mistake a
momentary impulse for a deliberate conviction. 'If
ye continue in My word, then are ye My disciples
indeed; and ye shall know the truth, and the truth
shall make you free.'

These words are taken up apparently by some of
the bystanders, who understand them partly in the
sense in which they were spoken, as having reference
not to national but to individual freedom, but miss
that spiritual sense to which their whole habits of
mind made them inaccessible. The Jewish pride of
birth naturally prompts their question. They were
descendants of Abraham; they had never been slaves
to any man; how could they be made free? But
there is something strange in the answer, direct and
appropriate though the main portion of it is: 'Verily,

verily, I say unto you, Whosoever committeth sin is the servant of sin. And the servant abideth not in the house for ever: but the Son abideth ever. If therefore the Son shall make you free, ye shall be free indeed.' We seem almost to be hearing an echo of the words of St. Paul (Rom. vi. 16–23), 'Know ye not, that to whom ye yield yourselves servants to obey, his servants ye are to whom ye obey; whether of sin unto death, or of obedience unto righteousness?' and again (Gal. iv. 30, 31; v. 1), 'Cast out the bond-woman and her son . . . . we are not children of the bondwoman, but of the free . . . . the liberty where-with Christ hath made us free.' Does or does not this resemblance imply a relation of dependence? Probably advocates would be found for both views. If the resemblance had been to the other division of the canonical Epistles, those of St. Peter, St. James, and St. Jude, there would have been no difficulty: we should have inferred at once that the similar passages had a common origin; in fact that the Johannean record was strictly authentic. But the 'revelation' which St. Paul claimed certainly would not include details of expression and phraseology such as these. It is possible that in Philo or the Rabbinical schools some such figure of speech may have been current. But it is not by any means in-credible that St. John should actually have seen the Pauline Epistles. The phenomena of the Epistles to the Hebrews, of St. Peter, and of St. James, seem to prove a somewhat free circulation and interchange of the Apostolic literature; and the fourth Gospel is later in date than any of these. We must notice however that the Pauline doctrine is not reproduced

crudely, but is assimilated with the rest of the Johannean system, and has received the genuine Johannean
stamp. This we see by the repetition of μένει (frequent in St. John, rare in St. Paul), and in the emphatic ὄντως ἐλεύθεροι.

Another argument that seems to throw doubt upon
the originality of the passage is found in the peculiar
transitions and ellipses of the thought. 'Whosoever
committeth sin, is the servant of sin. And the
servant abideth not in the house for ever: but the
Son abideth ever. If therefore the Son shall make
you free, ye shall be free indeed.' The connection
between the first two clauses is distant and subtle.
The qualification under which the figure of servitude
is introduced is dropped entirely. The servitude (of
sin) suggests the idea of servitude in the abstract:
and to this the idea of sonship in the abstract is
opposed. Then there is a further transition from
the abstraction of sonship to the Son in the concrete
—the Messiah. And in the inference there is a gap.
It is assumed that the Son must communicate His
own attributes to those whom He emancipates. The
thought is indeed throughout profound and instructive ; and to a Jew, always ready to picture to himself
the theocracy or the kingdom of heaven under the
form of a 'household,' it would be easily intelligible—
and yet I doubt much whether any clear parallel can
be adduced from the Synoptists. The difficulties that
we find in them ('Wisdom is justified of her children,' 'Make yourselves friends of the mammon of
unrighteousness,' 'Where the body is, there will the
eagles be gathered together') are quite different.
The mode of thought is rather Apostolic—essentially

Apostolic, Jewish, of the first century, but not of that universal elemental kind which distinguishes the 'words of the Lord.'

Does it follow from all this that the discourse, or at least the opening of it, is an ideal composition? I think not. It is difficult to escape the conclusion that in form at least it has been considerably modified. But there is much dramatic propriety in the Jews' appeal to their descent from Abraham. And the relations of social subjection are largely used in the Synoptic Gospels to illustrate ethical and spiritual truths. We seem to have here a combination and subtle development of two passages, 'No man can serve two masters' (Matt. vi. 24), and the discourse respecting the tribute-money (Matt. xvii. 25, 26, 'the children are free'). We may also see something of a parallel in Matt. xii. 29, the strong man armed (the tyranny of sin) subdued by one stronger. The ground idea is doubtless evangelic.

The next section, which extends from ver. 37 to ver. 47, is occupied by a different subject. From the liberty which belongs to the children of the kingdom, the argument passes to the Jews' claim to be considered children of Abraham. This is shown in its true light and character. After the flesh they are children of Abraham. But in spirit they have a very different parentage. Abraham would not have done what they are doing. Their actions show from whence they are. Their murderous designs, their rejection of the truth, can only come from him who was a murderer and a liar from the beginning.

Here again there is dramatic propriety, and we are reminded of Synoptic phrases, 'The wicked and

adulterous generation,' 'the child of hell' (Matt. xxiii. St. John viii.
15), 'the tares are the children of the wicked one'
(Matt. xiii. 38). Generally there are points of connection both with the dispute with the Pharisees in
Matt. xii. 22–30, and the denunciation of them in
Matt. xxiii. It is likely that dialogues of this sort
would be of not infrequent occurrence, especially just
at this time when the conflict is reaching its climax.
It is likely too that they would be of the nature of
dialogues broken by impatient interruptions on the
part of the Jews, and not always a continuous strain
of denunciation as in Matt. xxiii.

In the last section, from ver. 47 to ver. 58, the Jews vv. 48–59.
retort the charge of ver. 44, and they allude to the
counter-assertion as one that was current among
themselves, ' *Say we not well* that thou art a Samaritan and hast a devil?' Our Lord answers, first, by
asserting that His work has a far different character
from that which they attribute to it; and then by
appealing to that Divine testimony which He bears.
Not only so, but even Abraham himself bare witness
to Him. To him was accorded a prophetic vision of
the Messiah. And now that vision was fulfilled.
The discourse ends with an assertion of pre-existence,
at which the Jews are incensed to fury. And it was
with difficulty—almost, the Evangelist would seem to
suggest, by miracle—that Jesus escaped them.

The discourse as a whole seems to be a strange Mixed character of the discourse.
mixture of original and added elements. It contains
some singularly vivid flashes of reminiscence, among
which perhaps the most remarkable is that in ver.
48. Nowhere else do we find the designation 'a
Samaritan'; yet it would naturally—we might say

inevitably—be given to one who seemed to attack the exclusive privileges of the Jewish people. On the other hand, 'He casteth out devils by Beelzebub, the prince of devils' (Matt. xii. 24), was, according to the Synoptists, the way in which the Pharisees accounted for the influence that Jesus possessed over the unclean spirits. The crowning stroke is given by that vivid piece of dramatic reproduction, '*Say we not well?*' Doubtless these accusations formed part of the calumnies that were circulated among the people by the Pharisaic party. But the whole of the Jews' reasoning throughout the discourse is strictly what we should expect from them. These constant appeals to their descent from Abraham, these repeated imputations of diabolic possession, this narrow intelligence bounded by the letter, this jealousy of anything that seemed in the slightest degree to trench on their own rigid monotheism— all these, down to the touch in ver. 57, in which the age they fix upon in round numbers is that assigned to completed manhood, give local truth and accuracy to the picture; which in any case, we may say confidently, must have been drawn by a Palestinian Jew, and was in all probability drawn by a Jew who had been himself an early disciple of Christ.

For precisely at that very point where the record seems to deviate from the pristine standard of accuracy, we seem to see a further indication that its author was really an Apostle. There is a sensible difference between these discourses and their parallels in the Synoptists. Set them side by side with the denunciatory discourse in the first Gospel, Matt. xi. 20–24, xii. 38–45, and xxiii, and we cannot but

feel that another spirit has come over them. In
St. Matthew we have outpourings of righteous in-
dignation, the object of which is moral obliquity.
Even in the passage (Matt. xii. 38–42) where the
Messianic side is brought out most prominently, it
is *repentance* that is in view rather than *belief;* 'the
men of Nineveh *repented* at the preaching of Jonas.'
The call to repentance was universal, inexorable.
Belief was complicated by a thousand difficulties.
Hillel or Gamaliel might have been perhaps little
less severe upon their contemporaries than Christ;
but would Hillel or Gamaliel have believed? Yet
these personal claims are put forward almost exclusively by St. John. And the lash is inflicted
without tenderness, without mercy. There is none
of that yearning pity that the attentive ear may
distinguish as a deep sustained under-chord beneath
the most withering invectives of the Synoptists. 'Ye
are of your father the devil, and the lust of your
father ye will do.' . . . . 'O Jerusalem, Jerusalem!
thou that killest the prophets, and stonest them which
are sent unto thee, how often would I have gathered
thy children together, even as a hen gathereth her
chickens under her wings, and ye would not!'

Who is most likely to have introduced such
changes? Who but an Apostle? One to whom
his Master had been indeed all in all; his light;
his life; the giver of all truth, and the source of all
goodness. With what temper would he regard those
murderers who had slain the Holy One? If we can
conceive any one in whom bitter irreconcilable hate
would be at once natural and pardonable, it would be
in *him*. It was not the lapse of time or remoteness

of place, or the spirit of party, or any *à priori* system of philosophy, that implicated the nation in the sin of individuals, and dried up in part the milk of human kindness in a breast that by nature was singularly full of it. That which possessed this power was the recollection of a single scene enacted long ago upon the hill of Calvary. To the Apostle the darkness that hung over Jerusalem was never removed ; even in his old age, and in the peace of his Asiatic home, it still cast its shadow over his recording page.

We observe a certain rise and fall in the accuracy of the Apostle's recollections ; and this in proportion as he has some definite, visible, external fact, to which to attach them. The more completely his record is taken up with discourse, the less unreservedly is it to be trusted—and *vice versâ*. Accordingly in chapter ix, where the scene is frequently shifted and the dialogues are short and broken, we have admirably fresh and lifelike history. The question in ver. 2, 'Master, who did sin, this man or his parents, that he was born blind,' is thoroughly true to Jewish character[1], and the answer agrees with the Synoptic tradition. The continuation possibly may not have belonged to this context. With regard to the pool 'Siloam,' both the topography and the etymology are correct[2]. The scene, when the blind man returns seeing and is questioned by

---

[1] This is abundantly illustrated from the Talmud; cf. Lightfoot and Schöttgen, *ad loc.*

[2] 'Missio (aquarum)' appears to be the proper force of the word (Meyer).

his neighbours, is vividly described. So too is the
whole of that which follows, when the Pharisees come
upon the stage. We may accept it with little short
of absolute credence. If the opponents of miracles
could produce a single Jewish document, in which
any event, known not to have happened, was described
with so much minuteness and verisimilitude, then it
would be easier to agree with them.

St. John ix.

But, as it is, the dilemma seems to admit of no
escape. Either we must believe in an unparalleled
natural occurrence, or else we must believe in an
unparalleled phenomenon of literary composition. If
the work before us had been composed in Greece four
centuries earlier, or if it had been composed in England,
sixteen, seventeen, or eighteen centuries later; or if
it had been composed by a person of flexible, quick,
versatile mind who possessed the faculty of readily
sinking his own personality—it would not have been
so incredible. But the author of the fourth Gospel
stands out a single isolated figure, with a loftiness
and intensity to which there is hardly a parallel to
be found in history; with a force of character that
transmutes and transfuses all the more ductile matter
that comes within its range, and yet with a certain
childlike simplicity in the presence of external facts.
This is not the personality of great writers of fiction
in any country or time : least of all is it the personality of one writing under a feigned name, and
asseverating all the time that he records nothing but
that which he has 'heard and seen.' It must be
remembered too that if it is a fiction it is not
merely a fiction that would fit in equally well to
any point of space or time. It is a fiction which is

Difficulties
in the way
of treating
the Johan-
nean
miracles as
' fiction.'

Anachron-
isms
involved.

laid in definite localities, and in the midst of circumstances and a circle of ideas that are remarkably definite. It is written after a series of tremendous changes had swept away all the landmarks to which it might have been affixed. The siege and destruction of Jerusalem, together with the rapid progress and organisation of Christianity, caused a breach between the ages before and behind it, which could be crossed only by memory, not by imagination. Those who deny the Johannean authorship of the Gospel require the supposed author of it to transgress the conditions of his age and position, and to throw himself back into another set of conditions entirely different to his own. They do not indeed do this in words; but this is, as I have tried to show, and as I think we cannot but see, because they have failed to take in by far the larger part of the phenomena. The hypothesis of Apostolic and Johannean authorship satisfies these, while it satisfies also, as I believe, all the other phenomena as well. It gives a consistent and intelligible account of *all* the facts, and I venture to say that no other hypothesis as yet propounded has done so. When we come to look at them, not from the point of view of a system obtained *per saltum* from a few scattered particulars, but embracing the whole of the particulars and casting away all preconceived notions whatsoever, then we gradually find that a single and clear conclusion emerges, that the Gospel is really the work of the Apostle St. John.

Looking back over the ninth chapter in the light of this conclusion, there is little in it that needs comment or explanation. It is all veritable fact and history.

The means by which the miracle took place we cannot analyse. It is enough for us to know what were the actual objective facts, without attempting to penetrate behind them. Whether the miracle was caused by a suspension of existing laws or the introduction of a higher one, whether it was an acceleration of natural processes or a new and unknown process, what relation the natural means employed may have had to it, we have no data to determine ; at least none beyond the fact itself. The moment we leave that we embark on a field of speculation where there is little to guide us, and where indeed we do not need to be guided. The essential point is that the miracle was connected with the Personality of Him who claimed to be the Son of God. Having assumed that, we have a ' ratio sufficiens ' for all that is required.

We need not read into the blind man's confession in ver. 35, 38 more than is psychologically natural and probable. It would necessarily be determined by the characteristics of the Messianic idea as it was received and as he understood it. The special inspiration that Bp. Ellicott seems to introduce, is not in accordance with what we know respecting God's dealings with man. Inspiration, as we gather its nature inductively, is a heightening of natural conditions, not a production of unnatural ones. But why should we go beyond that which is written? The belief of the blind man is no measure for ours.

The concluding verses of the chapter contain a saying which is thoroughly in the manner of the Synoptists, and has a parallel as regards its substance in Matt. xi. 25, 26, and frequently as regards the metaphor ' blind ' applied to the Pharisees

St. John ix.

The process of miracles inscrutable.

(cf. Matt. xv. 14, xxiii. 16, 17, 24). It also supplies a warranty for ascribing a typical significance to miracles.

That the Synoptists do not relate this miracle of the healing of the blind man does not affect its historical character, as the whole of these events in Judaea are equally omitted by them. Almost all the miracles contained in the Synoptic Gospels are taken from a single document, but they derive a fictitious appearance of completeness from their repetition in a triple form. The vague and shifting outlines of the Synoptic narrative allow ample room for all the insertions that are made in them with so much precision by St. John.

CHAPTER IX.

THE ALLEGORY OF THE GOOD SHEPHERD.

St. John x.

vv. 1–21.

THE form of the discourse in the first half of chapter x. is remarkable. It resembles the Synoptic parables, but not exactly. The parable is a short narrative, which is kept wholly separate from the ideal facts which it signifies. But this discourse is not a narrative; and the figure and its application run side by side, and are interwoven with one another all through. It is an extended metaphor rather than a parable. If we are to give it an accurate name we should be obliged to fall back upon the wider term ' allegory.'

Allegory and parable.

This, and the parallel passage in chapter xv, are the only instances of allegory in the Gospels. They take in the fourth Gospel the place which parables hold with the Synoptists. The Synoptists have no allegories as distinct from parables. The fourth Evangelist has no parables as a special form of allegory. What are we to infer from this? The parables certainly are original and genuine. Does it follow that the allegories are not?

We notice, first, that along with the change of form there is a certain change of subject. The parables generally turn round the ground conception of the kingdom of heaven. They express its nature, its constitution, its laws, its spirit, and if we may say so, its history. But though it was always understood that the kingdom of heaven centred in the Person of its King, the Synoptic parables do not enlarge on the relation which He bears to the separate members. We have seen however in St. John how much more this particular side of the Evangelic teaching is thrown into relief. We have seen that it was by no means entirely wanting in the Synoptists. There are several isolated sayings which relate to it directly. The miracles, if we understand them rightly, have a typical reference to it. Some of the parables indeed border upon it nearly—such as that which contains the history of the foundation of the kingdom under the figure of the wicked husbandmen; or again, the marriage-feast. But though in these the royal dignity of the Son is incidentally put forward, there is nothing which expresses so closely and directly the personal relation of the Messiah to the community of believers, collectively and individually, as these two ' allegories ' from St. John. Their form seems in an especial manner suited to their subject matter, which is a fixed, permanent and simple relation,—and a *relation*, not a history of successive states, of growth and development, or a description of particular acts and phases of conduct or feeling. The form of the Johannean allegories is at least an appropriate one.

We notice next that even with the Synoptists the use of the parable is not rigid. All do not conform precisely to the same type. There are some, like the Pharisee and the Publican, the good Samaritan, and the Rich Man and Lazarus, which 'give direct patterns for action[1],' and are not therefore in the strict sense parables. They are not parables in the same sense in which the Barren Fig-tree, or the Prodigal Son, or the Ten Virgins, or the Labourers in the Vineyard are parables. They do not represent God's action under the figure of human action, or circumstances and conditions of human life in figures borrowed from external nature, but they are examples of conduct and character held up directly for avoidance or imitation. If, then, the parable admits so much deviation on the one side, may it not also on the other?

Lastly, we have to notice the parallels to this particular figure of the Good Shepherd that are found in the Synoptists. These are indeed abundant. We should have almost a direct parallel in the parable of the Lost Sheep, if it were not somewhat ambiguous who is meant by the Shepherd—though from the description of the Messiah's mission, 'I am not sent but to the lost sheep of the house of Israel,' we might be tempted to think that a Messianic reference was contained in it. In any case this appears in Matt. ix. 36 ('But when He saw the multitudes, He was moved with compassion on them, because they fainted, and were scattered abroad, as sheep having no shepherd'), which, when taken with Matt. xi. 28, 29 ('Come unto Me all ye that labour and are heavy laden'), gives almost an exact parallel to the Johannean allegory.

It has been observed however that in St. John we have really two separate parables mixed up together, the key to which is given in the one case by the expression 'I am the good shepherd,' in the other,

[1] Cf. Westcott, *Intr.* p. 456.

'I am the door.' For this we have fewer parallels in the Synoptists, though the figure is not unknown to them, e.g. 'the strait gate and the narrow way,' and 'the wide gate and the broad way' in the Sermon on the Mount. There the difference corresponds to that which we usually remark between the Synoptists and St. John. For nearer parallels of sense as well as of words we must go to St. Paul: Eph. ii. 18 ('Through Him we both have access by one Spirit unto the Father'); Rom. v. 2 ('By whom we both have access by faith into this grace wherein we stand').

The general conclusion at which we should arrive from these considerations would seem to be, that there is no sufficient reason for saying, that the discourse contained in the first half of this tenth chapter is otherwise than authentic and original in its main outline both as to form and matter. In the case of the first figure, that of the Good Shepherd, we can trace a gradual progression leading up to it naturally in the Synoptic Gospels themselves. In regard to the second figure this is wanting: but it is vouched for by its exact parallelism to the first. In no case does the Evangelist overstep the circle of Apostolic teaching, or the legitimate and necessary inference from premises that the Synoptists supply.

The peculiarities of form in this discourse are probably also in the main original. But supposing that they are not, the kind of modification which they exhibit suggests much more the unconscious action of an active mind upon matter that had been once faithfully committed to it, than the conscious invention or deliberate transformation of a forger. Why does the author keep so near to the old lines?

Having diverged from them so much, why should he not have diverged more? It is to me far more probable that he has been restrained by a fund of positive indissoluble memories, than that he is consulting proprieties of composition. The change, so far as there is a change, is the spontaneous and natural development of a basis of fact, not the conscious construction of fiction.

The first statement of the allegory in verses 1–6 is extremely tender and beautiful. If the words are in part those of an Apostle, they are the words of that Apostle 'whom Jesus loved,' and upon whom, more than upon any of the rest, the mantle of his Master had fallen.

Ver. 8 has caused some difficulty. 'All that ever came before Me were thieves and robbers.' These are not to be interpreted too definitely of false messiahs, traces of whom before these words were spoken are hardly sufficiently distinct[1]. They are exactly the 'wolves in sheeps' clothing' of the Sermon on the Mount. It is possible that the form of the saying may have been affected by the Apostle's actual recollection of false prophets. The πρὸ ἐμοῦ is difficult to understand, but is possibly not original. And the Apostle, looking back over a long life, need not have observed an absolutely accurate chronology. Still there may be a reference to personages like Herod and Judas the Gaulonite, who seemed or attempted to restore the kingdom to Israel, but in a wholly wrong way. We cannot tell how far the Messianic expectations may have been worked upon by political adventurers.

[1] Cf. Meyer *ad loc.*; but compare also Keim, i. 244, 245.

The universalism of ver. 16 ('other sheep I have'), which is so often quoted against the Gospel, seems rather to be exactly of the kind of which we have abundant evidence in the Synoptists: e.g. in Matt. viii. 11, 12 ('Many shall come from the east and from the west'); Luke xiii. 28, 29—according to Dr. Holtzmann, from the λόγια of St. Matthew; Matt. xiii. 24–30, the parable of the Tares, from the same document; Matt. xxv. 31 ('Before Him shall be gathered all nations'); Matt. xxviii. 19 ('Go and teach all nations'). A certain precedence is assigned to Israel, but the inclusion of the Gentiles is distinctly contemplated. There can be the less objection to the verse before us, as it is placed by the Evangelist in the latest portion of the public ministry, when similar utterances were doubtless plentiful. Neither can I see a sound objection in the fact that the Apostle St. John belonged at first to the Judaizing party. The exclusiveness of this party has been much exaggerated: but, supposing the Apostle to have held all that is attributed to him, by the time he wrote the Gospel the success of the heathen mission and the destruction of Jerusalem could not fail to modify his views, and to revive in him a number of latent reminiscences, convincing him that the more liberal doctrine of St. Paul had received in advance his Master's sanction. If other Apostles, e.g. St. Matthew, went through this process, there is no reason why we should not also attribute it to St. John. And there can be no doubt whatever that the evangelisation of the Gentiles, even if not directly commanded, was an immediate and inevitable consequence of the teaching of Christ. On the other hand, the amount and nature of St. John's universalism must not be mistaken. As laid down in this verse it is not only consistent with, but it implies, a privileged position on the part of the Jews. And that this is really maintained by the Apostle is proved by iv. 22, i. 11, viii. 29–40, &c. Reckless statements have been made with reference to this supposed universalism; but it is found to be in perfect harmony with the Apostolic teaching generally, and so far as it represents a development, it is such a development as would be caused simply by time and the progress of events. The Apostle's foot is firmly planted in the old dispensation. The new has, as it were, grown up round him, but he holds fast to the organic connection between them. Abraham prophesied of Christ; Moses, by the gift of manna, by the brazen serpent, by the stricken rock, foreshadowed Him. Moses too was a lawgiver, and his laws are not to be broken. Salvation is of the Jews. Christ cometh of the seed of David. He is the Jewish Messiah, and He fulfils the Jewish prophecies. To the Jews He first directs His call; and it is only when they do not receive it that He turns to the Gentiles. Yet even so they are the first occupants of the fold, and the others are but gathered in to them. 'Many shall come from the east and from the west, and shall sit down with Abraham, Isaac, and Jacob.' It is the same thing in other words.

The conception of verses 17, 18, though not the expression, is Pauline (cf. Phil. ii. 5–11), or rather Apostolic (cf. Acts ii. 23, 24; v. 31), with the exception that here the Resurrection is regarded as self-caused[1]. The voluntary nature of the sacrifice of Christ and its relation to the will of the Father is brought out in the Synoptic Gospels, especially in Matt. xxvi. 39 (parallels). It is possible that these verses, or the saying to which they correspond, did not originally belong to this context, but were suggested by the conclusion of ver. 11 and ver. 15. Again, the comments of the people are given in a very natural

form. Up to this point the events recorded appear to belong to the visit occasioned by the feast of Tabernacles in chap. vii. The last day of this feast would fall, according to Wieseler's calculations, on October 19[2]. But here there is a break in the narrative, and we are carried in ver. 22 to the Feast of Dedication (December 20, Wieseler), when our Lord is still or again in Jerusalem.

The feast of Dedication (Encaenia) was of comparatively recent institution, commemorating the purification of the temple by Judas Maccabaeus from the profanations of Antiochus Epiphanes. It is not a feast the name of which would be likely to occur to any one but a Jew; still less the accurate note of place in ver. 23 ('And Jesus walked in the temple in Solomon's porch'). Both these verses proclaim the eyewitness. So does the admirable question in the verse following. Attracted by His teaching and His miracles, but repelled by His persistent refusal

---

[1] As Meyer justly observes, the difference is that between the 'causa efficiens' and the 'causa apprehendens.' 'Das Wieder*nehmen* des Lebens, wozu der gottmenschliche Christus ermächtigt ist, die Wieder*gabe* voraussetzt. Diese Wiedergabe von Seiten Gottes, durch welche Christus ζωοποιηθεὶς πνεύματι wird (1 Pet. iii. 19), und jene ἐξουσία, welche Christus von Gott hat, sind die beiden Factoren der Auferstehung, von welcher aber der erstere die Causa *efficiens*, die ἐξουσία Christi hingegen, die Causa *apprehendens* ist.'—*Comm.* p. 405.

[2] Compare the tables, *Chron. Synop.* p. 435, Eng. Tr.

to assume the Messianic character such as they understood it, the Jews ask Jesus directly, 'How long
dost thou make us to doubt?' (τὴν ψυχὴν ἡμῶν αἴρεις,
'keep us in suspense') 'if thou be the Christ, tell
us plainly.'   It is such a question as at this period
of the ministry was inevitable, and the language in
which it is expressed exactly represents the real
difficulties and hesitation that the Jews would feel.

Our Lord is made to answer now as elsewhere in
St. John by appealing to His miracles.   And He
explains the unbelief of the Jews also as elsewhere
in St. John by the doctrine of Predestination and
Election.   This again is one of those few marked
recurrent themes which seem to displace so much
of the rich ethical material of the Synoptists.   We
have hardly yet had a single discourse in which it
does not occur; in the prologue, i. 12, 13; in the
discourse with Nicodemus, i. 3 (ἄνωθεν, 'from above');
the testimony of John iii. 27; the discourse after
the healing of the impotent man, ver. 21; that in
the synagogue at Capernaum, in the two parentheses, vi. 37–40, and 44; it is alluded to again in
ver. 65, and in the discourse we have been discussing,
viii. 44, 47; it occurs also in the later discourses.

This is, as we have seen, Apostolic doctrine both
Pauline and Petrine, but the nearest approximation
in the Synoptic Gospels is the much less dogmatic
expression '*revealed*' ('unto Peter,' Matt. xvi. 17;
'unto babes,' Matt. xi. 25).   We are led therefore
to think that, though the doctrine may be founded
upon sayings of our Lord Himself, still these were
hardly so frequent or so prominent as would appear
from St. John.   And this supposition is confirmed

when we observe that most of the passages in question have but little to do with their context. They are more like the reflections of an aged Apostle meditating on the wonderful course of the events through which he had passed, than the practical and ethical, or even the theological teaching of the Gospels. Still, in the verses before us, there is a natural reference to the preceding parable or allegory; just as in vi. 65 there was an allusion to the previous discourse, which can hardly have had other than a historical basis; it is possible therefore that these two may be amongst the passages that come nearest to the original.

The doctrine of Predestination and Election is joined with another Johannean doctrine, that of the unity of the Son with the Father. This too derives additional probability from the place which it holds at this advanced period of the history, and similar claims certainly formed the ground of accusation before the Sanhedrim. We notice, however, that in spite of this high Christology, St. John does not suppress the phraseology of subordination which is found alike in all the Apostolic writings. The theology of the prologue does not intrude into the historical portions of the Gospel. There we find a different set of conceptions, which, if they end in a conclusion that the Evangelist himself regards as equivalent, reach it by a different channel[1]. The Son is sent by the Father,

---

[1] So Phil. ii. 9 by the side of 8; Col. i. 15, *b* by the side of *a*; Eph. i. 20 by the side of 21, 22; 1 Cor. iii. 23, xi. 3, xv. 28; Acts ii. 36, v. 31; Rev. iii. 12, 14, 22, &c. Compare Schultz on Rom. ix. 8 in Jahrb. f. d. T. 1868, iii. [Dr. Keim's latest position is that the Evangelist contradicts not so much the Synoptic Gospels as himself, ii. 394, 395. The fuller discussion of this must be reserved.]

as the prophets were sent by Him. But the Son St. John x.
is sent in a peculiar and unique sense. The perfect
love and perfect obedience, the absolute surrender of
His own will to that of the Father, make Him in
return a peculiar object of the Father's love, and the
select organ of the Divine revelation. He is endowed
with the full Messianic powers and prerogatives, more
especially with the power over life and judgment. He
gives life, both spiritual and physical, to whom He
will. He judges men now, and will judge them hereafter. By the symbolical significance of His miracles
He establishes the plenipotentiary character of His
mission. It is indeed the Father Himself who works
them (xiv. 10), dwelling and abiding in Him as the
source of spiritual life (vi. 57). Thus the Son, both by
His works and by His person, is a revelation of the
Father, and no further revelation is needed.

The practical conclusion from this is, that 'all men
should honour the Son, even as they honour the
Father. He that honoureth not the Son, honoureth
not the Father that sent Him.'

But the origin and source, as well of the unique
commission which the Son bears, as of the unique
honours which are to be paid to Him, lies in His
perfect ethical union with the Father, His absolute
self-abnegation, and the love which the Father bears
to Him (v. 20; xviii. 23, 26).

In this the fourth Gospel is essentially at one with
the Synoptists, and with the Apostolic writers generally. By the title 'Son of God' the same ethical and
spiritual Homoousia is indicated. And in the voice
which accompanies the Baptism and the Transfiguration (Matt. iii. 17; xvii. 5) it is alleged as the ground

N

of the Messianic commission, just as in Phil. ii. 9, &c. it is alleged as the ground of the subsequent exaltation.

Throughout the New Testament the Son receives His commission, His powers, His glory from the Father. He is sent by Him, He is raised from the dead by Him, and by Him exalted to His own right hand. And therefore there is a sense in which St. John too, like the other New Testament writers, would accept the words, 'My Father is greater than I' (xiv. 28), and in this chapter, 'My Father is greater than all.'

This conception is strictly borne out by the remarkable *argumentum ad hominem* in vv. 34–36. In answer to the charge of blasphemy incurred by claiming unity with God, Jesus appeals to the language of Scripture in Ps. lxxxii. Certain unjust judges, understood here of the Israelitish judges as representatives of the theocracy, are there called 'gods.' *A fortiori* then, if they could without blasphemy receive this title, much more could He, whom the Father had sanctified and sent into the world, designate Himself as the 'Son of God.' It is noticeable that the accusation of the Jews is not admitted exactly as it is made; but that the term 'Son of God' is substituted in the reply. The predicate θεός is applied to the Son in the prologue i. 1, and also in Rom. ix. 5, but always as a predicate[1]. If we are to accept the reading μονογενὴς Θεός in i. 18, it is a ἅπαξ λεγόμενον in the New Testament. The argument, though essentially Jewish, is yet not without a universal value, because it is based upon the realisation of the theocracy of which the previous history

---

[1] Compare a passage quoted from Epiphanius (the synod of Ancyra) by Professor Lightfoot, *Commentary on Philippians*, p. 110.

and constitution of the Jews had been an imperfect St. John x.
and typical embodiment. If the Jews were not satisfied
with this argument from Scripture, they ought to be
by the argument from miracles, especially by miracles
so distinctively Messianic in their character.

The chapter ends with a note of place which is vv. 39-42.
evidently and certainly historical. No forger would
ever have thought of the periphrasis 'where John at
first baptized.' 'And Jesus went away again beyond
Jordan into the place where John at first baptized;
and there He abode. And many resorted unto Him,
and said, John did no miracle: but all things that
John spake of this man were true.' It would be impossible to find a stronger incidental proof that the
author of the Gospel had been originally a disciple
of the Baptist, or at least his contemporary, and also
that he is writing of things that he had heard and
seen. A Gnostic, writing in Asia Minor, even though
he had come into relation with 'disciples of John,'
would not have introduced the Baptist in this way.
In circles that had been affected by the Baptist's
teaching, and were hesitating whether they should
attach themselves to Jesus, this is precisely the sort
of comment that would be heard. Very likely the
Evangelist may be wishing to commend Christianity
to the disciples of John in the district in which he is
moving; but he would not have done so thus, unless
the suggestion had come from facts that he actually
remembered.

CHAPTER X.

THE RAISING OF LAZARUS.

St. John xi.

IT is right that we should bear in mind the impression which we carry over with us from the end of the last chapter, now that we come face to face with the one great, and I may say, crucial question of the Gospel—the Raising of Lazarus. I cannot estimate the amount of conviction produced in the reader by the argument so far as it has gone; but my own conviction, I confess, is strong. The theological, the literary, the historical data have all hitherto seemed to attest the Gospel as a work of the Apostle. On any other hypothesis it is difficult, I think impossible, to account for them. Are all these threads of proof to be suddenly unravelled, and the whole work undone, because we are brought into the presence of a fact, which, if a fact, is only explicable as a miracle? That will depend, it is true, partly upon the philosophical conception which the reader may have formed as to the antecedent improbability of miracles. But the subject ought not to be dismissed until some conception has also been formed of the weight of evidence for miracles from other sources.

'John did no miracles: but all things that John spake of this man were true.' If legend has been active upon the history of Christ, how is it that

Historical evidence for the reality of miracles.

it has left untouched the history of the Baptist which is so intimately bound up with it? In the Synoptic Gospels it is not one document or one set of traditions alone that includes miracles, but all without exception. The mass of the Synoptic literature can be proved to have been in existence at the time of the destruction of Jerusalem. At that time it appears in such a state of literary development as to throw back the date of original composition considerably earlier. The earliest documents of the Acts—documents which still present the politico-theocratic hopes in their crudest form (Acts i. 6, cf. Luke xxiv. 21), and are characterised by the most rudimentary Christology—bear witness to the same belief. Some of the miracles related in the Synoptists are of the most stubborn character, and refuse to yield as well to the rationalizing as to the mythical hypothesis. They are connected with sayings that bear the certain stamp of genuineness, e.g. in the case of the Syrophoenician woman, the paralytic, the centurion's son. The miracles are referred to in discourses which have never been disputed, e.g. Matt. xi. 20, 23, xii. 24. They are assumed in narratives like the Temptation, which have a deeper meaning than any of which the Evangelists were conscious, and therefore cannot be the product of invention. The great facts of the Resurrection and Ascension are assumed in the earliest epistles from the year 52 onwards. The possession of miraculous powers is treated by St. Paul as a matter of course, and he claims to have performed miracles himself [1].

Putting all this accumulated mass of historical proof

---

[1] Cf. Rom. xv. 19; 1 Cor. xii. 10, 28; 2 Cor. xii. 12; Gal. iii. 5.

together, with the observations that have already been made upon the exceptional nature of the Christian miracles themselves, the ease with which they admit of a typical and spiritual application, and the peculiar relation which they seem to hold as a pragmatic climax to the teaching; and further, looking to the unique and transcendent phenomenon presented by the personality of Jesus Himself, he will be a bold man who should ignore all this positive and sub-sidiary weight of proof in deference to an *à priori* conception of incredibility, which on philosophical grounds alone is far from certainly tenable. I prefer to abide by the ordinary canons of historical evi-dence; and if we confine ourselves to these, the evidence for miracles is abundant and conclusive.

vv. 1–46.

Not least so is it with reference to the miracle before us—the Raising of Lazarus. An unbiassed reader coming to this narrative, and putting its miraculous character for the moment out of sight, would, I think, naturally conclude that it was history of a very high order, and that it bore all the marks and signs of having been written by a person who had been present at the occurrence himself. The narrative begins with much circumstantiality. We are introduced fully to the personages who are to act in the drama that follows. A minute touch is thrown into the sister's message, 'Lord, he whom Thou lovest is sick;' and this is explained, 'Now Jesus loved Martha, and her sister, and Lazarus.' 'When He had heard therefore that he was sick, He abode two days still in the same place where He was. Then after that saith He to His disciples, Let us go into Judaea again.' The disciples naturally try

to dissuade their Master from returning into the midst
of danger that He had but lately escaped. The
answer breathes that calm divine resignation to the
Father's will, which was soon to undergo so sharp a
trial : 'Are there not twelve hours in the day ? Is
not My time appointed ? When it comes it will
come, and I shall fall into the hands of My enemies,
but till then their malice will spend itself in vain.'
Presently our Lord breaks to the disciples in a figure
the death of Lazarus, and when they fail to understand Him, He tells them plainly Lazarus is dead.
He motions to go, and Thomas, brave and impulsive
though desponding, springs to His side, 'Let us also
go, that we may die with him.'

They find upon their arrival that Lazarus has lain
in the grave four days. 'Now Bethany,' we are told,
'was nigh unto Jerusalem, about fifteen furlongs off.'
Thus the fact is accounted for that there were many
Jews there who had come to condole with the sisters
for the loss of their brother. The news comes that
Jesus is near, and Martha—as we should gather from
St. Luke—the more energetic and less sensitive of
the two, rises and goes to meet Him, while Mary
remains broken down by her sorrow in the house.
A very natural and beautiful dialogue follows, in
which we notice especially the way in which Martha
puts off the questions that are addressed to her.
The first is implied in the assurance, 'Thy brother
shall rise again.' To this she answers, 'I know that
he shall rise again in the resurrection at the last day.'
And then, when those lofty words are spoken, 'I am
the resurrection and the life,' and she is asked if she
believes them, she covers her failure to understand

them with the confession which was by this time common among the disciples, 'Yea, Lord, I believe that Thou art the Christ, the Son of God, which should come into the world.' The readiness and un-embarrassed vigour of her answers, combined with a not very profound intelligence, is all characteristic. So is the haste with which she returns and fetches Mary, who rouses herself by an effort to follow her sister. Jesus and His disciples have been by some cause or other delayed, and they are still at the place where Martha met Him. Mary no sooner sees Him than she falls down at His feet (we are not told that Martha did this), and exclaims in words similar to those of Martha, 'Lord, if Thou hadst been here, my brother had not died.' But, unlike Martha, this is all she can say. She is not ready with any profes-sions or protestations. Her heart is full, and it is with difficulty that she can speak at all. 'When Jesus therefore saw her weeping, and the Jews also weeping which came with her, He groaned in spirit and was troubled, and said, Where have ye laid him? They said unto Him, Lord, come and see. Jesus wept.' Once more He is heard to groan, and they come to the grave. We notice that the saying in ver. 39 is ap-propriately put into the mouth of Martha. The stone is taken away, and now the weeping and the groaning, by which even the Saviour Himself had been wrung, are hushed. A moment's prayer, and then He cries with a loud voice, 'Lazarus, come forth. And he that was dead came forth, bound hand and foot with graveclothes: and his face was bound about with a napkin. Jesus saith unto them, Loose him, and let him go.'

Such is the simple ending of a narrative that the highest art could not excel. Is there any other art than the unconscious touch of nature and truth? One most remarkable feature in the history is the coincidence between the characters of Mary and Martha as depicted here and in St. Luke. If it is a designed coincidence, if these characters are altogether a fictitious creation, we can only say with Meyer that instead of a historical miracle we have presented to us a literary miracle of the second century, 'a creation of the idea at a time which bore within itself the conditions for a very different class of creations [1].' To this century belong some of the earliest Apocryphal Gospels, and it is needless to say that those dry products of superstition do not afford the remotest parallel to the tender humanities of the Apostle.

The argument from the silence of the Synoptists, which is much insisted upon by some critics who have not formed for themselves a clear and accurate conception of what the Synoptic Gospels are [2], really counts for but little. We are accustomed to regard the Synoptic Gospels as three,—but for the outline and by far the greater part of their narrative they are virtually only one. The groundwork of them all is supplied by a single document, that document itself a compilation, and, as there is ample evidence to show, a very fragmentary one [3]. Considering that the Synoptists know nothing (though we have seen that they imply something) of events in Jerusalem before the last

St. John xi.

The character of Mary and Martha.

The silence of the Synoptists.

[1] *Comm.* p. 439 ad in.
[2] Even Dr. Keim still presses this argument, i. 132.
[3] In St. Mark's Gospel the only records of this period (four months, Keim, ii. 336) are comprised in forty-five verses, x. 1-45.

Passover, we cannot be surprised that they should omit an event which is placed at Bethany.

The raising
of the dead.

The significance of their silence too has been exaggerated by looking at it in the light of modern ideas. To us the raising of the dead stands apart from other miracles in a class by itself as peculiarly unexampled and incredible. But that it was not so regarded at the time when the Gospel was written appears from this very narrative, where the Jews are made to ask whether He who opened the eyes of the blind could not have prevented the death of Lazarus altogether. So, in the Synoptists, the answer that Jesus gives to the disciples of John groups together every class of miracle, the raising of the dead amongst them, without distinction. Similar narratives in the Synoptists, in the Acts, and in the Old Testament, are given without any special relief or emphasis. And if the fourth Evangelist himself does lay more stress upon them, this belongs rather to his own peculiar conceptions than to the circle of popularly current ideas.

Authentic
character of
the narra-
tive.

In a narrative of that high degree of authenticity that we have been led to vindicate for this, we must not look for much that is unhistorical. If there is anything, it is perhaps the repeated declarations according to which it would seem to be asserted that the circumstances had been from the first providentially ordered so as to lead up directly to the miracle. This might very well be the view taken after the event by an Apostle, and might easily affect to some extent his account of it.

The intense humanity attributed to Jesus, His affection, His visible suffering, the effort with which

He collects Himself, are all strong marks of authenticity, and the more so because they might be thought to conflict with the doctrine of the prologue. But this is one more proof how little that doctrine has disturbed the Evangelist's true historic recollection.

M. Renan[1] urges, in proof that the raising of Lazarus must have had some sort of reality, its intimate connection with the succeeding portion of the Gospel 'which contains an amount of minute information infinitely superior to that of the Synoptists.' 'If we reject it as imaginary,' he says, 'all the edifice of the last week in the life of Jesus, to which our Gospel gives so much solidity, crumbles at one blow.' We may doubt whether the reality contended for by M. Renan, who reduces the miracle to a *malentendu*[2], satisfies this condition; but the argument still remains valid.

As to the hypothesis of a *malentendu*, or the supposition that a didactic sentence, ('I am the resurrection and the life,') has been wrapped up in an ideal history, we can only say that, if this explanation is to hold good here, there is no reason why it should not all through the Gospel. There is no reason why the Gospel should not be, from first to last, what M. Renan so vigorously repudiates, a purely ideal composition. The raising of Lazarus stands or falls with the rest of the narrative. It presents precisely the same characteristics; the same circumstantiality

---

[1] p. 514.

[2] 'Le nom de Lazare, que le quatrième Évangile donne au frère de Marie et de Marthe, parait venir de la parabole *Luc* xvi. 19 et suiv. (notez surtout les versets 30-31). L'épithète de "lépreux" que portait Simon et qui coincide avec les "ulcères" de *Luc* xvi. 20-21, peut avoir amené ce bizarre système du quatrième Évangile.' *Vie de Jésus*, p. 354 n. 'There is a river in Macedon, and there is a river in Monmouth.'

(verses 1, 2, 6, 16, 17, 20, 28–30, 32, 38, 39, 44, 46), the same topographical accuracy (ver. 18), the same natural accessories (verses 8, 19, 31, 36, 37), the same tender breathing human life. The marks of authenticity, though strong, may not be so absolutely convincing as they are elsewhere, but still they are the same in kind as the other phenomena of the Gospel; and, if we put upon these one interpretation in one place, we must also in another. The Gospel is like that sacred coat 'without seam woven from the top throughout;' it is either all real and true or all fictitious and illusory; and the latter alternative is, I cannot but think, more difficult to accept than the miracle.

Controversies as to historical probability are always difficult to bring to a conclusion, and therefore I suppose it must remain an open question whether the final arrest and condemnation of our Lord find the best and fittest preparation in the Synoptists or in St. John. At any rate the Johannean narrative is consistent and consecutive in itself. It is not intended that we should suppose the meeting of the Sanhedrim to be called solely in consequence of the raising of Lazarus. It is only that, as coming at the end of a series of miracles, which determines the hierarchic party to take definite action. Ver. 48 throws singular light upon their motives, which the Synoptic Gospels alone would leave much in the dark; 'If we let Him thus alone all men will believe on Him: and the Romans will come and take away both our place and nation.' The Sanhedrim, especially the Pharisaic section of it, was a national and patriotic body. It was the inheritor and guardian of the Rabbinical theories as to the Messiah. There can have been no class in the nation in which these were so inveterately ingrained[1], and therefore none that was so little accessible to the teaching of Jesus. It was from first to last unintelligible to them. It seemed to abandon all the national hopes and privileges, and to make it a sin to defend them. If it were successful, it seemed as if it must leave the field open to the Romans. The national existence would be crushed without a struggle ; and the hierarchy itself would vanish with it. It is rarely in ancient literature that we find a highly complicated situation so well understood and described.

A point has been made by the Tübingen critics out of an expression in the next verse—'Caiaphas being the high priest that same year'; as if this implied a yearly tenure and change of office[2]. But this is not at all necessarily involved in the words. 'That fatal year' they probably mean ; but in any case the knowledge of Jewish customs and Jewish history displayed by the Evangelist is beyond question. This comes out indeed immediately in the peculiar oracular functions attributed to the High Priest, and in the conception of unconscious prophecy which the Evangelist applies here. It is also involved in the notice of ver. 55, 'And many went out of the country up to Jerusalem before the passover to purify themselves.' There is really no book of the New Testament which, so far as its matter is concerned, bears such clear and

---

[1] This is acknowledged on all hands, in spite of the fact that individuals like Philo ignored the Messianic prophecies, or like Hillel, supposed that they had been already fulfilled.

[2] Cf. Hilgenfeld, p. 297 n.; Schwegler, *Nach-apostolische Zeit-alter*, ii. 350. This point is given up by Keim, i. 133.

St. John xi.   unmistakeable marks of Jewish origin as the fourth
———   Gospel.

Ephraim.   The historical value of these last verses is very high.
                There is some difference of opinion among com-
                mentators as to the exact position of the city called
                Ephraim, but not for any want of data supplied either
                by St. John or by other sources. Eusebius says that it
                was eight, Jerome twenty miles from Jerusalem. There
                seems to be no sufficient reason why it should not be
                identified with the Ephraim mentioned in Josephus,
                B. J. iv. 9. 9, and in 2 Chron. xii. 19, as in the
                neighbourhood of Bethel[1]. According to Vaihinger
                the wilderness would then be that of Bethaven, though
                from the article ἐγγὺς τῆς ἐρήμου we should naturally
                take it as the wilderness of Judaea. There are many
                of these geographical identifications in which it is
                impossible to arrive at certainty. It is enough for us
                to be sure, as we may be here, that the writer had a
                precise and definite locality before him.

                     [1] Cf. Vaihinger, in *Herzog.* iv. 93.

CHAPTER XI.

THE TRIUMPHAL ENTRY INTO JERUSALEM.

WE are not told how long our Lord and His disciples stayed at Ephraim. If we are to put faith in the tradition contained in the Talmud, and in the inferences which Dr. Caspari draws from it, an actual verdict of death was passed at the recent meeting of the Sanhedrim, and was only waiting for its execution until an opportunity offered, and the legal period for the production of witnesses in the defence had expired. This would make the interval between the retreat to Ephraim and the Passover coincide more or less nearly with the forty days allowed. The data however are not such as we can build upon confidently.

St. John xii.

The stay at Ephraim.

The harmonistic combination of this later portion of the Johannean narrative with that of the Synoptists also appears to aim at an amount of accuracy which is unattainable. It is best to hold fast to the general scheme given by St. John, and to treat the Synoptic sections, especially those in St. Luke (ix. 51–xviii. 35) as fragments of a great picture which are more or less fortuitously thrown together, and are no longer capable of an exact reconstruction.

Chronological uncertainty.

Apparently, on what would be, according to our reckoning, the Friday evening, but according to that of

The arrival at Bethany.

St. John xii.

the Jews, soon after the commencement of the Sabbath before the Passover, Jesus and His disciples enter Bethany. We gather this as well from the law which prohibited a long journey upon the Sabbath day, as from the fact that time was allowed for the preparation of a supper on the evening of the same day, i.e. at the *end* of the Sabbath, and nearly twenty-four hours afterwards.

Superiority of the Johannean narrative.

We can have no hesitation in following here the very precise narrative of St. John in preference to that of the Synoptists, according to which this supper would seem to have occurred four days later. Looking at the synopsis of the three Gospels, St. John, St. Matthew and St. Mark, it is impossible to doubt on which side the superiority lies.

Its relation to that of the Synoptists.

The natural construction to put upon the words 'but Lazarus was one of them that sat at the table with Him,' certainly seems to be that Lazarus was a guest and not the host : but if so, there is no contradiction with the Synoptists, who place the feast in the house of Simon the Leper. There may have been some relationship or friendship between Simon and the family of Lazarus. St. John is alone in identifying the unnamed 'woman' of the Synoptists with Mary, Lazarus' sister. He is alone in calling attention to the rich odour of the ointment ; he is also alone in assigning the complaint, which the Synoptists agree with him in mentioning, definitely to Judas the traitor, and in the account which he gives of the position and character of the false Apostle. This is an extremely natural touch, if we suppose the Evangelist and Judas to have been Apostles together. The detestation in which Judas was held by the

Apostolic circle may well have had its origin further back in suspicions such as those which are here recorded. This trait in his character, too, gives peculiar appropriateness to his remonstrance. St. John is anxious to remove the imputation from the other Apostles, and fixes it upon its real author, explaining the motive by which it was prompted.

In some of the other details of the Johannean narrative there are remarkable coincidences with the Synoptists, which apparently rest upon a basis of actual fact, but in regard to which it is highly probable that the memory of the Apostle had been refreshed by a previous perusal of the Synoptic Gospels. Thus there is, in common with St. Luke, the statement that Martha served, and, in common with St. Mark, the remarkable epithet πιστικὴ, and the term τριακοσίων δηναρίων, in common with both εἰς [τὴν ἡμέραν τοῦ] ἐνταφιασμοῦ μου.

If this narrative had stood alone, we might have hesitated to say whether it had not been entirely constructed upon that of the Synoptists—though even then the number of details peculiar to St. John would involve a difficulty. They point, as I think, rather in the direction of original reminiscence, but do not in this particular instance lie so wide as to be beyond invention. While it is natural that an Apostle should recall his own early suspicions of the traitor, it is not so very unnatural that legend or fiction should fasten similar suspicions upon him.

But when it is remembered that coincidences of this sort are confined, so far as we have gone at present, to this narrative and the feeding of the five thousand, that along with them we have a greater

O

St. John xii.

Coincidences.

Independence of St. John.

St. John xii.

number of instances where the Synoptists are corrected, that the character of the Gospel in general is one of bold originality, and that all the narrative portions alike present this same accurate minuteness, it becomes clear that the only tenable hypothesis is that which we have accepted — that the Evangelist has not copied existing documents, but has only had latent impressions revived by them, which have served to lend additional distinctness to his description.

The narrative as a whole is vouched for by the saying in ver. 8 (' The poor always ye have with you; but Me ye have not always'), which is of indubitable authenticity. It also goes to confirm the Johannean Christology. Those who realize most deeply the true relation of Jesus to the poor, will feel how vast are the claims here enunciated — enunciated, too, with that calm and simple authority which is its own legitimation.

The entry into Jerusalem.

The entry into Jerusalem is also contained in all four Gospels. In St. John it appears in an abridged form, which however offers nothing that conflicts with the Synoptists. The acclamations attributed to the multitude are important, and deserve attention. We have these clearly in their fullest and most original form in St. Mark : ' Blessed is He that cometh in the name of the Lord : *Blessed be the kingdom of our father David*, that cometh in the name of the Lord ; Hosanna in the highest.' The allusion to the theocratic king is evidently original. St. Matthew has omitted it entirely. St. Luke has reduced it to the single word 'king.' St. John gives a shorter but fully equivalent form, ' the King of Israel.'

Once more, as in ii. 23, vii. 39, the Evangelist tells

us how the application of the prophecy of Zechariah | St. John xii.
was not apparent at the first, but gradually dawned
upon the disciples, as they afterwards came to reflect
upon the events they had witnessed. This coincidence
with Luke xxiv. 25, 26 is probable in itself, and
furnishes another not inconsiderable proof that it was
an Apostle who wrote the Gospel.

The composition of the crowd, and the motives by
which it was actuated, are well described by St. John.
We gather from ver. 12 that it consisted partly or
chiefly of pilgrims who had come up for the feast.
Many of these were probably Galileans who were
already prepared to acknowledge Jesus as the Messiah. Some, we see from ver. 18, were attracted especially by the great miracle that had taken place at
Bethany. M. Renan has noticed the repeated references to this miracle, and evidently feels that these
are inconsistent with his new theory of *malentendu ;*
he therefore exerts all his finesse and dexterity of
style to sustain as a possible alternative his earlier
view, which makes the miracle, in plain words, a
preconcerted fraud[1]. However much we may allow
for the peculiarities of Oriental character, this can
only be taken as an instance of the desperate re-
sources[2] to which those are driven who deny miracles
à priori, and yet are at once too clear-sighted and
too conscientious to underrate the historical evidence
for them.

Ver. 19 ('Perceive ye not how ye prevail nothing') | Survey of the position.
well marks the climax of the Pharisees' opposition,

---

[1] *Vie de Jésus.* Appendice, pp. 510-513.
[2] Compare *The Jesus of History*, pp. 177, 178 n.

and the climax also of the success by which it was provoked. Our Lord had probably more disciples now than at any other period of His ministry. The entry into Jerusalem, as if it were the beginning of the Messianic reign, would give fresh impulse to their enthusiasm—though there would be few in whom it would survive the 'stumbling-block of the cross.' This would be quite sufficient to account for the almost total desertion that followed His death, so that the Apostles had as it were almost to rebuild the Church from the foundation. The visible results of the life of Jesus might have been summed up in the definite and loyal attachment of the Apostles and some few others, and in the creation of a general susceptibility to Christian teaching. But in this small seed what wonderful powers of growth and expansion lay hidden!

Interview
with
Greeks.

In verses 20 foll. we have the account of an interview with certain Greeks, i. e. persons who, by birth Gentiles and heathens, were now apparently, from their having come up to the feast, proselytes in the remoter degree.

They are introduced, under circumstances that are closely narrated, by Andrew and Philip; and it speaks well for the historical truth of this episode that nothing further is said respecting them. The object of the Evangelist may be, probably is, that assigned by Bengel, Baur and Meyer, to indicate the transference of the kingdom of God to the Gentiles, and to bring out by contrast the unbelief of the Jews. But if the circumstance had not been originally historical it would doubtless have been more enlarged upon. Appropriate speeches would have been put into the

mouth of these proselytes, and they would have re- |
ceived a more directly appropriate reply.

The reply that St. John gives is not addressed so
much to the proselytes as to the disciples—perhaps
in particular the two, Andrew and Philip—and shades
off almost into soliloquy.   The approach of these
Greeks suggests to Jesus the thought of His death,
the great instrument through which the Gentiles were
to be gathered in.

Ver. 24 (' Except a corn of wheat'), there is every
reason to think, must be authentic.   Ver. 25 ('He that
loveth his life shall lose it') is found also in the
Synoptists in a different context, and perhaps a truer
one, though it is not unnatural that the Apostle
should refer it to this.

Ver. 27 foll. hardly excludes or takes the place |
of the agony in the Garden.   As the feeling there expressed was not momentary or transient, the scene
itself may well have been repeated in its essential
features.   That the voice from heaven was a real
objective fact is rendered probable by the comments
which are so naively given in ver. 29.

Ver. 34 adds to our already large collection a |
Rabbinical inference from passages like Isa. ix. 7,
Dan. vii. 14, which none but a Jew, and probably none
but an ear-witness, would have thought of introducing :
' We have heard out of the law that Christ abideth
for ever : and how sayest thou, The Son of Man must
be lifted up ? Who is this Son of Man ?'   Here too we
have the secret, unexplained by the Synoptists, why
even when the scale is seeming to turn for a moment
in favour of belief, it is continually swayed down
again by the discovery of some new particular in

St. John xii.

Retrospect.

which the current ideas respecting the Messiah are disappointed and contradicted. Therefore it is that the Evangelist, in bringing the first half of his Gospel to a close, and in reviewing the results which had so far been obtained, can only explain their comparative smallness by that judicial blindness of which Isaiah had prophesied when he saw and spake of the advent of the Messiah. 'And yet,' he adds with the candour of a historian, but with the bitterness of one who had been himself a confessor and apostle, 'even among the Sanhedrim many believed in Him; but because of the Pharisees they did not confess Him, lest they should be put out of the synagogue. For they loved the praise of men more than the praise of God.'

The conflict portrayed in the Gospel, not purely ideal ;

So far the subject of the Gospel may be brought under the categories of the prologue as the history of the conflict between 'light' and 'darkness.' We may, if we please, see in the various scenes of the drama which have been hitherto unrolled before us, so many typical representations of this contact of the 'light' successively with different portions of that chosen people to whom it came—sometimes entering in, but more often rejected, and at last compelled to throw its beams elsewhere, and illuminate regions that sat in darkness. But, if we do so, we shall not therefore recognise anything but the most *bonâ fide* history. The principle that the Evangelist has pursued is one of selection, not of invention. The latter hypothesis is by every class of considerations decisively excluded. On the contrary, when certain deductions have been made for a kind of monotony which results from the limited number of subjects put forward for dogmatic

exposition, the great opposition itself is portrayed in a
manner singularly lifelike and intelligible.   In the
fourth Gospel we see this opposition in its true
character as essentially national.   It is the conflict of
the Messianic idea as popularly understood and
authoritatively expounded, with its spiritual counterpart.   The interval was not one that could be crossed
in a moment.   And the higher our conception of that
idea which is embodied in Christianity—the more
lofty and pure we believe it to be—the more easily
shall we comprehend the difficulty that it found in
penetrating minds not dishonest, in the highest degree
brave and tenacious, but encrusted and overgrown
with narrow prejudices, and stunted and perverted by
false method.   Most curious indeed is it to trace the
efforts which under more favourable conditions the
Jew himself made to escape from his thraldom.
Alexandrinism was the refuge by which, with the help
of Greek culture, the higher spirits sought to free
themselves from Judaism.   But Alexandrinism in its
turn was apt to become vague and indefinite.   It lay
in too near proximity to the wild oriental mythologies.
The pure abstractions of its Platonic source were too
easily corrupted into genealogies and old wives' fables,
or worse.   At best it was speculative and unpractical.
It provided but a feeble and failing guide, and no
strong prevailing motive in active life.   It might have
held sway over a philosopher here and there, but
would never have had power upon the masses.   Something different was needed, and something different
was given.   'The Word was made flesh' is the key
by which the inspired Apostle unlocks the secrets of
the spiritual world, and sets in motion the springs of

St. John xii.

but con-
ceived in a
concrete
form and
with local
colour.

the practical.   By way of developing this great central proposition, he gives us, not a philosophical disquisition, but a simple history.   He sets this before the eye of faith, and he leaves it to work its work.   Its influence extends equally into both spheres.   It solves theoretical difficulties, but it has also a firm hold upon practice.   It is law, motive, and example in one.   It satisfies religious instinct and aspiration, as well as philosophical system.   While Judaism and Alexandrinism have both ceased to be living forces, the doctrine of the Logos has held on its way ; and though we may not perhaps recognise it under its old name, it is still to this hour the life of Christendom.

'Jesus cried and said, He that believeth on Me, believeth not on Me, but on Him that sent Me.   And he that seeth Me, seeth Him that sent Me.   I am come a light unto the world, that whosoever believeth on Me should not abide in darkness.'   So the Apostle summarizes the teaching of which he is the bearer ; so we may summarize the truth that his Gospel was written to prove and to proclaim.

CHAPTER XII.

THE DAY OF THE CRUCIFIXION.

St. John xii.

The Day of
the Cruci-
fixion and
of the Last
Supper.

THE next eight chapters of the Gospel are concentrated upon the events of four days, which
are treated with a fulness suited to their importance.
But before we enter upon these more closely, it may
be well to dispose of the main critical question arising
out of them—that which regards the date of the
Crucifixion and of the Last Supper. The literature
of the subject is notoriously large, and to state all the
different and conflicting theories would require a
treatise in itself; but it may suffice to put forward
that alone which appears to commend itself to a
careful judgment as resulting from the survey of
previous investigations, and to leave it to be ratified or
not by the verdict of general opinion.[1]

I. It is to me clear that St. John intends to place
the Crucifixion on the day when the Paschal Lamb was
slain, and *before* the Passover when it was eaten, i. e.
in the afternoon (or at the end) of the 14th Nisan.
The Last Supper he places in the first hours of the
(Jewish) day on which the Paschal Lamb was slain, i. e.
on the evening with which the 14th Nisan began.
Thus :—

[1] Compare with what follows,
esp. Wieseler, *Chron. Syn.* pp. 313–
352; *Beiträge*, pp. 230–283; Caspari,
Leben Jesu, pp. 164–186; Meyer
on *John* xviii. 28, &c.

St. John xii.

JULIAN DAY.		JEWISH DAY.
		13 Nisan.
Thursday, ?.....	6 p.m.	**14 Nisan beg.**
		Last Supper.
	Midnight.	Gethsemane.
Friday, ...		Judicial Examination before Annas and Caiaphas, then Pilate.
	πρωΐ.	
	9 a.m. (Mark), 6th hour (John), ...	Judgment finally given.
	12 — 3 p.m.	Crucifixion.
	3 — 5 p.m.	Slaughter of Paschal Lamb.
	6 — p.m.	**15 Nisan beg.**
		The Passover.
	Midnight.	
Saturday, ...		Great Day of the Feast.
		Jesus in the grave.
	6 p.m.	**16 Nisan beg**[1].

This result rests as regards St. John upon the following data :

a. St. John xiii. 1, 'Before the feast of the passover' (πρὸ δὲ τῆς ἑορτῆς τοῦ πάσχα, κ.τ.λ). The connection in which these words are to be taken is not precisely fixed, but I have no doubt whatever that they are intended to assign a date generally to the narrative of the Last Supper which follows. They can hardly be taken exclusively with εἰδὼς, ἀγαπήσας, or ἠγάπησεν, in the same sense : for we usually date facts and not feelings ; and I cannot think that it is admissible to take πρὸ τῆς ἑορτῆς grammatically with εἰδὼς, but virtually as if its sense were thrown on to the clause ἦλθεν αὐτοῦ ἡ ὥρα, ('*Before* the feast He knew that His hour was come'='He knew that *at* the feast His hour *would be* come[2].') There would

---

[1] This table is taken with some additions from Caspari, p. 170.

[2] Luthardt, whose view is endorsed by Wieseler, explains the passage thus :—'Der Evangelist hebt gern hervor, dass Jesus wusste, was ihm bevorstand. So denn auch hier : er wusste, was ihm wider-fahren sollte, ehe es ihm widerfuhr. Bereits vor dem Passahfeste wusste Jesus, dass die Stunde seiner Verklärung im Tode gekommen sei. Das hat einen Sinn allerdings nur dann, wenn Jesus eben an dem Passahfeste gestorben ist.' (ii. 274.)

appear to be a kind of anacolouthon at the end of ver. 1, as if δεῖπνον ἐποίησεν had followed—or the first εἰδὼς being carried on by the second without regard to the καὶ preceding (καὶ δείπνου γενομένου). But the meaning of the passage is evident, and only one meaning I believe to be possible : 'It was on the evening *before* the passover that Jesus sat down to supper with His disciples.'

β. St. John xviii. 28, '(The Jews) themselves went not into the judgment-hall, lest they should be defiled ; but that they might eat the passover.' If the words φάγωσι τὸ πάσχα are to be taken in their ordinary sense, this would clearly imply that the passover had not been eaten already. Accordingly those who place the Crucifixion on the 15th Nisan, endeavour to show, that they refer not to the passover proper (the eating of the paschal lamb), but to that of the Chagiga or thankoffering which took place on Nisan 15th, or one of the days immediately following. But the 'thankoffering' was not a rite confined to the passover ; it was also ordered to be made at the feast of weeks and of tabernacles (Deut. xvi. 16). It had therefore nothing specifically paschal in its character ; and it is difficult to suppose that it would be designated by the name of the most distinctive part of the paschal festival. The instances that have been adduced in support of this theory only tend to show that the term πάσχα might cover the whole of the seven days festival, including the offering of the Chagiga, not that it could be used,—still less that the phrase φαγεῖν τὸ πάσχα could be used, of this last singly and separately. For the eating of unleavened bread the condition of levitical purity was not required.

We seem therefore to be driven back to the most obvious and natural conclusion that the passover proper is meant; that the Jews had yet to partake of it; and thus that the date is the 14th and not the 15th Nisan [1].

γ. St. John xix. 14, 'And it was the preparation of the passover and about the sixth hour' (ἦν δὲ παρασκευὴ τοῦ πάσχα, ὥρα δὲ ὡσεὶ ἕκτη). Here a nice philological question arises, turning upon the history of the word παρασκευή. Can this mean not the preparation for the passover, but Friday in the paschal week? So far it seems to be clear that παρασκευὴ was at this time used independently, i.e. without τοῦ σαββάτου, for the day of the week that we call 'Friday,' and also that the phrases σάββατον τοῦ πάσχα (Ignat. Phil. 13 interpol.) and κυριακαὶ τοῦ πάσχα (Hippolytus, Chron.) were used later for 'the Sabbath' and for 'the Sundays in the paschal week' respectively. But whether or not these instances are sufficient to justify the interpretation given, we seem to be relieved from the necessity of deciding. For whatever might have been the case in regard to other days, it seems in the highest degree improbable that the great day of the feast itself should be called simply 'Friday in the paschal week.' Here we are again compelled to revert to the more natural interpretation.

δ. St. John xix. 31, 'Because it was the preparation ..

---

[1] I do not repeat here the argument used by Dr. Caspari (apparently following Bleek), that defilement contracted through entering the house of a heathen would only last until the evening of the same day, and therefore would not prevent the eating of the Chagiga, because the same fact, if it is true, would raise a similar difficulty in regard to the passover; but the fact itself is a doubtful inference. Cf. also Wieseler, *Beit.* p. 251 n.

for that sabbath day was a high day,' i. e. on the St. John xii.
ordinary view, because it was at once the weekly
sabbath and the first day of the feast, which had itself
the sanctity of a sabbath [1] (Lev. xxiii. 78). On the rival
theory the 'high day' is accounted for by the coincidence of the sabbath with the offering of the 'sheaf of
first-fruits' (Lev. xxiii. 10–14) which fell on Nisan 16.
Both these explanations would be adequate, though
the first is perhaps slightly the more attractive.

ε. An incidental argument occurs in xiii. 29, 'Buy
those things that we have need of against the feast,'
i. e. that of Nisan 15. From which it appears doubly
that the feast had not yet begun ; for then all business
and traffic would be suspended, and the buying of
necessaries would no longer be possible.

On each of these points the thesis is maintained,
and without straining the plain language of the Gospel
no other seems tenable—that the Crucifixion took
place at the end, the Last Supper at the beginning,
of the 14th Nisan, the one on Thursday evening, the
other on Friday afternoon.

II. But if this is the conclusion that we derive from The Synop-
tic date.
St. John it is no less clear that a different one was
intended by the Synoptists. In their narrative the
Last Supper is throughout identified with the paschal
meal, and is placed upon the first hours not of the
14th but of the 15th Nisan.

---

[1] The common explanation of
the word 'sabbath' in Lev. xxiii.
11, 15, is that the 'first day of the
feast' is meant, which had just
been described as kept sabbatically.
Knobel however (*Comm.* ad loc.)
combats this, and would make it
= the regular weekly sabbath.
Arguing on the supposition, that
the year always began on the first
day of the week, he would make
the offering of the sheaf fall always
on Nisan 15, thus cutting away
the ground from Dr. Wieseler; the
premises, however, for this conclusion are highly precarious.

St. John xii.
———

It was 'on the first day of unleavened bread when they killed the passover' (Mark xiv. 12), that the disciples came to Jesus to ask where they should prepare the passover. This must have been in the morning, when some twelve hours or more of the 14th Nisan were past.[1] The meal was not eaten until late in the same day, i. e. after the slaughter of the paschal lamb, just as the 15th Nisan was beginning, and precisely at the time when the passover was usually eaten (cf. Ex. xii. 6, 8). So far the Synoptists are explicit, and they describe the Last Supper consistently as the Paschal meal.

Inconsistencies in the Synoptic tradition.

III. Here then we can only say that there is a contradiction ; and the question is which of the two narratives is to be preferred. The Synoptists themselves decide for us by letting fall certain slight incidental indications, from which it appears that the original tradition agreed with the version of St. John, and that they have deserted this tradition in giving to the Last Supper the character of a passover. These indications are as follows. In Mark xiv. 2 (Matt. xxvi. 5), the Sanhedrim determines to arrest Jesus ; 'but,' they say, 'not on the feast day, lest there be an uproar amongst the people.' But, according to

[1] Canon Westcott (*Intr.* p. 318) reconciles the Synoptic and Johannean narratives, by supposing that the question of the disciples was asked, and the instruction to them given, immediately upon the sunset of the 13th. Calling attention to the epithet (ἀναγκαῖον) ἕτοιμον, he argues that the preparation need not have taken much time, and that therefore the supper may really have taken place as St. John represents it, on the evening of the 13th–14th But I cannot bring myself to think that this is consistent with the plain words of St. Mark. Taking Mark xiv. 12 and 17 together, it seems to me clear that an interval of some hours is implied between them, and also that the disciples' question was asked *before* sunset. The last words of ver. 16 show that ἕτοιμον cannot be taken to mean that further preparation was not necessary.

the Synoptic account, it was precisely on the feast day, and *after* the feast itself, that the arrest was carried out. We notice in confirmation of the suspicion that this cannot have been the case, that though the meal is described as a passover, there is no hint or allusion to its most characteristic feature, the paschal lamb.   Following the course of the narrative we find that Simon of Cyrene is met returning ἀπ' ἀγροῦ (Mark xv. 21, Luke xxiii. 26), from which we infer that it was a working day. Work did not cease until noon on Nisan 14th, but on the 15th it was suspended altogether. The haste with which the bodies were taken down from the cross is accounted for by the sanctity of a day that is about to begin, not of one that is just ending (Mark xv. 42).   If it had been the latter, Joseph of Arimathaea could not have 'bought the fine linen' that was used for the embalmment (Mark xv. 46).

St. John xii.

This unwilling testimony of the Synoptists can hardly be otherwise than conclusive ; but it is confirmed in other ways.

Other evidence.

(1) The difficulties of supposing that the meeting of the Sanhedrim, the Judgment, and the Crucifixion took place on the great day of the feast, are not indeed insuperable, but leave a certain weight of probability against it.

(2) Both St. Paul (1 Cor. v. 7) and the author of the Apocalypse (Rev. v. 6, 9, &c.) regard the sacrifice of Christ as representing that of the true Paschal Lamb ; which is the more natural if it coincided with it in point of time.

(3) Jewish tradition refers the death of Jesus to the 'vespera paschatis' (=ἡ παρασκευὴ τοῦ πάσχα).

St. John xii.

(4) And in this the great mass of Christian tradition that has come down to us, agrees with it. The Chronicon Paschale, a work of the seventh century, is prefaced by a number of quotations from the early fathers, in which it is expressly stated that the Crucifixion took place on Nisan 14, superseding once and for ever the offering of the paschal lamb. The fathers quoted are Peter of Alexandria († 311), Hippolytus, bishop of Portus (c. 230), Apollinaris, bishop of Hierapolis (c. 170), Clement of Alexandria († 220).[1] There is no ambiguity in any of this evidence, and to it may be added that of Irenaeus († 202), Tertullian († 220), Origen († 254), and Epiphanius († 403). A passage in Justin Martyr is open to some doubt, but from the extract it appears that he is no exception to the general rule ; for if he places the Crucifixion upon the ' day of the passover,' he shows that he means by it the day on which the paschal lamb was slain, and on the second evening of which it was eaten, the 14th Nisan[2].

Reservation in favour of the Synoptists.

In the face of all this we can hardly refuse to accept the Johannean date of the Last Supper and the Crucifixion as the right one. The Synoptists, however, have one real argument to allege in their favour ; that is, the way in which paschal forms are observed, not only in their own account of the institution of the Last Supper, but also in that of St. Paul (cf. Luke xxii. 17, 20 ; 1 Cor. x. 16, xi. 25). It may be therefore that the two accounts are partially at least to be reconciled ; and that perhaps in the way suggested by

---

[1] The quotations are given in full by Caspari, pp. 179-186. The names which follow are from   Steitz (*Herzog*. xi. 151).
[2] Cf. esp. Meyer, *Einl.* pp. 24, 25.

Dr. Caspari.   This clear and accurate writer endeavours to show from the Talmud, that the other paschal ceremonies were independent of the sacrifice of the lamb ; and these, he thinks, may have been attached to the commencement of the feast of unleavened bread on the 14th Nisan.   This does not answer the whole of the contradiction ; for the Synoptists state almost explicitly, that the Last Supper was held on the evening of the 14th–15th Nisan ; but, if true, it would make it easier to understand how the mistake had arisen.   The Last Supper would soon come to be identified with the Passover, and to this identification other portions of the history would be made to conform.   In the Synoptic narrative, as we have it, the work of re-adjustment is still incomplete, and traces of the original tradition are still visible.

In connection with the Christian tradition that has just been alluded to, we are brought into contact with the famous 'Paschal Controversy[1].' This was once one of the hottest centres of discussion in regard to the fourth Gospel, but it bids fair once more to retire into obscurity.   The argument of the Tübingen School was this.   Towards the middle of the second century a strife arose between the Eastern and Western Churches, as to the celebration of Easter or the point at which the fast of Lent was to be broken.   A diversity of custom had arisen. In the Roman Church the day of the week observed was fixed, the day of the month movable.   It was always the Friday that fell upon or immediately after

St. John xii.

The Paschal Controversy.

---

[1] The view taken below is mainly that of Steitz, art. 'Pascha' in *Herzog*.   Cf. also Bleek, *Einl.*   §§ 74, 75.   Compare on the other side Hilgenfeld, *Evang.* p. 341 foll.

St. John xii.

the 14th Nisan. In the Churches of Asia Minor, on the contrary, the day of the week was movable and the day of the month fixed—the 14th Nisan. The Christian and Jewish festivals were observed upon the same day. Now the Asiatic Churches professed to base their practice upon that of the Apostle St. John. 'He,' they said, 'while living at Ephesus, had always observed the 14th Nisan.' And this contention of theirs does not seem to have been questioned.

Argument of the Tübingen School drawn from this.

Baur and his school therefore, assuming that what the Apostle celebrated was the institution of the Last Supper, use this as an argument against the genuineness of the Gospel, in which, though the Last Supper is placed according to the Jewish reckoning on the first hours of the 14th Nisan, according to the ordinary reckoning it would fall upon the evening of the 13th. Without pressing this ambiguity it will be seen that the whole argument depends upon the assumption that the Apostle and the Church of Asia Minor after him celebrated, not the Crucifixion, but the institution

Insufficiently proved.

of the Lord's Supper. This, however, is neither probable in itself, nor does it admit of historical proof. The one passage that might seem to deserve this title is from the testimony of Apollinaris cited above. He says 'that certain persons from ignorance captiously urge that on the 14th the Lord ate the lamb with His disciples, and that on the great day of the feast He Himself suffered [1].' But even supposing (what there is no evidence to show) that Apollinaris though an Asiatic bishop, was not a Quartodeciman himself, it

---

[1] Εἰσὶ τοίνυν οἳ δι' ἄγνοιαν φιλονείκουσι περὶ τούτων . . . καὶ λέγουσιν, κ.τ.λ. Can this possibly be the way in which Apollinaris, an Asiatic bishop, designates the opinion of Polycrates of Ephesus, Melito of Sardis, Sagaris, Papirius, and Polycarp himself?

still would not be natural that he should speak of the St. John xii.
main body of the Church to which he belonged in this
slighting way. It is on all grounds more probable
that he is alluding to some side issue in the main
controversy; and precisely such a side issue appears
to have been raised in the Church at Laodicaea [1]
(Euseb. iv. 26). The history of the Paschal Contro- Inconclusiveness of the Paschal Controversy.
versy is, however, too obscure for any positive
conclusion to be built upon it; and there is the less
reason for attempting to make it carry more than
it will bear, that it can in no case affect the
argument for the genuineness of the Gospel. For the
external evidence shows that the Gospel was received
in Asia Minor, and received there at the very time
when this controversy was raging [2].

The real cause of difference in the practice of the Probable origin of the difference of practice.
Churches of Rome and Asia Minor appears to have
been not so much a conflicting interpretation of the

---

[1] Eusebius quotes the preface to a work of Melito's upon the Passover, ἐπὶ Σερουιλλίου Παύλου ἀνθυπάτου τῆς Ἀσίας ... ἐγένετο ζήτησις πολλὴ ἐν Λαοδικείᾳ περὶ τοῦ πάσχα. Surely it is some *local* controversy that is here described, and not that which Polycarp, as the representative of the Asiatic Churches generally, maintained against Anicetus. Something is perhaps to be said on the other side, and I cannot think that any conclusion is to be asserted positively; but supposing it could be proved that Apollinaris was an isolated advocate of the Roman practice in Asia Minor, and that the 14th Nisan was really put forward by the whole Asiatic Church not as the day of the Crucifixion but as that of the institution of the Lord's Supper, it still would not follow that this had been the

original source of the custom. The theory stated below (that of Bleek) seems to me distinctly the more natural and probable.

[2] It is curious that Dr. Hilgenfeld seems to have forgotten that the only point of alleging the Paschal controversy is to show that the fourth Gospel was not recognised in Asia Minor. He himself admits (*Evang.* p. 345) that it was recognised not only by Apollinaris, but also by Melito and Polycrates. We may add, by Tatian the pupil of Justin, and by Irenaeus the pupil of Polycarp. This is indeed certainly the case; but if it is, the Paschal controversy ceases to have any importance. [I am indebted for the above observation to a few minutes conversation that I once enjoyed with Professor Westcott.]

St. John xii.

Gospels (the discrepancy in which had not yet been noticed), as an accident in their respective circumstances and position. The 'pillar-apostles' remaining in Jerusalem and living for some time on amicable terms with their fellow-countrymen, did not at once open a breach with Judaism. They continued to observe the Jewish festivals; and that the more readily because they found it easy to give them a Christian signification. And the usage of the Mother-Church was carried by St. John, its last surviving representative, into Asia Minor. Meantime in other parts of the empire where Jewish customs were not so predominant the week was taken as the unit, which the yearly festivals followed. Sunday was celebrated (rightly) as the day of the Lord's Resurrection, and Friday (also rightly) as the day of the Crucifixion; and the Easter festival preserved and intensified this distinction. Thus was gradually formed the usage which was adopted by the council at Nicaea as the law of the whole Church. But its growth was accidental, and any dogmatic meaning that might be read into it was an afterthought.

Defects of the Tübingen theory.

So far as a conjectural reconstruction of the Paschal controversy is possible, this seems an extremely plausible one. On the other hand, that propounded by the Tübingen critics, though ingenious, is far too much dominated by theory. It supposes the several parties in the Church to have been conscious of their own ideal tendencies to a degree which all experience contradicts. And, like so many other theories of that school, it is only obtained by inverting a great part of the scanty materials of fact. It was really invented in order to prove on ideal grounds the

rejection of the fourth Gospel by the Church of Asia, | St. John xii.
whereas on historical grounds it is little less than
certain that that Church (at least at this date,
170 A.D.) received and acknowledged it.   But the
fundamental fallacy by which all the Tübingen
reasoning has been vitiated in regard to the Gospel,
is the fictitious Anti-Judaistic character which was
imagined for it.   The fourth Gospel is above
Judaism; but it has grown out of it by an organic
and natural process.   Its author, as we have seen, had
been brought up in the midst of Jewish customs and
practices and habits of thought.   They are part of
himself, and he cannot disengage himself from them.
So far from writing his Gospel to *oppose* them, he
unconsciously displays, and, we might almost say,
consciously justifies them.   He has shown—more,
perhaps, than any other Apostle, more even than
St. Paul—that inner unity in which Jew and Greek
become one by becoming Christian.

CHAPTER XIII.

THE LAST SUPPER.

St. John xiii.
vv. 1–17.

TENDER and touching is that brief preface with which the Evangelist introduces the second great division of his Gospel.

'Now before the feast of the Passover, when Jesus knew that His hour was come that He should depart out of this world unto the Father, having loved His own which were in the world He loved them unto the end.' We can see here the traces of that reciprocal feeling by which the Apostle himself was animated, and which it is difficult to believe to have been assumed.

It was the custom for slaves to wash the feet of the guests before sitting down to meat; and we are tempted to suppose that the symbolical act, which our Evangelist relates here, took the place of this custom. The supposition would be confirmed, if γινομένου for γενομένου (which is adopted by Tischendorf, and sanctioned by Ellicott and Meyer) were the correct reading in ver. 2. But the expression in ver. 4, ἐγείρεται ἐκ τοῦ δείπνου hardly seems to favour this. It is best therefore to leave it an open question, at what part of the supper this incident occurred, and how it is to be fitted in with the narration of the Synoptists. It will be noticed, that the narrative of St. John touches that of St. Luke (xxii. 24–27) in a remarkable manner at vers. 14, 16, ('The servant is not greater than his lord'). If we are to combine these two narratives it must be in some such way as that proposed by Bishop Ellicott[1]. We must assume that the dispute among the disciples 'which was to be greatest,' had taken place on the way to the upper chamber, and that this menial act on the part of their Master was intended as a tacit rebuke to them. But there are three objections against this : (1) that the dispute itself, in the position accorded to it by St. Luke in the midst of the final pathetic leave-taking, seems singularly out of place ; (2) that precisely such a dispute has occurred before ; (3) that the Johannean version does not seem to recognise or agree with it. There it would seem as if the act were quite spontaneous, and had no occasion or suggestion from without. It seems most probable then to suppose that St. Luke has confused two separate traditions, that which St. John has preserved in its original form, and that which properly belongs to the place indicated in Matt. xx. 20. One thing is clear, that St. John, if he has read St. Luke's Gospel at this point, has not copied or followed it. He proceeds with the same peculiar independence which we have noticed in him all through. Perhaps in some dim remote way St. Luke's narrative may have helped to recall to him a few sentences towards the end. But it has not done more. It does not give a hint that could lead to the construction of the scene as a fiction. 'He riseth from supper, and layeth

St. John xiii. vv. 1-17.

Relation of St. John's narrative to St. Luke's.

---

[1] *Huls. Lect.* p. 324.

St. John xiii.
vv. 1–17.

Its striking
circumstan-
tiality.

aside His garments, and took a towel and girded
Himself.   After that He poureth water into a bason,
and began to wash the disciples' feet with the towel
wherewith He was girded.'   This is the realism of
history indeed.   The very mode of using the towel is
especially described.   The words addressed to Peter,

And psy-
chological
truth.

'What I do thou knowest not now, but thou shalt
know hereafter,' do not read as if they belonged to an
ideal scene.   If it is, the illusion is wonderfully kept
up.   What interest would the readers of the Gospel
have in the mental development of a single Apostle?
To suppose that it was intended as a type of their
own would make it an incredible subtlety.   Peter's
remonstrance, and then the impetuosity with which he
rushes into the opposite extreme, are very true to his
character as delineated elsewhere.   The carefulness
with which here, as we saw in the account of the
cleansing of the temple, the successive stages in the
action are described, proclaim the eye-witness.   And
if here and there fragments of other discourses or
fragments of imperfect authenticity find their way in,
this is still not incompatible with the work of an eye-
witness describing what he has seen after years of
reflection.

Symbolical
character of
the act.

The action is real, but it is also symbolical ; just as
again in xx. 22 (the 'afflatus') ; and there is something
not altogether dissimilar in Matt. xviii. 2 (the little
child taken as a pattern).   Symbolical action probably
played a larger part in our Lord's teaching, than we
should directly gather from the Gospels.   It attaches
itself naturally to the method of drawing lessons from
the circumstances of the passing moment (Matt. iv. 19,
viii. 22 ; John iv. 10, &c.) ; and holds a place midway

between the parable and symbolical miracle.   It is a parable acted, but without miraculous accessories. St. John xiii.

There is a touch of the Galilean fisherman as well as of the impetuous Apostle in Peter's request that his hands and his head may be washed, and not only his feet.   He at once imagines that the act must have some physical virtue.   It is explained to him where the symbolism lies.   He who has once bathed still needs to wash, but only that part of him which is soiled by the dust of the way.   So he who has once undergone the decisive crisis of conversion, must still exercise daily repentance, but only for his daily transgressions.   Perhaps we may regard this as a secondary application of the foot-washing suggested by Peter's conduct; its first intention must have been to teach simply a lesson of humility, or rather the higher lesson of ministering love. vv. 8-10.

A saying like this in ver. 10 (the reply to Peter) bears the strongest internal marks of its own authenticity. It is perfectly in the manner of the Synoptists, though not even remotely suggested by them.

There is no reason whatever to suppose, with some critics, that the foot washing is intended to take the place of the institution of the Eucharist.   The random guesses that have been made to account for the omission of the latter, are sufficient to refute the theories of which they form a part.   The simple explanation is that the subject was too familiar to need repetition.   We gather as well from the Acts as from 1 Cor. xi. that Eucharistic feasts were common in all Christian Churches.   No doubt the history of the rite and the rite itself were both well known and understood.   And we may imagine that a thorough reform The institution of the Eucharist.

of the Agapae would follow upon St. Paul's Epistle to the Corinthians. But if the practice of the Church generally was in this respect in a satisfactory condition, St. John naturally would not think it necessary to refer to the subject further. At the same time we can hardly help inferring that he did not assign to it that cardinal and almost exclusive importance which some are found to claim for it in the present day. Otherwise he would not have shrunk from repetition, as we see from his minute treatment of the events of the Passion.

The Evangelist relates, however, an episode which is necessary to keep up the thread of the narrative—the discovery and exit of the traitor. And he does this with singular vividness and exactness, as the synopsis of the four Gospels is enough to show. The fourth Gospel is the fullest, the most minute, the most lifelike, the most intelligible. It tells us that Jesus was troubled in making the announcement. ' Then the disciples looked one on another, doubting of whom He spake.' And the passage that follows has a precision which is imperfectly preserved in the English version. This has been well brought out by Professor Lightfoot in his recent work on Revision[1]. St. John was reclining on the bosom of his Master, and he suddenly threw back his head upon His breast to ask a question. The change of posture is emphasized and illustrated by a change in each of the words, verb, preposition, noun ; ἀνακείμενος—ἀναπεσὼν, ἐν—ἐπὶ, κόλπῳ—στῆθος. The exactness of this is wonderful. And the mode in which the announce-

---

[1] p. 72. Cf. also Meyer, *ad loc.*

ment is made is much more delicate and natural than | St. John xiii.
in the Synoptists. Our Lord does not say aloud who
it is that shall betray Him. If He had really done so,
would it not be strange that Judas should immediately
commit himself to the act which was to be his own
exposure? In an undertone He conveys to St. John
the sign by which the traitor shall be indicated. St.
John tells St. Peter, who had at first prompted the
question. But from what follows it appears that the
warning does not go all round the table. Meantime
another communication is seen to pass between our
Lord and Judas, who immediately goes out. Then
the reader is carried farther into the interior of the
room, and hears the whispered comments and con-
jectures of the disciples : 'He has gone to buy the
necessary provisions for the passover, which was to be
the next evening,' or 'to give money to those who are
too poor to provide for themselves.' ' But the traitor,' it
is added, with a single, profoundly though unconsciously tragic, stroke, ' having received the sop went out,
and it was night ! '

　In the brief interlude which follows it is perhaps | vv. 31–35.
probable, though a matter of conjecture, that we have
words which do not all equally belong to the present
context. The glorification of the Son in and by the
Father is a peculiarly Johannean theme, and the
transitions of subject are abrupt ; at the same time
the remaining discourses are given at such length that,
with the Synoptic matter to insert besides, there does
not seem to be room for much condensation ; verses
34, 35 (the 'mandatum') come in curiously as a parenthesis. But the matter of them is attested in the
amplest manner by the Synoptists and in the

St. John xiii.

Apostolic Epistles. Neither is it at all improbable that the charge should be repeated as a parting address to the disciples. The passage is important as showing how essentially St. John occupies the same standpoint as the other Apostles. If ethical questions seem to be subordinated in his Gospel, it is from no theoretic difference as to their place and value or as to their adjustment with other parts of the Christian system ; it is only that the natural bent of his mind leads him to lay stress rather on the theological side of Christianity—a side which all the Apostolic writers recognise, and to which St. Paul at least has given a development little less complete and profound.

vv. 36–38.

The account of Peter's protestation, and the prophecy of his fall, coupled with that of the Resurrection and Appearance in Galilee, seems to have been in the Synoptic Gospels slightly coloured by the event. The account in St. John is simpler and more vague ; though the phrases, ' Whither I go ye cannot come,' ' Thou canst not follow Me,' seem to be almost a Johannean formula (cf. vii. 34–36, viii. 21, xiv. 4). It has doubtless a basis of authenticity, as appears from the direct reference here to the previous discourse ; but how this is to be apportioned among the several passages where it occurs, it is beyond our power to determine.

CHAPTER XIV.

THE LAST DISCOURSES.

WE come now to the last great discourse, which constitutes a striking and peculiar element in the fourth Gospel. It is apparently intended to be conceived of as only momentarily broken at ver. 31. Our Lord and His disciples arise from the table as if to go. But we see from xviii. 1 (ἐξῆλθε) that they had not yet left the house, or at least the city. We must therefore suppose that the contents of chh. xv and xvi, with the prayer of ch. xvii, were still spoken in the upper room, though after the first motion for departure.

The argument would not have any great weight, but yet we should be led in some degree to infer from this that the Evangelist had enlarged upon his original. And the whole character of the discourses goes to strengthen this conclusion. They have been freely reproduced; probably portions of other discourses, though all belonging to these last days, worked up in them. It is a well-known psychological fact that words, conversations, are apt to attach themselves to occasions different from those which in the first instance gave rise to them. This is especially

Present and original form of these discourses.

the case where the original occasions have had nothing very marked or distinctive about them, and where some great and impressive event is found in near proximity to them. The lesser moments are gathered up and drawn as it were into the greater, so that it represents an aggregate of parts that once had a separate existence.

Some such process seems to have been at work in the mind of the Apostle. And not only has he mixed together portions of different discourses, but he has also shaped, moulded, developed their substance in such a way that we are no more able to draw the line at the point where the old ends and where the new begins. But it is clear that he has done this in perfect good faith and quite unconsciously. He sees the scene, the place and the actors, vividly before him. And the discourses are all no doubt repeated under the impression that they represent what was actually spoken. But it is impossible for an active mind to retain the exact recollection of words over a space of perhaps fifty years. Little by little the products of its own individuality will filter in and disturb the clear element of objective fact. But this will take place so gradually and insensibly, that there will be no consciousness of change. The continuity of recollection will seem to be as perfect as that of personality. And indeed the one will be a very near figure of the other. There will be an inner soul of unity while the tissue and composition of the outward particles has changed.

The wonder is indeed less that the Evangelical discourses have undergone modification, than that they should be preserved so perfectly as they are.

It would not have been so in modern times. But a Jew was thrown much more entirely upon his memory; and we have evidence quite apart from the Evangelical tradition that the Jewish memory was singularly tenacious. A great part of the Talmud was preserved orally, and it has 'all the appearance of notes taken down at short-hand [1].'

The reason why the Synoptic discourses surpass those of the fourth Gospel in accuracy, in spite of the greater number of hands through which they have passed, is, first, because they were so much sooner fixed in writing (the greater part of them at least twenty years), and secondly, because of the inferior mental capacity and moral authority of those who bore and transmitted them. A strong mind and character is much less likely to retain a faithful recollection of words than a weak one. Its natural impulse is to creation. Its faculties are too active to rest. They work unconsciously upon the material to which they have access; and when it comes to be brought out again after a long period of incubation, there is nothing to tell that it is different, but it is not really the same.

We shall then renounce the attempt to discriminate closely between the subjective and objective elements in this parting discourse. We will first give a running abstract of its contents, and then endeavour to group them as much as possible under a few heads, observing what amount of confirmation they receive from the Synoptic Gospels or other sources.

Our Lord turns from Peter to the other Apostles. xiv. 1–7.

---

[1] Renan, *Vie de Jésus*, pp. xlvi. xciv. (thirteenth ed.). Compare Westcott, *Introd.* p. 154.

They now knew that the time of His departure was near at hand. And He cheers their spirits with words of comfort and of promise. He bids them not to be troubled, but to have faith in Himself and in the Father who sent Him. He is but going to prepare them a mansion in His Father's house. He would soon return 'with power and great glory' and take them to dwell with Him for ever.

But what is the way to these mansions above? asks the honest but slow and unapprehensive Thomas; he knows not whither his Lord is going, and how should he know the way? He is reminded of the nature of that kingdom that had been so long and so fully put before him. It is centred in the person of its King. He is the Truth, in that He has revealed its nature, and that of all the conditions which lead up to it and which it fulfils. He is the Life, inasmuch as He is the source of that eternal life, which is only another name for the blissful possession of the Kingdom itself, and which is only to be obtained through faith in Him. And therefore He also is the Way, because it is by entering into a certain relation to Him that both Truth and Life, i. e. the Kingdom in its fulness of illumination and glory is to be appropriated. The way to the Son is the way also to the Father. To know the Son is to know the Father, nay, to see Him.

These last words are taken up by another disciple, Philip. He is a Jew, and has inherited all the traditions and ideas of a Jew. His thoughts at once run to the Old Testament theophanies. These especially signalized and accompanied the giving of the first Law by Moses. Philip was by this time aware

that he was in the presence of another and greater
Lawgiver than Moses—that Prophet whom Moses
had foretold. He looked, like all the Jews of his time,
to see the wonders of the old dispensation repeated.
Hence his question, 'Lord, show us the Father and
it sufficeth us.' How touching is the Lord's reply!
'Have I been so long time with you, and yet hast thou
not known Me, Philip?'—Are not these Jewish prejudices yet broken down? Are you still so far below
that high and true conception to which I have tried
to raise you?—'He that hath seen Me hath seen the
Father.' The Son of God had come into the world
to reveal the Father to man. His own assurance of
the fact ought to be enough. But if not, it was confirmed by His works. These at least afforded proof
that the Father dwelt in Him who performed them.
As revelations of the divine love, and as manifestations of the divine power, on both sides they pro-
claimed their origin.

Yet the believing disciple shall do in one sense
even greater works than these. They had been confined to a little corner of the earth and to a short
space of time. But the Apostles and their successors
should spread them through all the world. The
return of the Son to the Father was to be a signal
for the diffusion of the Gospel, and that diffusion
would be itself a further testimony to the glory of
the Son.

Meanwhile to the Apostles in their labours a two-
fold assistance would be accorded; on the one hand
through prayer to the Father in the name (i.e. in
complete devotion to the cause and Person) of the
Son; and on the other hand through the gift of the

Paraclete, who should take their Master's place after He was gone, and should abide with the Church perpetually—with the Church and not with the world.

vv. 18–21.

Through the Paraclete, the Lord Himself would return to His own, and then their communion with Him should be full. The Triune God should dwell in them and reveal Himself to them.

vv. 22–24.

The Apostle Jude, supposing that the revelation would be a visible one, asks how it could be made to the Church and not also to the world? He is told in reply, that it will be a spiritual revelation, and that a certain spiritual susceptibility will be needed in order to receive it. This spiritual susceptibility is shown by love, and obedience to the divine commands. Those who do not exhibit these necessarily can have no part either in the Son or in the Father.

vv. 25, 26.

Then follows a somewhat further definition of the office of the Paraclete. He shall instruct or teach the disciples. He shall tell them new things, and call to their remembrance old.

vv. 27–31.

And finally the discourse returns to the point from which it started. Its object had been to reassure the sorrowful disciples against their Lord's departure, and with words of reassurance and consolation it concludes. These are thrown into the form of a leave-taking or farewell. 'Peace I leave with you' is the usual benediction at parting in the East. But this was no common benediction, such as the world gives. Why should the disciples be troubled? Their Master goes but to return. He goes to a state of greater power and glory, whence He would advance His kingdom more effectually. If their love was real, and really bound up in their Lord and in His glory,

this would be a cause of rejoicing, not of dismay. St. John
A time would come when these words would prove xiv.–xvii.
themselves to be true. But now they must cease, for
the end is near.

There is a short break or pause, during which the ch. xv. 1–11.
company rises as if to go. But as they are rising the
discourse is resumed. It opens this time with an
allegory similar to that which we found in chap. x.
The meaning is simple. Christ is the vine. Those
who believe in Him are the branches or fruit-bearing
shoots. He is their life, and it is through Him alone
that they can bring their fruit to maturity. Without
Him they are barren and wither, they are cut off and
cast into the fire. With Him and in Him they bring
forth fruit abundantly. This is a cogent reason for
seeking to abide in Him. The conditions of abiding
in Him are obedience and love. Through these the
disciples would come to share the joy of their Master's
victory over sin and death.

In love He was to be their pattern. No love could vv. 12–17.
be greater than His. He was even now to die for
them, as a man would die for his friends. They were
His friends, the partners of His confidence, chosen by
Him out of the whole world, and drawing their life
from Him. Once more let them imitate His love.

The love of Christ is enmity with the world. There- vv. 18–27.
fore the world will persecute those who love Him.
They will deal with the servant as they dealt with the
Master—and that because they are blinded and in-
fatuated. They cannot plead the excuse of ignorance.
They have heard the words and seen the works of the
Messiah. But they have 'hated Him without a cause,'
that the Scripture might be fulfilled. Only in contrast

with the hatred of the world shall be the testimony that is borne by the Paraclete through the disciples and by the disciples, from their own experience.

Thus the disciples have received a distinct fore-warning of what is to happen to them, so that they will be armed against their fate when it comes.

And they are sorrowful; yet it is expedient that their Master should leave them. When He is gone, the Paraclete will come. He will be the champion of the faithful against their enemy the world. He will convince, convict, expose, call to account and put to shame the world with respect to three things; first, with regard to its own sin in rejecting the Son of God; secondly, with regard to His righteousness, signed and sealed by His glorious Ascension—glorious even though for a time it causes the pain of loss to His disciples; thirdly, with regard to the judgment which is thereby meted out to the Prince of darkness. In respect to all these three things will the Paraclete hold up a mirror, as it were, before the world, and make it see them in their true colours. They will either repent in dust and ashes, or their sin will be the greater. Besides this office of conviction as against the world, the Paraclete shall dispense instruction to the disciples. To them He shall be the Spirit of Truth. The hidden things of the future and the mystery of Christ and God He shall reveal, and that shortly, when at His (the Spirit's) coming, Christ Himself should return to His disciples.

Soon they were to be separated, but soon again the parting was to end. In answer to the perplexed enquiry which Jesus sees upon the faces of His dis-ciples, He does not explain the words further, but merely gives them emphasis and vivid reality by the Old Testament figure of the woman in travail.   Now they have sorrow, but then their sorrow shall be turned into joy.   When the Paraclete is come they shall ask no questions; they shall put up no prayer that is not answered: for then their faith will be ripe.   They will make no more random petitions, such as Philip's but a moment ago.   They will know what spirit they are of, and they will ask accordingly. They will pray in the name and spirit of the Son, in complete devotion to and reliance upon Him, as identified with His cause and glory.   And they shall receive what they ask for.   It shall be no longer as when their Master was with them 'in the flesh' and told them divine things in parable and figure.   Then, through the Paraclete, He shall tell them of the Father, not in figures but in plain words.   Then they shall know more fully, what indeed already they believe, that from the Father He Himself was come, and that to the Father He returned.

St. John xiv.–xvii.

This provokes from the Apostles a profession of faith, which is however damped by the announcement of their approaching desertion.   Yet no desertion of theirs can touch Him, who is one with the Father, and with whom the Father continually abides.

vv. 29-33.

One more parting word.   The peace that Jesus leaves to His disciples is the peace that He has won by His own victory over the world—a peace which no earthly tribulations can shake, and which they shall share.

Touching and sublime as this is, and much as we may hesitate to exercise criticism upon it, we cannot but recognize a change from the simple compact lucid

Criticism of the Discourse.

addresses and exposition of the Synoptists. They too can be profound, and St. John too can be simple. But both the profundity and the simplicity are different. This appears not so much in single verses as when we look at the discourse as a whole. In all the Synoptic Gospels, imperfectly as they are put together, there is not a single discourse that could be called involved in structure, and yet I do not see how it is possible to refuse this epithet to the discourse before us as given by St. John. The different subjects are not kept apart, but are continually crossing and entangling one another. The later subjects are anticipated in the course of the earlier ; the earlier return in the later.

For instance, the connection in xiv. 12–17 is difficult but real. The Son is glorified, borne witness to, as well by His own works as by those which the disciples shall do in His name after He is gone. They shall do them through prayer and the help of the Spirit. But there is hardly a place in this connection for ver. 15, 'If ye love Me, keep My commandments.' It seems to have strayed in from the section below, verses 20–24. We can trace perhaps the subtle association of ideas which has led the Apostle to introduce it, but it is an excrescence upon the argument, to which no parallel is to be found in the Synoptists.

Again, on a larger scale, we see that the description of the functions of the Paraclete is broken up, we cannot but think unnecessarily, into five fragments—xiv. 16, 17 ; xiv. 25, 26 ; xv. 26 ; xvi. 8–15 ; xvi. 23–25. It would surely have gained in clearness and perspicuity if these fragments had been thrown together. The personality too of the Paraclete and His functions in relation to the Son need further definition. This is

seen from the disagreement among commentators as
to the interpretation and application of a great part of
the passage from xvi. 8–25. The coming of the
Paraclete is spoken of in terms which seem to identify
it with the promised return of the Son ; the return of
the Son is connected with attributes which seem to
belong specially to the Paraclete. And yet the two
are categorically distinguished in xiv. 16.

Again, another main subject of the discourse, the
relation of the Church and the world, is intersected
just in the same way. One portion of it is found in
xiv. 22–24, another in xv. 18–25, a third in xvi. 1–3,
besides scattered references in single verses. We are
strongly tempted to suppose, in spite of xv. 20—which
however refers to the earlier occasion in Matt. x.
22-25—that all this section is simply the discourse in
Mark xiii. 9–13 transposed. The allegory of the vine
and the branches also appears to belong to a different
and more didactic period. It breaks the thread, and
has little bearing upon the object of the discourse
here, which is to comfort the disciples in the prospect
of their Lord's departure.

Conjectural reconstructions are precarious things,
but there seems reason to suppose that the elements
of the original discourse were somewhat simpler than
they appear, and it is open to us at least to mark out
those which have most coherence in themselves, and
seem best to suit the situation.

But the question how far the original matter of the
discourse was grouped in its present connection, is
subordinate to that other question how far the discourse in its present state is to be traced back to an
objective original at all. We may consider it perhaps

under these heads :—(1) the departure and the return,
(2) the Paraclete, (3) the vine and its branches, (4)
the disciples and the world.

Departure
and return
of the
Saviour.

(1) Now the conception of the departure and the
return is not very fixed and definite.   There is indeed
but one point of departure, but there may be three
different modes of return—the Resurrection, the
Second Advent or Parousia of the Son, or the Gift of
the Holy Ghost.   The Evangelist, as we have said,
has not quite clearly distinguished between these.   In
the first place where it is mentioned, the return is
apparently the Parousia : 'If I go and prepare a
place for you, I will come again, and receive you unto
Myself.'   Elsewhere it seems to have reference rather
to the coming of the Paraclete, through whom the
Saviour Himself would be restored to His own,
though in spiritual presence.   So in xiv. 19–24, and xvi.
17–25.   To the return of the Saviour in the Paraclete
there is no immediate parallel in the Synoptists ; but
it is remarkable how close is the logical development
from them.   In the ground-document of the Synoptists the function of the Holy Ghost that is most
prominently brought forward, is precisely this which is
ascribed to him by St. John as the champion of the
Church after the departure of its Master. (Cf. Mark
xiii. 11 par. : 'Take no thought what ye shall speak,
for it is not ye that speak, but the Holy Ghost.')   But
at the end of St. Matthew's Gospel, in a passage of
doubtful originality, but at all events not later than
70 A.D., the risen Saviour promises to be with His
Church Himself in person, to the end of the world.
Putting these two passages together we have clearly
all the materials of the Johannean conception.

(2) But it will be said, 'St. John is the first to speak of the Holy Ghost in terms so distinctly expressive of personality.' Language seems almost to fail when we attempt to characterize the conception of the Holy Spirit contained in the earlier books of the New Testament. It is not yet that of a Person, and yet it is more than the poetic personification of the Old Testament. It seems to waver between this and the metaphysical personification of intermediate agencies in the Alexandrine philosophy. The Spirit is distinguished from other manifestations of the Divine Essence more by its functions than by its nature. Even with St. Paul the conception is still fluid. Speaking of the Spirit as the animating principle of the new dispensation, he does not hesitate to say 'the Lord is that Spirit' (2 Cor. iii. 17). There is exactly the same ambiguity as in these chapters of St. John. There too the Paraclete is at one moment a separate 'hypostasis' and at the next merged in the person of Christ. The conception is not yet capable of rigid definition.

When we think how much of this conception all the New Testament writers have in common; how marked is the interval which separates them from the Old Testament, and how slight on the other hand is that which separates them from one another; how easy is the transition from the early portions of the Acts and the other Apostolic Epistles to St. Paul and St. John,—it seems impossible not to look for the common basis on which they stand to the actual teaching of our Lord. And the Synoptic Gospels give us traces of that teaching sufficiently distinct to warrant us in asserting its existence, and, I think we may add, its essential identity with the Apostolic doctrine.

We shall enter perhaps more completely into St. John's delineation, if we look at it psychologically, from the point of view of his own mental history and experience. Supposing, what I think we have a right to suppose as something more than a mere hypothesis, that St. John was really the author of the Gospel, a great deal of light seems to be thrown on these chapters. The functions assigned in them to the Paraclete, are those of Comforter, Champion, Instructor. The Paraclete was to console the disciples for the loss of their Master ; He was to be their stay in the midst of persecution ; He was to teach them all things, and bring all things to their remembrance whatsoever their Master had said unto them. Now what had been the experience of the Apostle ? He, like the rest of his colleagues, had been dismayed and broken down by his Master's death, but like them he was suddenly raised to new hope by the Resurrection. Then came the gift of the Spirit (to which there was certainly some objective fact to correspond, whether exactly that described in Acts ii. or not). He, like the rest, felt himself carried away by a strange exaltation and enthusiasm, which is still reflected in the pages of the Acts (iv. 23–30, v. 41, vi. 15, &c.) He found his sorrow actually turned into joy. He found himself actually sustained before mobs and councils and kings. He found, both at first and as time went on, that the full significance of his Master's mission, the nature of His Messiahship, the value of His sufferings, became much clearer to him. One by one the sayings of his Lord came back into his memory, seeming to explain both past and present, and also to give a key to the future.

All this he would connect with the gift and promise of the Holy Ghost, and all this would help him to fill in or to retrace the outline of the promise itself. The Apostle ascribed to the Paraclete those changes which he was conscious had been supernaturally wrought in himself. The functions thus indicated may have been, and probably were, foreshadowed in the discourse of which these chapters are the reproduction; but the autobiography of the Apostle lent them additional distinctness and individuality.

St. John xiv.–xvii.

(3) The allegory of the vine and its branches belongs to the same class as the miracle of the multiplied loaves and fishes with its explanation, and has probably an equal degree of authenticity; though, as we have said, its place in this particular context may be doubtful.

The Vine.

(4) In like manner the predictions of persecution, if our theory has any claim to be considered a true one, not only nearly resemble the parallel discourse in the Synoptists, but were originally identical with it, and have come to be incorporated here by a slight transposition of time and occasion. In any case they belong to the last week of our Lord's ministry. The association of ideas which led to their introduction appears to have had its rise in the conception of the Paraclete as Champion or Protector.

The disciples and the world.

The prayer which follows the last discourse as its fit crown and conclusion has been designated by an old tradition the prayer of the High Priest, now about to take upon Him His office, and to offer Atonement for the sins of the people. It falls naturally into three divisions. It is a prayer, (verses 1–5)

ch. xvii. Oratio Summi Sacerdotis.

for the Speaker Himself, (6–19) for the disciples then present, (20–23) for those who should be joined to the Church in after times — with a summary (25, 26) gathering up with deep emotion the relations of the Saviour to His own, their nature and their end, as embodying a revelation of God, and through that revelation realizing the Divine Love.

Here again we feel that we are upon ground where criticism might well be silent. But our object is to determine how far the fourth Gospel is a truthful historical record, and in order to do this no part of it must be exempt from investigation. Criticism, however, has in this instance little to do. We have recognized distinctly the fact that the discourses contained in the fourth Gospel have received a colouring from the mind and style of the Evangelist. I cannot but think that an impartial reader, coming to the study of the Gospel with the intention to form his opinion by strict induction from the facts, will inevitably arrive at this conclusion ; and it will not be otherwise than confirmed in him by this chapter. But having said this we shall not attempt to go further, and separate the Johannean form from the original substance. For such a step the data are not sufficient. We shall simply leave the chapter as it stands, with that caution or proviso.

Objections.

On the other hand, it cannot be allowed that there is anything in the chapter that is incompatible with its Apostolic and Johannean authorship. The points that have chiefly been noticed as indicating such a conclusion are these [1].

1. The combination Ἰησοῦν Χριστὸν as if it were a

---

[1] Cf. Scholten, *Ev. Joh.* p. 296.

proper name, and had slipped in inadvertently from the later use. If it were so, this would not prove that the words were not written by an Apostle. But Χριστὸν is rather a predicate than a proper name. Without going so far as to say, with Dr. Alford and Luthardt, that we can see here the particular source of the use as a proper name, we may yet fairly say that we see an example of the *process* by which that use arose. The epithet is emphatic. Eternal life consists in knowing the only true God, and Jesus His Anointed Son.

2. A supposed harshness in ver. 9, ' I pray not for the world,' which is thought to point to a system of Dualism. But the words merely mean that the world is not the subject of this particular prayer. And there is no Dualism : for in ver. 21 the possibility of the world's conversion is distinctly contemplated, as else-where (cf. xvi. 8–11, and especially iii. 16, 17 : 'For God so loved the world, that He gave His only-be-gotten Son, that whosoever believeth in Him should not perish, but have everlasting life. For God sent not His Son into the world to condemn the world, but that the world through Him might be saved'). The unbelief and opposition of the world is not invincible ; and that, I presume, is what Dualism would mean.

3. The doctrine of Pre-existence appears more than once in the course of the prayer (verses 5, 22, 24). But if there is reason on other grounds to believe that the Gospel was really written by St. John, this at least does not afford sufficient for thinking otherwise. The incomplete and comparatively popular character of the Synoptic Gospels is enough to account for its omission in them.

4. Lastly, it is urged that the triumphant elevation of this prayer is inconsistent with the Synoptic account of the agony in Gethsemane. But the liability to fluctuations of feeling and emotion is inherent in humanity, and was assumed with His manhood by Him who was perfect man. If we had another version of the prayer besides St. John's, we should probably find the elements of depression somewhat nearer the surface; but that they were subordinate, though breaking out from time to time, is seen from the whole both of the Johannean and Synoptic narratives. St. John himself, we cannot doubt, underwent a reaction. In common with all the disciples, the Crucifixion was to him at the first a stumblingblock and a shock to his faith. But the Resurrection, and the events that followed, with the rapid success of the Gospel from that moment onwards, carried his enthusiastic nature to the opposite extreme of joyful exultation. This was the permanent impression left upon him, by which the earlier and transitory one was obliterated. And it dominated his whole conception of the history, both that anterior to as well as that succeeding the Crucifixion. There is probably in the prayer before us a proleptic element which is derived from the consciousness of the Apostle; but it acquires a peculiar probability and appropriateness when we refer it to that consciousness, and look at it in the light of the Apostle's mental history.

CHAPTER XV.

THE PASSOVER.

St. John xviii.

Character of the narrative.

WE return once more from discourse to narrative, which preponderates in the whole of the remaining portion of the Gospel. Accordingly, as we have found hitherto that in the narrative portions the marks of an eye-witness at once begin to multiply, so here especially they occur in such large amount and in such rapid succession that it appears impossible to resist the conviction that from an eye-witness and no one else the account proceeds. Not the least argument in favour of this, is the special pleading to which the opponents of the Johannean authorship are driven in order to support their conclusion. An example is to be seen in the work of Dr. Scholten, p. 296 foll., who takes up argument after argument in such a way as to make it clear that—though perhaps unconsciously—he is trying to make the worse appear the better cause. Critics like M. Renan, with less bias and a finer historical sense, freely acknowledge the excellence of the Johannean narrative.

It opens with a piece of precise topography and probable history. 'When Jesus had spoken these

vv. 1-3.

words, He went forth with His disciples over the brook Cedron, where was a garden, into the which He entered with His disciples. And Judas also, which betrayed Him, knew the place : for Jesus oft-times resorted thither with His disciples.' The garden ($\kappa\hat{\eta}\pi\sigma$) exactly corresponds to the $\chi\omega\rho\acute{\iota}\sigma\nu$ of the Synoptists, of which it is a further definition. An objection has been drawn from the reading $\tau\hat{\omega}\nu$ $K\acute{\epsilon}\delta\rho\omega\nu$, which, as in so many other instances, turns out upon examination to be favourable to the view against which it is directed. Arguing from the plural article, which has the authority of a majority of the Mss., it has been inferred that the Evangelist was ignorant of the true derivation of the name Cedron or Kidron, which does not stand for 'cedars,' but is a Hebrew word meaning 'black' or 'dark.' But the Codex Sinaiticus reads $\tau\sigma\hat{\upsilon}$ $K\acute{\epsilon}\delta\rho\sigma\upsilon$, and a respectable minority of Mss. read $\tau\sigma\hat{\upsilon}$ $K\epsilon\delta\rho\grave{\omega}\nu$, which may be restored to the text with little hesitation. If the original reading was $\tau\sigma\hat{\upsilon}$ $K\epsilon\delta\rho\grave{\omega}\nu$, it is easy to understand how each of the two corruptions came to be substituted for it by copyists knowing only Greek. But on the other hand it is difficult to see how either $\tau\sigma\hat{\upsilon}$ $K\acute{\epsilon}\delta\rho\sigma\upsilon$ could be corrupted into $\tau\hat{\omega}\nu$ $K\acute{\epsilon}\delta\rho\omega\nu$ or *vice versâ*, or how either of them could sink into such a monstrosity to a Greek eye and ear as $\tau\sigma\hat{\upsilon}$ $K\epsilon\delta\rho\acute{\omega}\nu$. To suppose that this last was a correction on critical grounds would be a mistaken modernism [1]. Even

---

[1] So Renan, Meyer, and Lachmann, and the argument is certainly attractive. It ought however to be noticed that a majority of the best professed critics (Tischendorf, Tregelles, Westcott) retain $\tau\hat{\omega}\nu$ $K\acute{\epsilon}\delta\rho\omega\nu$; and the niceties of text-criticism are such, that a positive opinion ought not to be expressed except by those who are thoroughly conversant with them. The genuineness of the Gospel, however, is not affected, whichever way the decision may go.

upon the supposition that τοῦ Κέδρου or τῶν Κέδρων was the right reading, it would still be credible that a person who was thoroughly acquainted with Hebrew, might yet be struck by the similarity in form (he might think also in meaning) of the Greek word, and so be led to use it as a translation. I suspect that the history of geographical nomenclature would furnish analogies to such a case.

Our English version gives little idea of the exactness of the description in the verse which follows. ' ὁ οὖν Ἰούδας λαβὼν τὴν σπεῖραν καὶ ἐκ τῶν ἀρχιερέων καὶ [ἐκ] τῶν Φαρισαίων ὑπηρέτας ἔρχεται ἐκεῖ μετὰ φανῶν καὶ λαμπάδων καὶ ὅπλων.' σπεῖρα is a Roman cohort, ἡ σπεῖρα that which garrisoned the citadel of Antonia. It is probable that part only was present; but it is called ἡ σπεῖρα from its being under the command of the chief officer or Chiliarch of the cohort, who is mentioned in ver. 12. The ὑπηρέται are the servants or apparitors of the Sanhedrim. Dr. Scholten raises another objection, which only recoils upon his own theory, founded on the introduction of the Roman soldiers. He thinks they were unnecessary and that their presence is improbable. But it is obviously accounted for by the fear of the chief priests that the arrest of Jesus would 'cause an uproar among the people.' At a time when 3,000,000 people were assembled in and round a city which usually held about 50,000, it must have been easy to collect a crowd anywhere; and Josephus testifies to the excitable condition of mind and frequent disturbances and bloodshed among the pilgrims attending the passover. A little spark might easily set so much inflammable material into a blaze, especially if it arose from the Messianic expectations.

R

Thus we read that 3000 men were slain in a sedition at the time of the passover on the accession of Archelaus in B.C. 4. A little later there is an outbreak against Sabinus at the feast of Pentecost, in putting down which Varus crucified 3000 men. Under the oppressions of Pilate the Jews were constantly upon the verge of insurrection, and the great centres of sedition were the religious feasts[1]. The presence of the Chiliarch and his soldiers was therefore a natural and necessary precaution. This particular instance might serve as a warning of the futility of *à priori* arguments from probability, as against positive testimony—especially when such arguments are grounded upon merely general considerations, without regard to the special historical conditions involved[2].

We may see a further confirmation of St. John's statement that the band was mainly composed of Roman soldiers in the account of the Synoptists, from which it would appear that the person of Jesus was unknown to them. The Synoptists also indicate that the band was a large one by their use of the word ὄχλος (ὄχλος πολὺς, Matt.).

The Judas kiss,—if it took place, and I do not doubt that it did,—must come in at verse 4 between ἐξελθὼν and εἶπεν. After it had been given the traitor would retire back into the crowd, or to one side of it, where the Evangelist sees him standing (ver. 5).

The description in ver. 6 is probably that of a natural shrinking from a presence at once so majestic and so

---

[1] Cf. Joseph. *Ant.* xvii. 9. 3, 10. 2 ; xviii. 3. 1, 2.
[2] A great number—I had almost said the greater number,—of

Sir Richard Hanson's arguments, though stated with much ability, have no higher value.

gentle. To the excited imagination of the Apostle it might well appear as a miracle: and this impression may have unconsciously heightened his recollection of the circumstance. To suppose a real miracle is both unnecessary and derogatory to the true dignity of our Lord.

In regard to the episode which follows, we notice that St. John knows the name both of the disciple who struck the blow, and of the high priest's servant who was wounded. He has also, in common with St. Luke, the remarkable touch that it was the *right* ear that was cut off. This agreement might have seemed suspicious, but for two considerations: (1) that St. Luke has evidently had special documents or a special tradition all through this scene; (2) that this minute and unimportant point is the only one on which St. John does agree with him, while he differs, or at least does not agree, upon a number of others, e.g. Luke xxii. 47, 48, 49, 51; Luke xxii. 53, 'I was daily with you in the temple,' St. John assigns to a different occasion (John xviii. 20). It therefore appears that the coincidence is independent and 'undesigned.'

The rebuke in ver. 11 stands in competition with that in Matt. xxvi. 52–54; and both seem to have equal claims to be considered original. Probably the second clause given by St. John ('the cup which My Father hath given Me, shall I not drink it?'), should take the place of the verse Matt. xxvi. 54 ('how then shall the Scriptures be fulfilled?').

We now come to a series of well-known difficulties and complications, which, however, it is clear, have their ground rather in our own want of knowledge

than in any vagueness or indecision on the part of
the Evangelist. We have sufficient guarantee for this
in the character of the narrative itself.

The questions raised are these. Before whom was
the interview described in verses 19–23 held? If before
Caiaphas, how are we to account for ver. 24? If before
Annas, why is he called the high priest? In what
house or apartment was the interview held? If two
separate interviews before Annas and before Caiaphas
are described, how is it that the scene is not changed
but is throughout laid in the house of the high priest?
Lastly, how is the Johannean account of Peter's denials to be harmonized with that of the several Synoptists?

I will once more simply state my own conclusions,
and leave them to an impartial consideration. They are
these.

(1) The correct reading in ver. 24 is probably
ἀπέστειλεν without any connecting particle. There
appears to be a nearly even balance of authorities for
οὖν and against it[1]; but the scale is decisively turned
by the fact that some Mss. and versions read καὶ and
others δὲ, so that these, together with οὖν, must be
taken to represent various attempts to supply what
seemed to be an omission.

(2) ἀπέστειλεν is strictly aoristic, but practically it
comes to have the force of a pluperfect. The verse is

---

[1] The evidence stands thus:
BC (first hand) LXΔ, 1, 33 (important cursives), copies of the old
Latin designated by Tregelles, a
b f ff, the Harcleian Syriac and
the Armenian read οὖν. Sin., the
important cursive, 69, the Peshito
Syriac and the Thebaic read δε.
AC (third hand) D (second hand)
Y, the rest of the MSS. and versions including the Memphitic, omit
the connecting participle altogether. The Vulgate, old Latin
c and g, and Aethiopic have 'et
misit;' the Gothic 'tunc misit.'
Westcott, Lachmann and Tischendorf retain οὖν, Tregelles brackets,
Griesbach and Meyer omit.

in fact an explanatory parenthesis *put in too late* at the point where the Evangelist happened to bethink himself of it. It merely states that Annas sent Jesus bound to Caiaphas without saying 'when.' The time was really before the preceding interview, about the middle of ver. 15. (συνεισῆλθε). In a classical composition such an explanation would of course be inadmissible, but the general *naïveté* ('Schlichtheit und Unbeholfenheit,' Keim) with which the Gospel is written, seems to leave room for it. We may suppose that the pluperfect was avoided on account of its awkward and irregular form.

(3) The interview in verses 19-23 was therefore held before Caiaphas, who is strictly and rightly designated throughout ἀρχιερεύς. With the express language of verses 13 and 24 before me I cannot conceive that in the intermediate verses the title could be given to another person, even though it might legitimately be applied to Annas as president of the Sanhedrim. The alternatives being either to force ἀρχιερεὺς or to force ἀπέστειλεν, I feel bound, contrary to the usual custom, to accept the latter as the less violent of the two [1].

(4) The house in which Peter's denial takes place is also that of Caiaphas. Annas either lived near, or else he may have held his preliminary examination in one of the rooms of the high priest's official residence, and the formal hearing may have taken place in

---

[1] The view here expressed is, of course, no new one, but is merely a return to what may be called the popular theory as against that which is held by the more accurate scholars. This is just one of those places where scholarship (i. e. that which is formed upon classic models) seems to be allowed more than its due weight. That the 'high priest' of verses 19, 22, and of 13, 15, 16, 24, &c., are different persons, is to me *incredible;* that ἀπέστειλεν should have practically a pluperfect force, at most improbable.

another. This assumption however is not necessary on the theory that we are adopting.

(5) St. Peter's three denials took place exactly as St. John describes them. The first question is put by the portress ; the second by several persons in the group round the fire at once ; the third by Malchus' kinsman. Nothing could be more sure and precise than the way in which these persons are singled out. No forger would have hit upon 'his kinsman whose ear Peter cut off.' St. John was standing by in obscurity, or sheltered perhaps by his acquaintance with the high priest, and saw all that passed. It is possible that, as M. Renan suggests, this acquaintance with the high priest merely means acquaintance with some of the upper servants : though from Mark i. 20 (the 'hired servants') it would seem that the family of Zebedee was not a poor one, and manual labour such as that described in Mark i. 19 had a different signi-ficance with the Jews and in other parts of the ancient world.

The narrative continues with the same admirable distinctness. 'Then led they Jesus from Caiaphas unto the hall of judgment *(praetorium)* ; and they themselves went not into the *praetorium* (as the residence of a heathen), lest they should be defiled ; but that they might eat the passover. Pilate then *went out* unto them, and said, 'What accusation bring ye against this man ?' Pilate comes out in front of the *praetorium*, while Jesus is led within.

The explanation in ver. 31 ('It is not lawful for us to put any man to death,') is confirmed, according to Dr. Caspari, by a passage in the Talmud, in which it is stated that the power of inflicting capital punishment was taken from the Jews forty years (in round numbers) before the destruction of Jerusalem [1].

St. John
xviii.

The accusation that the Jews bring against Jesus is exactly what from the historical situation we should expect it to be. 'They laid information against Him before the Roman government as a dangerous character; their real complaint against Him was precisely this, that He was not dangerous. Pilate executed Him on the ground that His kingdom was of this world; the Jews procured His execution precisely because it was not[2].' In no other Gospel do the motives and characters of the different actors in the scene stand out in such sharp relief. On the one hand is Pilate, guided throughout by a certain Roman sense of justice, shrinking from no extremity of punishment, but not wishing to inflict it without some clear cause; evidently suspicious of the Jewish hierarchy; despising their religious disputes, but at the same time not without fear of their turbulent spirit, and anxious not to give them a ground for accusing him before the Emperor; throwing out his far-reaching question 'What is truth?' not indeed in a spirit of 'jesting,' nor yet in that of earnest enquiry, but in the way in which stern practical men with much experience of the world do sometimes throw out a question that goes to the root of speculative difficulties. On the other hand the Pharisees, studiously keeping up the part of loyal subjects of the empire; at first seeking to escape the necessity of bringing any definite charge at all, then insisting upon the particular charge of treason, and finally compelled to fall back upon their

The historical position.

---

[1] Cf. *Leben Jesu,* p. 157.   [2] *Ecce Homo,* pp. 28, 29.

own religious law, though still holding the threat of a complaint of disloyalty *in terrorem* over Pilate's head; satisfying their consciences by the allegation of blasphemy, and urging this no doubt to some extent sincerely, but yet revealing their deeper motives by clamouring for the release of Barabbas, a robber, or bandit, but also—as we learn from the Synoptists, and as was frequently the case at that time—a leader in one of the patriotic risings. Such a meeting of parties in the Roman and in the Jews; and then above them all the object of their contention—'My kingdom is not of this world; if My kingdom were of this world, then would My servants fight that I should not be delivered to the Jews; but now is My kingdom not from hence[1]!'

We ought to be just to the Jews as well as to Pilate. 'They knew not what they did.' Their crime was the necessary outcome of the last four or five centuries of the national life. A series of intellectual mistakes had deepened into moral perversion. Brought up as they were in the school of Rabbinical tradition, with Pharisaism as their highest ideal of thought and action, they were almost constrained to act as they did. It was not the first time or the last that innocence and goodness have suffered through mistaken religious and patriotic zeal. It was terribly mistaken. There may have been not a little pure malignity mixed up in it; but we cannot doubt that it was to a

---

[1] Sir Richard Hanson's reconstruction of this part of the history I can only call an arbitrary caprice. Why destroy a picture that is perfectly consistent and intelligible, rich in detail, and in the finest shades of characterisation, in order to substitute for it another that is taken entirely out of the air, that might be true or that might be false, but rests upon no evidence of any kind—in fact, a mere romance.

great extent sincere.   The crime of the Jews was the
same in kind (if greater in degree) as that of Marcus
Aurelius, Innocent III. and the Dominicans, Loyola
and the Inquisition, Calvin and Cranmer and the Re-
formers, and indeed of all persecutors for religion.
So much indulgence as we accord on principle to one
we must accord to all.

However, this is not the place to go further into this
subject. For our present purpose it is enough to
notice that the Johannean narrative is in itself essentially consistent and credible, and agrees with all that
we know both of the Jews and the Romans and of the
origin and nature of Christianity.

The examination before Herod, which is almost
certainly historical[1], it seems should be inserted in
the course of xviii. 38. The Evangelist has apparently forgotten or overlooked it. This is one of
those passages which show that he did not write with
the Synoptic Gospels, and St. Luke's in particular, to
which we have noticed several points of affinity, actually lying open before him; but that in the cases
where they agree in minute detail, his memory has
probably been freshened by perusing them at some
greater or less distance of time.

The specification of the place where Pilate gave
judgment as the (tesselated) 'Pavement,' called in the
Hebrew (from its being upon the rising ground)
'Gabbatha,' (and therefore, we may add, from its

The exam-
ination be-
fore Herod.

ch. xix.
13-15.

[1] St. Luke has evidently had access to special information with regard to Herod's court, probably
through the circle to which belonged Joanna, the wife of Chuza;
cf. Luke viii. 3, xxiii. 7-12, xxiv.
10. From the same source I
should be tempted to derive parts
of vii. 1-10, and the narrative of
the Walk to Emmaus.

having a Hebrew name, a fixed spot, and not the portable mosaic work which the Roman generals sometimes carried about with them,) has been urged in favour of the view that Pilate's residence was not in Herod's palace, but in the tower of Antonia; because Josephus tells us that the whole of the temple hill, on part of which the tower of Antonia stood, was covered with this tesselated pavement. There seems, however, to be direct evidence for the statement that the procurators of Judaea occupied the palace of Herod when in Jerusalem; and it would hardly be likely that, supposing the whole of the hill to be covered with mosaic, a particular portion of it should be singled out to bear the name. The space in front of Herod's palace may have been laid down with mosaic; or it is possible, as Dr. Wieseler supposes, that there may have been a permanent and not portable '*suggestum*' (= 'Gabbatha') so decorated [1]. In any case we cannot but notice the accuracy of St. John's description, and the improbability that it should have been the work of a forger.

There is a considerable difficulty in regard to the note of time in ver. 14. If we are to follow the Jewish mode of reckoning, this will be clearly opposed to Mark xv. 25, and also, it is generally assumed, to Matt. xxvii. 45, Luke xxiii. 44. St. John places the final delivery of Pilate's verdict at the sixth hour, i. e. 12 o'clock in the day; St. Mark places the Crucifixion at 9 a.m., and the darkness is made by all the three Synoptists to last from 12 to 3 p.m. Dr. Caspari is perhaps right in calling attention to the fact, that the

---

[1] Cf. Wieseler, *Beit.* p. 249, n. Ellicott, p. 346, n. 1.

darkness ceases precisely at the ninth hour (3 p.m.), at the moment of our Lord's death. It might be inferred from this, that it was meant to be coterminous with the Crucifixion. The narrative of St. John might so be said to be confirmed roughly by the Synoptists, though the discrepancy with St. Mark would still remain, and the language of St. John himself would have to be somewhat strained[1]. If this is not satisfactory we may have recourse to the supposition that St. John has adopted the Roman mode of reckoning from midnight. Yet even this, if it removes some difficulties, raises others; for the interval between the time indicated by πρωί and 6 a.m. is hardly sufficient to allow for all the events recorded in John xviii. 28—xix. 14 together with the examination before Herod, Luke xxiii. 6–12. In spite of these multifarious difficulties, I should hesitate much to suggest that either of the two notes of time was unhistorical. This is not the way in which writers of fiction are wont to embellish their narratives; least of all writers of fiction in those times. The most honest and authentic testimony will admit of considerable discrepancies; and by allowing a certain latitude to the expressions used, those before us would appear to be not insuperable. If a choice is to be made, I should incline to the hypothesis that Roman time has been followed, the more so as it seems to give greater continuity to the sequence of the events generally; but at best the question cannot be left otherwise than open.

---

[1] Dr. Caspari adopts the—I must think—quite unjustifiable measure of altering the reading in St. Mark from τρίτη to ἕκτη (*Leben Jesu*, pp. 193–5).

St. John
xix.

vv. 16-24.

The distance of the hill Golgotha from the city [1], the title upon the cross, the remonstrance of the Jews, with Pilate's grim reply, the behaviour of the four soldiers on guard, are all told with greater exactness by St. John than by the Synoptists. Doubt may seem to be thrown upon the act attributed to the soldiers on account of the Messianic prophecy, of which the Evangelist sees in it the fulfilment. But the Synoptists notice the same circumstance, though its correspondence with the words of the Psalm has escaped them. It is by no means improbable that the incident of the tunic being without seam had a foundation in fact. It would be far-fetched as an invention, and would not be necessary to account for the lot-drawing, which the Synoptists mention without it. Besides, if it is a fiction, how did the writer know that the garments were divided exactly into *four?* So casual an indication of the number of the soldiers must be taken as a strong mark of authenticity.

vv. 25-27.

In regard to the women at the foot of the cross there is a discrepancy between St. John and the Synoptists similar to, but not so insoluble as, that in regard to the time of the Crucifixion. The picture is taken at different moments, that in the Synoptic Gospels somewhat later than that in St. John. The Apostle and those with him have withdrawn—

---

[1] The bold and striking view propounded by Mr. Fergusson (art. 'Jerusalem' in *S. D.*) according to which the site of Golgotha and the original Church of the Holy Sepulchre is that now occupied by the Mosque of Omar, appears to be gaining ground. It has lately found an adherent in Dr. Caspari, who seems to have arrived independently at the same result (cf. *Leben Jesu, Appendix on Topography of Jerusalem*, pp. 219-263). It would be a slight argument against this view, if, as above, the praetorium is to be taken as Herod's Palace, and not the Tower of Antonia.

perhaps been driven away by the soldiers or the Jews. It may be that they have rejoined a larger knot of disciples collected in the distance. Statements of this sort may legitimately be harmonised, where (1) they are equally precise in both documents, and (2) the process of harmonising them involves nothing far-fetched or unnatural. At the same time it would be wrong to press any particular theory as to the *way* in which they are to be harmonised, unless it is peculiarly self-evident and convincing. The most that can be done is to point out *how* a harmony may be possible. The combinations of events are so various that the actual harmony may have been different from any that we may imagine.

I have little doubt that there were *four* women at the foot of the cross. Bp. Ellicott, who thinks there were only three, does not notice the obvious improbability that two sisters should bear the same name. And the two arguments that he himself uses are far from equally cogent. 'The sister of Mary' would be sufficiently explicit to the Apostle and his contemporaries; and it is quite a plausible conjecture that this sister was Salome, the Apostle's own mother—in which case it would accord with his practice to introduce her indirectly. As to the use of καὶ I cannot help asking how wide an induction Dr. Ellicott has to go upon? Such nice literary arguments are very precarious. But the identification of the wife of Alphaeus with the sister of the Virgin stands or falls with the Hieronymian theory as to the 'brethren of the Lord;' and that I must regard as untenable [1].

---

[1] Cf. *Huls. Lect.* p. 354, n. Compare Lightfoot, *Excursus on Galatians*, pp. 247–282; Meyer, *ad loc.*; &c.

The Tübingen theory as applied to this scene receives its logical completion, and critical ingenuity its climax, in the suggestion of Dr. Scholten, that the mother of Jesus here stands for 'the Church,' which is significantly committed to the charge of the beloved disciple instead of to St. Peter[1]! If the circumstances are not too solemn to admit the question we should be tempted to ask, in what relation to 'the Church' the *other* personages are to be conceived as standing, the sister of Mary, Mary the wife of Cleopas, and Mary Magdalen?

———

But we must draw aside for a moment from these debates and questionings, and be mindful of the presence into which we have been brought.

On that terrible canvas with which Tintoret has covered the end of the last room in the school of San Rocco, the Magdalen is seen lying at the foot of the cross. She lies motionless, as if in a swoon.

In the Pietà or Deposition of Perugino the very air seems hushed and still with holy sorrow—but it is sorrow that does not show itself by tears. A tremor of the lip or a silent compression of the hand are the only signs by which it is revealed.

And we too, if we are true Christians, shall follow these examples. We shall stand with bowed head, and turn away with reverent step. But our words, if there are any, will be wary and few.

———

If in the history of the last moments of the Passion

[1] Cf. Scholten, p. 383.

and in those which follow we observe the peculiar care
with which the Evangelist points out and insists upon
the fulfilment of Scripture, this ought not really to
prejudice us against his narrative. In ver. 28, ἵνα
τελειωθῇ ἡ γραφὴ goes with the words that precede, and
not with those which follow. And with regard to verses
36, 37 it should be noticed (1) that the *crurifragium*
was a Roman custom though not *necessarily* connected
with crucifixion [1]; (2) that in this case both the
crurifragium and the lance-thrust are naturally
accounted for; (3) that no prophecy or precedent is
quoted for the remarkable phenomenon described in
ver. 34; (4) that none of the Synoptists allude to these
prophecies, from which it would appear that they had
not been generally noticed, and that it was not very
obvious to apply them literally. It is therefore, we
conclude, not only equally probable and natural but
more so, that the facts should have suggested an
application of the prophecies than that the prophecies
should have suggested an invention of the facts.

The issue of blood and water seems to be capable
of a natural explanation, as caused by a rupture of
the vessels about the heart [2]. As a pure allegory it
would be very far-fetched and extraordinary. Here
again it is the more credible hypothesis that the
facts came first in order of time, and that the symbolism is an after-thought engrafted upon them.

---

[1] Cf. Plautus, *Poen.* iv. 2, 64; *S.D.*
art. 'Crucifixion,' and Meyer, *ad loc.*
[2] Cf. Ellicott, p. 361, n. 2;
Meyer, pp. 635, 6; Ewald, p. 414,
n. When we think of the intensity
with which every detail of the Passion must have imprinted itself
upon the Apostle's mind, we shall
not be surprised if he should in some
respects have magnified slight and
accidental phenomena, especially
where they seemed to fall in with
his own peculiar symbolism.

For the rest we cannot but notice the strong asseveration of the Evangelist that he had himself seen that which he records, and that his record is true. It is not easy to believe that this asseveration was made in bad faith. When the details and sequence of events in the description are examined closely they will be found to be quite consistent with autoptic testimony. The mark of time in ver. 31 especially confirms this. At sunset the Sabbath would begin: and that Sabbath was one of peculiar sanctity. In addition to that which it possessed simply as a Sabbath it was also the first great day of the Passover, the night in which the Paschal lamb was to be eaten. The day on which the Crucifixion had taken place was itself the preparation for it, on which, if possible, work was suspended. The Jews therefore hastened to have the bodies taken down from the cross, and for the same reason that of our Lord was interred in the nearest appropriate spot, a garden situated on the hill where the crosses stood. All this is told with the greatest precision. And we have seen reason to think that the whole chronology of which it forms a part is accurate. It is difficult in the extreme to believe either that it was put together by any one but a Jew, or that even a Jew would have kept it so constantly and vividly in mind if he had not been himself actually present.

The circumstantiality of the narrative seems to increase as it proceeds. The Jews apply to Pilate and receive the necessary order for the bodies to be

taken down. This however could not be done till life was extinct. And while the soldiers are waiting for the *crurifragium* to take effect, Joseph of Arimathaea also goes to Pilate, and, having received permission, takes the body of Jesus, which he with Nicodemus embalms, and lays in a new tomb, possibly his own, which was near at hand. There are two slight coincidences to be noted here. One is the epithet τολμήσας in Mark xv. 43 (the original document), the emphasis on which becomes more intelligible when taken in connection with the statement in St. John that he was a disciple, but 'secretly, for fear of the Jews:' this boldness therefore was the more remarkable in him[1]. The other is the association of Joseph with Nicodemus. We learn from different places, and with regard to the latter quite incidentally, that they were both members of the Sanhedrim, and would thus naturally be acquainted.

We gather from St. John's account a singularly clear picture of the Jewish mode of burying. The body was first embalmed, and embalmed simply by the spices being wrapped in between the folds of the linen cloth or clothes in which the body was bound. Here as a mark of special honour, and as coming from wealthy men, the spices reach the large amount of 100 lbs.

[1] Cf. Ellicott, p. 362, n.

CHAPTER XVI.

THE RESURRECTION.

St. John xx.

Relative value of the different accounts of the Resurrection.

I T does not lie within the scope of this enquiry to determine the exact relation of the four different reports of the Resurrection to one another; but it may throw some light upon that which it is our duty to investigate, if we state briefly the results that seem to be given by a critical examination of the other three.

(1) That of St. Matthew is of these the least trustworthy. It is comparatively late in date, and it is highly probable that legendary matter has been mixed up with it [1].

(2) That of St. Mark appears to be imperfect, ending abruptly with ver. 8. It is now held by a majority of the best editors that the rest of the chapter did not originally form part of the Gospel, though it was an early addition to it and represents an early tradition [2].

---

[1] Cf. Bleek, *Evangelien*, ii. 475, 476, 494. Meyer, *Comm. on Matt.* pp. 601, 607, 608, 610, 613.

[2] At the time when this was written, there seemed to be a clear balance of authority against the verses — Tischendorf, Tregelles, Meyer, Alford, Westcott. The question has since been re-opened by the elaborate work of Mr. Burgon (*The Last Twelve Verses of St. Mark Vindicated:* Parker, 1871), with what success it is for the professed text critics to decide. One of the most competent of these, Mr. Hort, has declared against Mr. Burgon's view, in *The Academy*, No. 36, p. 519. Without any right to speak as a text critic, there are still one or two points that I should like to remark. (1) Mr. Burgon notices certain points in which he thinks that the Lectionaries have affected the Mss.;

St. Mark's narrative, to the end of ver. 8, appears to be drawn from the ground document of the Synoptists.

St. John xx.

(3) St. Luke has also adopted this, but he has had access to a special document or tradition besides, which is of early date and high value. It is marked by the introduction of Joanna, and, in the account of the walk to Emmaus, by an early Christology, and in ver. 21 by a vivid reproduction of the politico-theocratic hopes, which must have entirely disappeared some time before St. Luke wrote. This document has, especially in ver. 12, a certain affinity to St. John ; not such, however, as to admit the supposition, either that the verse has been interpolated from St. John, or that the Johannean version has been constructed out of it : κείμενα should probably, on textual grounds, be omitted.

This document or tradition to some extent confirms the narrative in St. John, but the best witness to that is itself. We have had before narratives remarkable for beauty and for lifelike minuteness of detail, but here they reach their climax. It is old ground that has been often trodden, but no one would

vv. 1-18.

---

is it not equally possible that the Lectionaries (which all appear to belong to the Eastern Church) merely reflect the phenomena of the family of Mss. used by that Church ? (2) Can we consider it proved that the note τὸ τέλος in the Mss. had, *at the time of Eusebius,* a liturgical object ? (3) If it had, are we to suppose that Eusebius himself was ignorant of that object, and did not know that in calling attention to the mark τὸ τέλος he was merely pointing to the end of an ecclesiastical lection ? (4) Mr. Burgon assumes that Eusebius is merely putting an assumed case or alluding to some more ancient writer without approving of the omission of the verses himself; but do not his 'Canons' prove that he *did* himself deliberately omit them ? (5) Is it after all so incredible that the Gospel should, for some unknown reason, have ended abruptly? What would Mr. Burgon say to the ending of the Acts as compared with the formal end of the third Gospel and the very formal openings of both books ? Accident (i. e. unknown causes) plays a large part in all human affairs.

weary of treading it again, of following the Magdalen as she hastens to the tomb while the streaks of dawn are barely breaking in the east, as she then hurries back frightened at what she had seen, and tells her strange story to the two disciples;—or again, of going with those two disciples to the sepulchre, watching how the youthful St. John outruns his older companion, but when he reaches the tomb dares not enter alone; how on the other hand St. Peter, less active in limb but bolder and not so finely strung in spirit, no sooner arrives than he goes in, and coming out describes the position of the linen clothes which are now lying empty, and the napkin 'that was about His head' folded in a place by itself; how then and not before the beloved disciple enters and the truth begins to dawn upon him, notwithstanding its suddenness and the want of preparation; and lastly, most beautiful scene of all, how the disconsolate Magdalen, lingering near the tomb, first sees bright forms within, which she questions, and in the midst of her questioning hears a step, or is conscious of a presence behind her, and turning round, between her tears and her abstraction does not look to see who it is, but concluding that it is the gardener, asks what has been done with the body of her Lord—in reply she hears but her name, and she too has but one word, but in that is concentrated all the depth and transport of her joy—'Master!'

I doubt whether we can really lay stress upon the plural οἴδαμεν in ver. 2 as an allusion to the narrative of the Synoptists: not so much because of οἶδα in ver. 13, where the situation is different, as because the Apostle's memory, close and accurate as it is, could

hardly retain so fine a point as a mere termination.
This would be to assume a more than verbal, a *syllabic*
inspiration. But it does not therefore follow that the
two accounts are altogether incompatible. We need
not suppose that Mary has hastened on before her
companions, but only that she breaks away from them
in order to bear the tidings to the Apostles[1].

It is not perhaps incredible, though it is improbable,
that a forger should have been so careful in his
description of the state of the tomb and its contents,
but it is in a high degree improbable that along with
this he should have preserved so accurately the character and individuality of the Apostles.

We notice that neither St. John nor St. Peter has
the vision of angels. It would be simplified in the
case of Mary if we were to suppose that the first
question, 'Woman, why weepest thou?' was an echo
(in her imagination) of the second. Then there might
be room to conjecture that what Mary saw was only
the morning light shining upon the white winding
sheet, as it lay within the tomb. But there is considerable evidence for the reality of angelic appearances, among which these in connection with the
Resurrection are not among the least well attested;
we may therefore hesitate to assert a negative with
regard to a sphere which is so entirely removed from
our knowledge. The line which separates the proven
from the unproven will always be uncertain, and there
will be a number of facts and propositions which some
minds will place upon one side of it and others upon
the other. For the rest, the vivid presentation of the
scene is only equalled by its psychological truth and

---

[1] Cf. Ewald, p. 415, and Meyer's objections.

delicacy. The words 'Touch me not,' etc., seem to have reference to an impulsive passionate motion on the part of Mary, prompted as such a motion would be by a mixed feeling of affection, adoration, and the desire for sensible proof of that which she saw, to convince herself whether it was a spirit or no. It is especially to this implied enquiry that the answer is addressed. 'Touch Me not—it is needless to touch Me. A spirit hath not flesh and bones as you see Me have. I am not yet ascended, though My ascension is indeed begun.' Though I thus in the main follow Meyer as to the connection implied by $\gamma\grave{\alpha}\rho$, I cannot but think that there is still something of withdrawal from mortal touch hidden under $\mathring{\alpha}\nu\alpha\beta\acute{\epsilon}\beta\eta\kappa\alpha$ compared with $\mathring{\alpha}\nu\alpha\beta\alpha\acute{\iota}\nu\omega$. 'I have entered on My return to the Father, though it is not yet complete.' So in ver. 27, the bodily touch is only allowed in answer to doubt, and with a certain reproof that it should be necessary. Still the first object in both passages is to insist upon the reality—the corporeal reality—of the Risen Body.

St. Luke's account of the appearance on the evening after the Resurrection appears to contain traces of all the three separate appearances recorded in St. John. 'Handle Me and see,' is a vaguer reminiscence of 'Reach hither thy hand and thrust it into My side.' So in Mark xvi. 14, ' He upbraided them with their unbelief and hardness of heart,' compared with ' Then were the disciples glad when they saw the Lord,' John xx. 20 (though this is perhaps partly an extension of the Evangelist's own feeling to the rest of the Apostles), seems to find its counterpart rather in ver. 27, ' Be not faithless but believing.' Then Luke xxiv. 42, ' Have ye here any meat? And they gave Him a piece of broiled fish'—especially if we may omit the addition καὶ ἀπὸ μελισσίου κηρίου—appears to be a reminiscence of the later scene, John xxi. 5, 9. From the English version the resemblance would seem to be closer than it is in reality: ἔχετέ τι βρώσιμον ἐνθάδε and μή τι προσφάγιον ἔχετε being translated by the same word, as it is not impossible that they may represent the same word in Aramaic.

It is clear in any case, that in the narrative of St. Luke several separate incidents have coalesced into one, as the Ascension itself is placed upon the same evening (that of the day of the Resurrection), a statement which the Evangelist found it necessary to correct when he came to write the history of the Acts. It would seem as if the narrative had in the first instance come to him in the form of proof of the reality of the Resurrection, the different 'moments' being marked by vv. 36, 39, 42.

It might be thought that perhaps St. John, or the author of the fourth Gospel, had constructed his narrative out of these materials. But, as in all other cases where some definite nucleus such as this is suggested, it is found upon examination that it really comes in more or less incidentally, and not in such a way as it must have done if the other details encrusted round it had really been fictitious.

A strong argument in favour of the Johannean version throughout is its psychological truth. In spite of the fact that the resurrection has been intimated beforehand, the disciples are not prepared for it, do not understand it, and at first find difficulty in believing it. Neither is their unbelief and the gradual formation of their faith described in the same rough and wholesale manner as in St. Luke and St. Mark, but with many fine touches of individuality. When Mary Magdalen finds the sepulchre empty, she has but one idea—'They have *taken away* the Lord out of the sepulchre, and we know not where they have laid Him.' She has no other way of accounting for it than that which occurred to the hostile Jews (Matt. xxviii. 13). So when the two disciples come to verify her report, one of them believes—but what? It must have been a very rudimentary belief, as it is added, 'For as yet they knew not the Scripture, that He must rise again from the dead.' At the first appearance after He had displayed His hands and His side, 'the disciples were glad when they saw the Lord.' But still they did not all believe. There was one at least who refused to be convinced without the evidence of his senses.

The character of Thomas is very delicately drawn. He is an honest plain man, cautious in his beliefs and not disposed to credulity, but standing fast upon the ground of common sense; and yet, when once his reason is convinced, filled with strong and deep enthusiasm,—no very gifted nature, but an earnest, loyal, steadfast soul. When the Lord invites him to touch His hands and His side, he does not wait to obey the invitation, but breaks out into the passionate cry, 'My Lord and my God!' His unbelief is gone for ever.

There is deep truth and appropriateness in the gentle reproof which follows: 'Blessed are they that have not seen, and yet have believed.' They are blessed, happy—μακάριοι.

'Serene will be our days and bright,
 And happy will our nature be,
 When love is an unerring light,
 And joy its own security.'

But this is not the only type of faith, and our Lord's words still leave room to question whether it is always the higher.

CHAPTER XVII.

THE APPEARANCE IN GALILEE.

St. John xxi.

A Supple-
mental
chapter.

IS the last chapter part of the original or first draft of the Gospel? Is it by the same hand? The first of these questions I think we shall answer in the negative; the second in the affirmative.

Apart from the slight differences of style which are noticed by the commentators, and which *possibly* may be sufficient to mark a different date of composition, the last two verses of the preceding chapter are so evidently adapted for a conclusion that we cannot doubt that the Gospel originally ended with them. Chap. xxi. seems to have been added specially with a view to correct the misconception mentioned in ver. 23; but how long after the completion of the rest of the Gospel, and under what other circumstances, we are not in a position to say. The arguments that have been brought to prove that it had a different origin from the main portion of the Gospel seem to be wholly insufficient. On the other hand, those which have compelled us to see in the latter the immediate work of an eye-witness and an Apostle, are equally valid here. There is the same distinctness of specification as to place and persons, verses 1, 2; the same

vv. 1–14.

wonderful minuteness of description, verses 7, 8, 9, 11, 13, 20; the same truth of character. It is almost a repetition of the scene at the tomb. John is the first to recognise his Master, but Peter throws himself impetuously into the water to reach Him. No one but an eye-witness would have thought of the touch in ver. 7 ('he girt his fisher's coat unto him, for he was naked') which *exactly inverts* the natural action of one who is about to swim, and yet is quite accounted for by the circumstances.

I strongly suspect that the miraculous draught of fishes in Luke v. really belongs to this place. St. Luke, not being an eye-witness, would naturally piece together the floating fragments of tradition that came to him very much by conjecture. Accordingly, he has been caught by the expression, 'Follow Me, and I will make you fishers of men' (Matt. iv. 19), and he has attached to it, not unnaturally or inappropriately, the miraculous draught, which is quite foreign to the Synoptic original. In order to introduce the situation he has made use of Mark iv. 1 (= Matt. xiii. 1, 2), which, it is to be noticed, in its proper place he has omitted (cf. Luke viii. 4). For the rest the features of the two narratives—the toiling all night, the command, the auxiliary boat—are remarkably similar.

We might be even tempted to suppose that the episode in Matt. xiv. 28–31 originally sprang from the action attributed to Peter by St. John. That too is recorded by only a single Evangelist—*not* the Apostle St. Matthew, who wrote only the 'collection of discourses,' but the compiler or editor of the first Gospel, who cannot have been an eye-witness. It is not implied, but is rather excluded or significantly

St. John xxi.

ignored in the parallel narrative of St. Mark and St. John. And it resembles the incident related in this last chapter of the fourth Gospel both as being the sequel to a miracle and as to the spirit by which the ardent Apostle was animated. Other traits in the Matthean version would seem to be derived from the earlier storm at sea—'O thou of little faith'—the wonder of the disciples. But, given these materials, there is nothing essential added in the first Gospel : it is not difficult to imagine a coalescence of the two incidents in the process of oral transmission ; and the marked silence of two witnesses of the first order, like St. John and the fundamental document of the Synoptists, must be taken to outweigh the secondary evidence on which the narrative rests.

I know that these combinations will appear hazardous to many minds. They are not of course to be pressed at all dogmatically. A certain slight degree, perhaps we may say, of *probability* is the most that can be claimed for them. But when we come to weigh document against document and to consider the relative position of the writers, I think they will commend themselves with some force to an impartial judgment. If they really held good they would only tend to throw out still more conspicuously the authentic and original character of the fourth Gospel.

Ver. 12 ('None of the disciples durst ask Him, Who art Thou?') is another instance in which the feelings of the Apostolic circle are represented from within. It gives a graphic picture of the hushed wonder and awe with which the Apostles beheld what had passed.

vv. 15–23.

In ver. 15 we have once more a touch of exquisite psychology. It is Peter's modesty that speaks, and

his sense of shame at his own shortcomings. He cannot appeal to his proved constancy, because he knows
that his constancy had been tried and found wanting.
He has indeed nothing to appeal to, and yet he is
conscious that his affection is not unreal or insincere,
and he trusts to Him who searches the hearts : 'Yea,
Lord, Thou knowest that I love Thee,' 'Thou knowest
all things ; Thou knowest that I love Thee.' This is
truly Johannean, as indeed is the whole passage, with
its tender pathos and delicate changes, ἀγαπᾶν—
φιλεῖν, βόσκειν—ποιμαίνειν, ἀρνία—πρόβατα.

St. John xxi.

The prophecy of Peter's death is attested as historical precisely by its vagueness. 'Thou shalt stretch
forth thy hands' is the only part of the description
that can be taken to refer directly to crucifixion ;
and it is not clear that it does not refer merely to
stretching out the hands before the judges. If it does
refer to crucifixion, it would be a curious inversion of
the order of events, for 'another shall gird thee'
clearly refers to the loading with chains, and 'carry
thee whither thou wouldest not' to the leading to the
place of execution ; yet these come *after* not before
the outstretched hands. It speaks well for the con-
scientiousness of the Evangelist, that writing certainly
after the death of St. Peter he has not accommodated
his description more closely to the circumstances of it.
Passages like Luke xix. 43, 44, xxi. 20, 24, compared
with the parallels in the other Synoptists, show how
easily details taken from the actual fact slipped into a
prophecy recorded after the event.

If we accept the supposition (for which, as we have
seen, much is to be urged) that this chapter was written
by, and therefore during the lifetime of the beloved

disciple himself, then we have in verses 22, 23, a further confirmation of its Apostolic origin. It was a belief universal in the Apostolic times, and naturally confined to them, that the second advent would take place before the first generation of Christians had passed away. It is clear that both ver. 23 and ver. 24 suppose the author of the Gospel to be still living at the time of its publication, and to have been an original disciple of the Lord. Can we believe that this is deliberate fiction? or that if a fiction it would have been so well preserved?

It is quite possible that the amanuensis who wrote this last part of the Gospel inserted ver. 24, as speaking for himself and for the whole Asiatic Church ('*we* know that His testimony is true'). But the hyperbole of ver. 25 is peculiarly natural in an Apostle. With his thoughts and memory full to overflowing of his Lord's acts and his Lord's words, he might well say that the world itself could not contain the record of them. In the mouth of any other person such an expression would be strained and affected.

It will be seen that I have assumed throughout the foregoing the reality of the Resurrection and of the appearances which followed upon it. The reader may take it, if he will, merely as an assumption; though as such I believe it is necessary to make the narrative intelligible, and without it the whole mass of evidence that has hitherto been accumulating before us will be resolved into a tissue of illusions. Just as it follows that if the Gospel was written by an eye-witness, the Resurrection must be true, so also does it follow that if the Resurrection is not true, the Gospel has not been written by an eye-witness. But that, with the facts before us, is extremely difficult to believe. And when we pass from this single Gospel, and take in the whole of the evidence from other sources, from the Synoptic Gospels, from the Acts, from the Apocalypse, from St. Peter, but above all from the Epistles of St. Paul, it acquires such force and such dimensions as even a prejudiced reason can hardly withstand. When, leaving the precise manner of the Resurrection and the precise nature and sequence of the appearances that follow upon it, we fix our attention solely upon the fact itself, the evidence for it is found to stand out in a variety and with a volume equal to that for any event the best attested in history. In the face of this, and taking into account the whole character of the phenomena in connection with which the Resurrection stands, I cannot refuse credence to it merely on the strength of an induction ' by simple enumeration,' based upon present experience, i.e. upon a range of facts existing under conditions that may not be, and indeed are not, the same[1]. For, looking at the broad

St. John xxi.

[1] It is strange that a writer of M. Renan's acuteness should have been betrayed into an argument so shallow and illogical as that on p. xcvii of his Introduction. No one supposes that miracles such as took place at the origin of Christianity, take place now. It is therefore a wholly irrelevant challenge to demand that miracles should be submitted to the test of experiment. As well say that Phidias did not carve the Olympian Zeus, because no one can carve an Olympian Zeus now. The real question is, what kind of presumption does the non-occurrence of miracles at the present time afford against the alleged fact that 1800 years ago miracles actually happened. The strength of this presumption will depend upon the identity of the conditions prevalent at the two periods. But, apart from the enormous tax upon our ignorance involved in the assertion that they are identical, the mere fact of the origination of Christianity shows that they are not. When we think of what Christianity is, and from what it sprang, it will not seem unreasonable to interpose a divine agency in the act of its production. At least, until M. Renan and his fellow critics have succeeded in accounting for it by natural causes, the world at large will not cease to account for it by supernatural.

St. John xxi.

features of the case ;—looking, that is, at the conditions out of which Christianity arose, and in the midst of which it was established and grew ; looking moreover at the phenomena of Christianity itself, as compared with all other religious manifestations, and even with its own very imperfect historical realisation ; looking at its place in the history of the world and the power that it still retains over the spirits of men,—we are obliged to take it out of the category of ordinary effect and cause, and the harmony of things is rather preserved than broken, when we attribute to it an origination which is miraculous and divine.

CHAPTER XVIII.

CURRENT ARGUMENTS AGAINST THE GENUINENESS
OF THE GOSPEL.

WE have now traversed the Gospel from begin-Objections.
ning to end, testing at each step the data that
seemed to be presented to us, and seeking to determine
their exact bearing upon the subject of our enquiry—
the question, that is, who was its author, and what
amount of credence we are to give to its contents.
But as yet these data are scattered indiscriminately
over the surface, and it is time that they were collected
in a form somewhat more compact and systematic.
We may do this perhaps best by first running through
briefly the arguments that are usually brought against
the Johannean hypothesis, and then by drawing out
the chief of those by which it seems to be established.
For the first half of this process we will not trust our
own statement, but will give the arguments as they are
urged by the latest writer who has taken this side of
the question, Dr. Keim[1].

Dr. Keim begins by remarking that the question as
to the authorship of the fourth Gospel hangs closely
together with that as to its historical character, and by

[1] Cf. *Geschichte Jesu von Nazara*, i. 121–133.

T

showing that a low view must be taken of the latter, he thinks, very rightly, that the Johannean hypothesis must be directly negatived. Accordingly he sets himself to prove that the Gospel is unhistorical, and this in three ways : (1) by the nature of the Gospel in itself ; (2) by its relation to the writings of St. Paul ; (3) by its relation to the Synoptic Gospels.

It is unfortunate, however, that this is far from the best part of Dr. Keim's learned and valuable work. It is rhetorically written, and consequently wants much of that precision which in treating of such a subject is especially necessary.

I. We see this at the outset. Dr. Keim's first argument is derived from the nature of the Gospel in itself.

From the character of the Gospel.

(a) 'Das Auswahl-Evangelium ist ein einseitiges Evangelium.' 'A Gospel which does not profess to be a complete history, but gives only certain select passages, is a one-sided Gospel.' Perfectly true ; in fact the proposition is almost a tautological one, so long as it is kept within its proper limits. The fourth Gospel is certainly a Gospel 'of selections,' though what the principle of selection has been we cannot in every case exactly say. No doubt it was written in the main to assert the Divinity of Christ, and the discourses especially seem to have been chosen with reference to this. But in the Synoptic Gospels, too, the same, or very similar claims, are put forward. And there is nothing whatever to show that the other Synoptic matter is excluded. When Dr. Keim extends his proposition so as to make it say this, he is alleging much more than can be proved. There is ample room in the Johannean narrative for that of the

Synoptists to be inserted. The very points in which
the two agree show how easily the agreement might
have been extended. But the fallacy is to suppose
that the Synoptists give us a complete history or anything like it. How many points do they touch only
to leave! Some of these the fourth Gospel has
cleared up, but many others still remain, and the
thoughtful student of the Synoptic Gospels cannot
but feel, that there was room for more 'supplementary'
Gospels than one.

(β) 'Not only is the fourth Gospel one-sided, but it
is also in a high degree subjective, i. e. historically
unreliable,' (willkürlich). This, Dr. Keim says, is confessed as regards the discourses. But the question is
entirely one of degree, and in examining the discourses
one by one we have come to the conclusion that they
are not so far subjective as that they cannot have been
written by an ear-witness and an Apostle, or so as
essentially to misrepresent the originals of which they
are the reproduction.

(γ) A particular mark of this subjectivity, Dr. Keim
sees in the ' system of triplets,' which is his own peculiar discovery. 'Three times is Jesus in Galilee,
three times in Judaea, twice three feasts fall in the
period of His ministry, especially three Passovers, at
the beginning, in the middle, and at the end, which
either prophesy or bring on His death : He performs
three miracles in Galilee, three in Jerusalem. Twice
three days He moves in the vicinity of John, three
days mark the history of Lazarus, six that of the
last Passover, three words upon the Cross, three
appearances after the Resurrection.' Who ever before
suspected a deep mystical meaning in notices that

seem so natural and so incidental? But the whole of this elaborate scheme is a pure fancy. It will not bear examination. It is not merely three times that Jesus is in Galilee, but Galilee is His home and the centre of His mission. The three visits to Jerusalem have to be very roughly reckoned—the third at least is broken by a retreat of not less than a month's duration to Ephraim and Peraea. There is nothing to lead us to class together the three feasts which are not passovers, and of those which are, one has no bearing upon the history and is only noticed casually in the course of events that are laid in Galilee (vi. 4). There are not six miracles but seven, of which four are in Galilee, that at Cana, at Capernaum, the feeding of the five thousand, and the walking upon the water. Three days are mentioned during which our Lord is for the first time in the neighbourhood of John, though more are implied. The second time there is no mention of days at all. The history of Lazarus takes up four days, not three; the words upon the cross are not counted; and besides the appearances to the disciples there is also that to the Magdalen. On the same principle it would be just as easy to discover other numbers besides three, two disciples of John, two days in Samaria, two firkins in the pitchers; five disciples first called, five barley loaves, five porches in Bethesda; and fours, sixes, sevens in the same way; how Dr. Keim would deal with the larger numbers I hardly know, e.g. v. 5, vi. 7, 19, xi. 18, xii. 5, xxi. 8, 11.

(δ) 'The subjective freedom of the author being thus shown to penetrate to the very marrow of the history and discourses,' it remains to see how it is applied.

This appears from the doctrine of the Logos, and of the opposition between light and darkness, which has been carried out in the history with 'mathematical accuracy.' We should like to see the author who, with no other data, constructed out of them the fourth Gospel. The doctrines of the Logos, and of light and darkness, are the most general of abstractions which do not affect the history at all. What outline could be simpler than that which they supply? Would not the narrative of the Synoptists, we might almost say the Epistles of St. Paul, fit into it equally well? If a historian were to describe the political history of England as a conflict between the principles of Order and Progress, should we therefore at once set down his work as constructed *à priori?* Not one whit more is suspicion justifiable against the fourth Gospel.

(ε) Lastly, it is argued that the figure thus constructed out of the doctrine of the Logos is not human. The Figure that we find in the Synoptists, in St. Paul, and indeed in all other Christian documents, is in some respects not human, and it is true that the author of the fourth Gospel has insisted especially upon these. But the fact, that he has thus been led, in the discourses especially, to turn the light upon a particular aspect of his subject, gives to his treatment of it an appearance of monotony which does not really exist. What can be more tenderly or beautifully human than the character of Christ as portrayed by St. John? There is nothing in the Synoptists that would take the place of the raising of Lazarus, the washing of the disciples' feet, the last discourses, the appearance to Mary in the garden, the discourse with Peter by the shore of the lake. If Gethsemane is omitted, the interview with the Greeks is given ; if the spiritual agony of the cross retires into the background, the physical anguish comes out no less than with the Synoptists. A writer who was merely embodying the doctrine of the Logos could not have written more than the last verses of the history of Lazarus. Neither would he have written xiv. 28, ' My Father is greater than I.'

II. But Dr. Keim does not seem to set very much store himself by the arguments hitherto brought forward, for he introduces the next section thus : ' But how much stronger are the objections derived from the oldest documents of Christianity, the Epistles of St. Paul and the Synoptic Gospels.' And yet the objections drawn from these are hardly such as can be called strong. No doubt St. John does exhibit a certain advance on St. Paul. But we must be careful to distinguish between portions where the Evangelist is speaking in his own person, such as the Prologue, and those which form part of the objective history, and in this again we must distinguish between the main substance of fact and that outward colouring of presentation in which the individuality of the writer necessarily displays itself. Bearing these considerations in mind, I do not think we shall see anything in the relations of St. John to St. Paul which serves to discredit the Gospel as history. The points that Dr. Keim has noticed are these :—

(*a*) The Christology. But if our examination of the Johannean discourses is sound, it will appear that the Christology to which they give expression is not peculiar to St. John, but is fundamentally that of the

rom its relation to the writings of St. Paul.

Synoptists and of Christ Himself.   The one part of
the Johannean Christology that is found in St. Paul
but not in the Synoptists is the doctrine of Pre-existence.   But the fact that the Synoptists do not allude
to it creates but very slight presumption against its
originality.   And as it is found both in St. John and in
St. Paul, the hypothesis lies quite as near that they
took it from a common source, or at least inferred it
from common premises.

(β) The Law.   Dr. Keim argues, chiefly from a
single expression, 'your law,' which is found in three
places ; but in each case, as we should expect, in an
argumentum ad hominem.   St. John does indeed to
some extent hold a more objective relation to the
Law and to the Jewish people than St. Paul ; but this
is accounted for simply by his removal from them in
space and time, and by the fact that the destruction
of Jerusalem had cut, more than anything that
preceded it, the connection between Jewish institutions and Christianity.   In spite of this we have
seen that St. John's relation to the Law is really less
negative than St. Paul's, and is not otherwise than
in accordance with the historical facts.   Dr. Keim
exaggerates very much when he says, 'Jesus is
represented as having abolished the Law while still
upon earth, and as having called heathens by the
side of Jews.'   On the contrary, it is precisely in the
fourth Gospel that the Law is represented as most
scrupulously observed[1] ; the prerogative position of
Israel is throughout recognized ; the Samaritans are
not in the general sense heathen, and the Gospel is

[1] 'The journeys to the stated
festivals at Jerusalem serve only to
discredit the old religion' (der

Entwerthung des Alten gelten)!
Keim (after Hilgenfeld), p. 124,
ad in.

preached to them in an incidental and occasional manner, the account of which is confirmed by a well attested document in St. Luke. The Greeks mentioned in chap. xii, from the fact of their attending the Passover, must have been proselytes, and were probably 'proselytes of the covenant': besides, we are only told that they were presented to our Lord, not that they were distinctly admitted into the Christian circle. The Johannean narrative contains nothing that goes so far as the Synoptic healing of the Syrophoenician's daughter; whereas, if it had really been a forgery written from the point of view that Dr. Keim contends, there can be little doubt that it would have gone much further. There was a place already made for such narratives in the history, which legend or invention might have easily filled.

(γ) 'The kingdom of heaven' with St. John lies in the present, with St. Paul in the future. St. John also looks forward to a second Coming and to a final establishment of the kingdom in the future; cf. v. 27–29, xiv. 1–3, xxi. 22. But so far as there is a difference between the two Apostles it corresponds to the different points of view which they occupy while they are writing, and is a further proof that the Gospel was written by one 'who had seen the Lord.' The key to the Johannean conception is to be found in the Synoptists (Mark ii. 19 par.), 'Can the children of the bridechamber fast while the bridegroom is with them? As long as the bridegroom is with them they cannot fast.' The Apostle throws himself back into the time when he had felt that the kingdom of heaven was present with its King. There was no need to look forward to the future 'in those days.'

(δ) Dr. Keim notices a single fact, the institution of the Lord's Supper, in regard to which the Synoptists are supported by St. Paul. But the omission of this is even less an argument against the fourth Gospel than other omissions, as the circumstance was so notorious and so constantly brought to the memory of Christians that to repeat it would have been superfluous and contrary to the principle which the Evangelist had proposed to himself.

In all these objections brought from the writings of St. Paul I can see nothing that furnishes a substantial reason for rejecting the Gospel as the work of an Apostle.

III. Neither does this appear any more conclusively from a comparison with the Synoptists.

From its relation to the Synoptic Gospels.

(α)⎱ The first two items of this, the Christology,
(β)⎰ and the relation to the Law, we have already considered. There is no essential difference. The Christ of the Synoptists is the Jewish Messiah, the Son of Man, the Son of God, the Centre round which the Kingdom of Heaven revolves, the Object of faith, the Source of spiritual life, refreshment, and peace, the Author of salvation. He is the Shepherd of the sheep, the Son of the Great King for whom the marriage supper is made. He is Himself the King of the Messianic community, its Founder, and its Head. He has power to forgive sins, to heal diseases, to cast out devils, to raise the dead to life. At His coming Satan falls from heaven. He will one day return in the majesty of His Father to judge the quick and the dead. And it will be by the services that they have rendered to Him that men will be judged. During His sojourn upon earth He is the Revelation of the Father. All

power is delivered unto Him. 'No man knoweth the Son but the Father, neither knoweth any man the Father, save the Son, and he to whomsoever the Son will reveal Him.' There is no reason to say with Dr. Keim that this consciousness of union with the Father is confined to certain exalted moments—it is stated as absolutely and as entirely without qualification in the Synoptic Gospels as in St. John[1]. The single particular that is wanting is the pre-existence, and in place of that we are presented with the 'Son of a pure Virgin.' What else is there in St. John that this description will not include? What is there that the compilers of the Synoptic Gospels might not have written if they had had access to all the facts? True, the fourth Gospel is a 'Gospel of selections'—it presents one side more prominently than the other; and this prevents it from exhibiting the same variety, the same many-sidedness, the same openness to all that is in the world and in man; but it does not therefore follow that it is not historical, or the soundest and the truest history.

(γ) Among particular statements in which St. John is at variance with the Synoptists, Dr. Keim naturally singles out 'the time and place of the ministry of Jesus.' But there is no thoroughly impartial critic at the present day who does not regard the advantage in this respect as on the side of St. John. This subject has been treated so exhaustively by Dr. Weizsäcker[2] that I need not do more than refer to his work and to the investigation in the body of the present enquiry. It is shown that the Johannean version is not only in

[1] See above, p. 109 n.
[2] *Untersuchungen*, pp. 306–311. Compare also pp. 54–58 above.

accordance with historical probability, but also that it is not excluded by the Synoptic Gospels, but is rather on a number of minute points implied and confirmed by them. M. Renan calls this a 'signal triumph' for the fourth Gospel, and I cannot think that he is wrong. When two historical documents are distinguished, the one by vagueness and uncertainty of outline, the other by marked precision, we naturally conclude that the author of the latter stood in nearer relation to the events, and in this case such a conclusion is abundantly confirmed.

(δ) It is noticeable that the rest of Dr. Keim's instances are taken entirely from the last division of the Gospel. They are (1) the way in which the last events are introduced, (2) the miracle at Bethany, (3) the day of the Crucifixion. All these we have discussed in their places. (1) is a question of historical probability which cannot be otherwise than inconclusive, as it has to be measured by a subjective standard. Naturally the commentators and critics divide themselves into two camps. Renan, Ewald, Weizsäcker, think that the Johannean version is the more probable, and that in that of the Synoptists the deadly hostility of the hierarchic party in Jerusalem is not sufficiently accounted for. Dr. Keim, on the other hand, with those who agree with him, inverts this. He maintains that in the fourth Gospel the motives by which the conflict is brought to a crisis have long been 'used up,' and that therefore the miracle of Bethany is invented to take their place. The opposite opinions cancel each other, and we must leave the question where it stands. (2) Our acceptance of the raising of Lazarus will depend partly on the conception we may have formed as to the *à priori* improbability of miracles, and partly upon the importance we attach to the silence of the Synoptists. This last, as I have endeavoured to show, arises from the way in which they were composed, and is part of the general fact that they are silent as to all the events that take place in Judaea before the triumphal entry. The former question is properly suspended until the weight of the historical evidence for miracles is determined. (3) The day of the Crucifixion we have shown to be rightly fixed by St. John. And here again unprejudiced critics like Renan, not to speak of Lücke, Bleek, Meyer, and Ewald, are all of the same opinion. We wait to see what Dr. Keim will have to say when he comes to this part of his history, but it is with the expectation that he will find it extremely difficult to prove his point.

Miscellaneous objections.

'This,' he adds, 'shall be enough, and as to the rest we will say nothing. In this we do not include the rubric of general, historical, or geographical errors, which it is the fashion to prove from other sources than the Synoptists, from the Old Testament, Josephus, Eusebius, or Jerome. These supposed errors with regard to Bethany and Bethesda, Kana and Kidron, Salem and Sychar, with regard to the "high priest of that year," and the distance of Cana from Capernaum, Bethany, and Peraea, there is the less reason to believe (braucht man desto weniger zu glauben), as the author otherwise displays a fairly accurate knowledge of the country, and the most difficult cases are explained by special intention. The high priest "of that fatal year" is emphatic, and does not at all betray the sense of yearly change ; Sychar

is a vernacular or mock name for Sichem ; Salem and
Ain are situated in Judaea, or perhaps rather in
Samaria, up to the borders of which the Forerunner
made his way from Jacob's well ; the enhancement of
distance[1] must correspond to the enhancement of the
miracle.' So Dr. Keim disposes of the ordinary
arguments against the fourth Guspel. But are his
own any more substantial ? Do they not all rest upon
vague generalities and probabilities which give way
when they are put to the proof ? Are they enough to
prove a negative conclusion, or to overthrow the
weight of positive evidence that can be brought
against them ? My own conviction is that they are
wholly insufficient to do this, and I cannot but think
that it will be shared by the reader.

---

[1] There is no enhancement.
With regard to Capernaum, see p.
102 above ; with regard to Peraea,
there are many parts of that district
which would be at least four days'
journey from Bethany.

CHAPTER XIX.

SUMMARY PROOF OF THE GENUINENESS OF
THE GOSPEL.

The crucial question.

THE ground is now sufficiently clear for us to put to ourselves definitely the crucial questions by which the result of our enquiry must be determined. Was the author of the fourth Gospel a Jew? Was he a Jew of Palestine? Was he a member of the original Christian circle? Was he an eye-witness? Was he the son of Zebedee[1]? Incidentally the evidence on all these points has been already discussed,

[1] The same questions are asked, and *opposite* answers given, by Dr. Scholten (*Ev. Joh.* pp. 376-399, 406-414). This will not however mislead any one who examines the process by which Dr. Scholten reaches his conclusions. Most of the points, especially the Paschal controversy, on which great stress is laid, have been discussed above. A specimen of the reasoning followed may be seen in the three pages (408-410) which are devoted to the Johannean topography: (1) the instances in which the accuracy of the Evangelist is authenticated beyond question are ignored; (2) wherever the authentication (from the scanty sources accessible) is imperfect, it is at once assumed that the Evangelist is wrong, however precise and credible his statement may be. With regard to the language and style and the quotations from the Old Testament, we must set against Dr. Scholten, who is not specially a Hebraist, the evidence of those who are (see pp. 28, 29, above, and add Bleek, *Einl.* p. 210, Westcott, *Intr.* 287, 288). The multitudinous instances of acquaintance with Jewish ideas and customs pass unnoticed. Of the few objections brought (p. 407 *ad fin.*) only one ('out of Galilee cometh no prophet') has any kind of validity.

and I will not weary the reader by repeating it in detail; but in order that he may be able clearly to appreciate its weight, it is now presented in a summary form under each of the several heads to which it belongs.

I. The author of the fourth Gospel was a Jew, and a Jew of Palestine. This appears from his intimate acquaintance—

(a) With *Jewish ideas.* Of these the most prominent is the Messianic idea, of which we find a singularly clear and accurate apprehension. Cf. i. 19–28, 45, 46, 49, 51; iv. 25 (the Samaritan Messiah); vi. 14, 15; vii. 26, 27, 31, 40-42, 52; xii. 13, 34; xix. 15, 21.

Besides this, we notice—baptism, i. 25; iii. 22, 23; iv. 2; purification, purifying, defilement, ii. 6; iii. 25; xi. 55; xviii. 28; xix. 31; relation of Jews to Samaritans, iv. 9, 20, 22; viii. 48; *ad hominem* arguments couched in Rabbinical form, vii. 22, 23 (circumcision on Sabbath); viii. 17, 18 (testimony of two men); x. 34 ('I said ye are gods'). *Current Rabbinical and popular notions,* besides those with reference to the Messiah—iv. 27 (conversation with a woman); vii. 15 (Rabbinical schools—'how knoweth this man letters?'); ix. 2, 3 (connection of sin with bodily affliction); ix. 16 ('can a sinner do such miracles?'); ix. 28 (Moses' disciples); viii. 52, 53 (Abraham and the prophets); viii. 57, ix. 23 (Jewish division of age).

(β) With the *Jewish Feasts,* which are used as landmarks :—ii. 13, 23 (Passover); v. 1 ('a feast of the Jews'); vi. 4 (Passover); vii. 2 (Feast of Tabernacles); vii. 37 ('The last day, the great day'); x. 22 (Dedication); xiii. 1, etc., xviii. 28 (Passover); xix. 31, 42 (the preparation, the high day).

The author a Palestinian Jew.

(γ) With *Jewish topography* We notice in connection with many of the places mentioned some exact specification :—i. 44 (Bethsaida, native place of Philip, Peter, and Andrew) ; i. 28 (Bethany, beyond Jordan = Tell Anihje ? cf. p. 45 n. above)[1] ; i. 46 (Nazareth, its local reputation) ; ii. 1, xxi. 2 (Cana, distinguished as 'of Galilee,' the native place of Nathanael = Kana el Jelîl) ; iii. 23 (Aenon, 'near to Salim, because there was much water there,' = Sheikh Salim) ; iv. 5 (Sychar, 'a city of Samaria, near to the parcel of ground that Jacob gave to his son Joseph. Now Jacob's well was there' ; either a vernacular name for Sichem or = Askar : cf. p. 93 above ;) v. 2 (Bethesda, 'a pool by the sheep gate, having five porches,' mentioned by Eusebius and Bordeaux Pilgrim, A.D. 333) ; viii. 20 (The Treasury in the Temple, cf. Mark xii. 41) ; ix. 7 (Siloam, 'a pool, which is by interpretation Sent '; ' missio aquarum,' Meyer : cf. Neh. iii. 15) ; x. 23 (Solomon's porch or ' cloister,' Jos. Ant. xx. 9. 7) ; x. 40 ('the place where John first baptized') ; xx. 18 (Bethany, fifteen furlongs from Jerusalem) ; xi. 54 (Ephraim, near to the wilderness, cf. 190) ; xviii. 1 (the brook Cedron, cf. p. 240) ; xix. 13 (the place that is called the Pavement, but in the Hebrew Gabbatha) ; xix. 17 (the place of a skull, which is called in the Hebrew Golgotha—near this is the

---

[1] These brief notes are added in order that the reader may be reminded of the extent to which the Johannean topography can be authenticated. It is strange that this authentication should be most complete where the landmarks had been most effaced—in regard to Jerusalem and the Temple. Nothing more is needed to prove that the Gospel was written by one who was intimate with Jerusalem as it was before the year 70 A.D. Allusions to the Temple services occur, e.g., in the Epistle of Clement, §§ 40, 41, but none to its architectural plan and history so precise as these in St. John.

Sepulchre, xix. 42). The passage ii. 13–16, gives an accurate description of the state of the temple ; and ii. 20, of its history.

(δ) We may notice, in addition to these marks of Jewish origin, the philological evidence derived from the language and style in which the Gospel is written (cf. pp. 28, 29). I extract from M. Wittichen a few instances[1] of *Hebraistic words and phrases :* σκανδαλίζειν (xvi. 1), γενέσθαι θανάτου (viii. 52), φαγεῖν τὸ πάσχα (xviii. 28), ὑψωθῆναι ἐκ τῆς γῆς (xii. 32), ἐντεῦθεν καὶ ἐντεῦθεν (xix. 18), σφραγίζειν, 'approve' (iii. 33), σημεῖα καὶ τέρατα (iv. 48), ὁ ἄρχων τοῦ κόσμου (rabb. xii. 19), ἄξιος ἵνα (i. 27), περιπατεῖν trop. (viii. 12). *Figures of speech :* the woman in travail, xvi. 21 (cf. Is. xxi. 3, Hos. xiii. 13) ; the good and the bad Shepherd, x. 1 foll. (cf. Ezek. xxxiv. 7, Jer. ii. 8, Zech. xi. 5) ; living water, iv. 10 (cf. Ecclesiasticus xv. 3, Baruch iii. 12) ; the lamp, λύχνος, v. 35 (2 Sam. xxi. 17, Ecclesiasticus xlviii. 1). *Special theological terms :* σὰρξ καὶ πνεῦμα (iii. 6), κόσμος οὗτος (viii. 23), φῶς καὶ σκοτία (xii. 35 foll.), βασιλεία Θεοῦ (iii. 3 foll.), ζωὴ, θάνατος (iii. 36, viii. 51), ὀργὴ and κρίσις (iii. 18 foll., 36), δικαιοσύνη (xvi. 8), ἁγιάζειν (xvii. 19), πατὴρ in ethical sense (viii. 41 foll.). I suspect that this list might be readily extended.

(ε) An equally convincing argument is drawn from the use which the author makes of the Old Testament. He quotes it almost as often in proportion to the length of the Gospel as the most Jewish of the Evangelists, the editor of our present St. Matthew. He appears to be equally familiar with the Hebrew

---

[1] Approved by Dr. Holtzmann, art. ' Johannes der Apostel ' in *S.B.L.* iii. 336. The subject is discussed more fully on pp. 28, 29 above.

text and the LXX. Two of the quotations, xiii. 18 = Ps. xli. 9, xix. 37 = Zech. xii. 10, agree with the former and not with the latter (Westcott, p. 287); also xii. 40 = Is. vii. 9, 10 (according to Bleek, p. 210).

All these points taken together seem to afford convincing proof that the author was a native of Palestine.

A contemporary.

II. But there are some among them that tend also to give an affirmative answer to the second great question—Was he a contemporary of our Lord and a member of the original Christian circle? There is one point especially which seems to decide this; that is, the way in which the conflict is described between the Jewish and Christian conception of the Messiah. Only the first generation of Christians could represent this accurately. The breach between the two conceptions was soon so wide that it became impossible for the writer to pass from the one to the other as easily and readily as the fourth Evangelist has done. The Jewish conception of the Messianic reign was that of a political theocracy, in which Jerusalem was to be the capital and mistress of the world, and all nations were to flow to it. We see from all the earliest and most authentic documents of Christianity how long the disciples themselves clung to this idea, and what a fruitful cause of misunderstanding it was among the Jews: it was in fact the one main cause of their rejecting the true Messiah. But the recollection of this can only have lasted in the consciousness of the Christian community up to the taking of Jerusalem. That event cut a sharp line between its past and its future. All hope and expectation of a political reign was at once and for ever abandoned, and we cannot doubt that it soon came to be forgotten that such a hope had ever existed. The only persons who retained the memory of it must have been those who had themselves assisted at the foundation of Christianity. And it is proved, I think we may say almost to demonstration, that the author of the fourth Gospel was one of these. Nathanael hails our Lord as the King of Israel. After the miracle of the multiplication of the loaves the multitudes would fain take Him by force and make Him king. At the triumphant entry they salute Him as the King of Israel. He is brought before Pilate as a leader of sedition. And the Jews make loud professions of their loyalty to Caesar in order that they may not be suspected of abetting Him. They remonstrate against the apparent recognition of His claim to be the Messiah in the title upon the Cross. But it is not only in this respect; the Evangelist is quite as familiar with other aspects of the popular idea. Could the Christ come from Nazareth? or from Galilee? Was He not to be born in Bethlehem, David's city? Was not the Christ to come suddenly out of obscurity? Was He not to abide for ever? When He came He was to do miracles, but could He do more than these 'which this man hath done?' Only at one time and to one generation of men was such easy and precise delineation possible, and that to those who had grown up in the midst of this popular idea and these popular expectations themselves, and had heard them constantly canvassed all about them. Jewish customs in the general sense were permanent, and a Jew in the second century might be as well acquainted with them

as a Jew in the first ; but the *relation of a Christian* to
this particular set of Jewish ideas rapidly and totally
changed, so as to be quite beyond the power of a
later age to revive.

Of similar importance and bearing is the knowledge
which the Evangelist displays of the state and condition of the temple, the buyers and sellers in its courts,
the particular articles in which they trafficked, the
position of the treasury and of Solomon's porch—nay,
of the precise point of time at which the events
recorded happened from the date at which the restoration of the temple commenced—'Forty and six years
was this temple in building.' I repeat that I am
wholly unable to conceive this statement to be the
work of a forger. With our modern habits of research
and careful reproduction of past ages such a thing
might have been credible, but at that time and in that
condition of literature it is not. A miracle (taken
with the whole class of circumstances to which
miracles belong) would be less surprising, because
in such a phenomenon there would be a miracle without an adequate cause.

These considerations are confirmed when we come
to observe the fondness of the Evangelist for throwing
himself back into the position of the original disciples,
and repeating their reflections or comments, these
being such as, though appropriate at the time, would
not be likely to have occurred to one who had not
been himself a disciple. Cf. ii. 11, 17, 22, iv. 27, vi. 60,
vii. 39, xii. 6, 16, 33, xiii. 28, 29 (cf. xiii. 7), xx. 9,
20, xxi. 12, 23.

In connection with this is the distinct character-
ization of many of the disciples, especially the

beloved disciple, Peter, Thomas, Philip, Judas Iscariot.

We may notice too that the Apostle throws himself
with almost equal facility into the feelings, doubts,
difficulties, plots, hostility, the conflicting motives and
the overt action of the Jews. Cf. vii. 11–13, 40–53,
ix. 8, 12, x. 19–21, 41, xi. 47–53, xii. 9–11, xviii. 30, 31,
xix. 7, 12, 15.

An incidental confirmation is afforded by the peculiar familiarity which the Evangelist shows with the
Baptist and all that concerned him, justifying the
supposition of M. Renan and others that he was once
numbered among the Baptist's disciples.   This comes
out indeed in the early chapters, but especially in that
remarkable periphrasis in x. 40, 'And he went away
again beyond Jordan into the place *where John at
first baptized:* and there abode;' along with what
follows, 'And many resorted to him and said, John
did no miracle ; but all things that John spake of this
man were true.'   The curious contrast, 'John did no
miracle,' and the easy natural way in which the whole
passage is introduced show that it is not premedi-
tated.

III. Thus we are prepared for that by which the
previous arguments are riveted, as it were, together—
The Gospel is the work of an *eye-witness*. This is
proved by the number of minute and precise details
which none but an eye-witness would have preserved.

These are:—

(*a*) Notes of time, *days*, i. 29–35, 43, ii. 1, 13, iv. 40,
xi. 6, 39, xii. 1 ; *hours*, i. 39 (tenth), iv. 6 (sixth), iv. 52
(seventh), xix. 14 (sixth).   It is to be observed that in
each case the time is given *approximately*, ὥρα ἦν ὡς

An eye-wit-
ness.

ἔκτη. This is characteristic of a genuine eye-witness, just as the more precise assertion would be of a forger. *Feasts*, ii. 13, 23, v. 1, vi. 4, vii. 2, x. 22, xiii. 1. *Years*, the date forty-six years from the commencement of the temple restoration, ii. 20 ; the thirty-eight years during which the cripple at the porch of Bethesda had suffered from his infirmity, v. 35.

(β) Among the *notes of place* already mentioned some show signs of an eye-witness, e.g. iii. 23, iv. 5, 6, v. 2, x. 23, x. 40.

(γ) The particular mention of *persons*. Where the other Evangelists speak generally of the 'disciples' or 'one of the disciples,' St. John almost invariably singles out the person, and frequently with some individualizing trait of incident or character. Cf. i. 35–51, the five Apostles; iii. 1, Nicodemus; vi. 5, Philip; vi. 8, Andrew; vi. 68 foll., Peter; vii. 3, 5, the Lord's brethren; xi. 1 foll., Mary and Martha; xi. 16, Thomas; xi. 49, Caiaphas; xii. 2, 3, Mary; xii. 4, 7, Judas Iscariot; xiii. 6 foll., Peter, 23, 26, Peter, the beloved disciple, and Judas, 36, Peter; xiv. 5, Thomas, 8, Philip, 22, Judas; xviii. 10, Peter and Malchus, 15 foll., Peter and the beloved disciple, Annas and Caiaphas; xix. 25, the women at the Cross, and the beloved disciple, 38, 39, Joseph and Nicodemus; xxi. 1 foll., Mary Magdalene, Peter and the beloved disciple; xx. 24, Thomas; xxi. 2, the seven disciples, 15 foll., Peter and the beloved disciple.

(δ) Lastly, a certain *minute picturesqueness and accuracy of description* which is peculiarly characteristic of an eye-witness (points which have already been mentioned under the head of 'time,' 'place,' 'customs,' 'persons,' 'reflections,' are not repeated, though they have the same bearing). Cf. ii. 13–17, iv. 6, 20, 28, 39, vi. 7, 9, 10, 19, 22, 23, vii. 10, 27, 37, chapters ix. and xi. generally, xii. 2, 3, 5, 13, xiii. 4, 5, 12, 23, 25, xviii. 1, 3, 10, 13, 15–18, 25, 27, 28, xix. 4, 5, 8, 9, 13, 14, 20, 23, 39, xx. 4, 7, 11, 15, 16, xxi. 8, 11, 20.

(ε) We must add to these the implied assertion of i. 14, 16 (cf. 1 John i. 1 foll.) and the express assertion of xix. 35, xxi. 14, in which the Evangelist himself claims to have been an eye-witness.

These phenomena admit of only two explanations. If they are not the work of an eye-witness they imply an amount of genius, remarkable as judged by any standard, and wholly without parallel as compared with the other literature of late Judaism and early Christianity. But even this hypothesis will not account for the whole of the phenomena. Shakespeare himself, if he had been born after the taking of Jerusalem, could not have written the fourth Gospel as it is. He might have produced the touches of an eye-witness,—though a Shakespeare would not at the same time have written the Johannean discourses. But there are points where the fiction must have inevitably betrayed itself, i.e., such as the allusions to the Jewish Messianic idea and its relation to the Christian. 'Can any good thing come out of Nazareth?' 'Shall Christ come out of Galilee?' 'Hath not the Scripture said that Christ cometh of the seed of David, and out of the town of Bethlehem where David was?' 'We have heard out of the law that Christ abideth for ever.' 'Howbeit we know this man whence he is: but when Christ cometh no man knoweth whence he is.' 'We are Moses' disciples.' 'Thou art a Samaritan and hast a devil.' 'Why baptizest thou then if thou be not the Christ, neither Elias, neither the prophet?' 'Forty and six years was this temple in building.' 'He departed to the place where John at first baptized.' These are touches that would not have been given even by a Shakespeare, and that prove, it is not too much to say, beyond possibility of question, that the hypothesis of an actual eye-witness is the only tenable one.

The Apostle St. John.   IV. But if the author of the fourth Gospel was an eye-witness there can be little doubt that he was also the son of Zebedee, and St. John. He is identified in ch. xxi. directly with the beloved disciple. But the beloved disciple was one of the most prominent among the Apostles, and in particular a close companion of Peter, cf. xiii. 23, 24, xviii. 15, 16, xx. 2–10, xxi. 20, 21. This tallies exactly with the position assigned to St. John in the Synoptic Gospels and in the Acts (iii. 1), and is confirmed by the ecclesiastical tradition.

The arguments which have been drawn from the Synoptists against the identification of the author of the fourth Gospel with the Son of Zebedee, proceed from a hasty and imperfect psychology. There is nothing to prevent the 'Son of Thunder' from being also the 'Apostle of Love,' but rather strong reason to see in them the same person. Intensity of nature is the common ground in which strong affection meets with strong antipathies. Dante is another St. John, but embittered by the world's opposition instead of being purified by the spirit of Christ. The only trait that is wanting in the Evangelist that had been pre-

sent in the youthful Apostle is a certain impetuosity—not indeed an impetuosity like St. Peter's,
but of finer tone and more surbordinate to the
main bent of his character. By the time the Apostle
came to write the Gospel it had been further softened by age.

CHAPTER XX.

THE HYPOTHESIS OF MEDIATE JOHANNEAN AUTHORSHIP, AND CONCLUSION.

The hypo-
thesis of
mediate
Johannean
authorship.

IF the foregoing considerations prove anything, they prove that the Gospel proceeds at first-hand from the Apostle St. John himself. And the other hypothesis, that it is to be attributed to the Apostle mediately, i.e. to a disciple in possession of the Johannean tradition, is not only unnecessary, but serves to confuse and neutralize the clear indications that determine our conclusion. 'All the grounds,' says Dr. Weizsäcker, 'which speak for the apostolic origin of the Gospel remain untouched when it is assumed that the Johannean tradition was strictly followed in its composition[1]'? If the intervention of second persons is reduced to merely mechanical assistance in the transcription of the Gospel[2], then this may be so, but not otherwise. The marks of an eye-witness and contemporary are either genuine and original, or else they are pure fiction, and these marks are scattered so promiscuously over the whole surface of the Gospel that it is a vain attempt to separate them. They will

[1] *Untersuchungen*, p. 298.　　[2] As apparently by Ewald, *Johann. Schriften*, p. 50.

be found in every chapter and in every section of the narrative from the beginning of the Gospel to the end. Any one may see this who will follow carefully the course of the preceding investigation, or who will cast a glance over the summary lists of instances collected in the last chapter.

Not only so, the hypothesis of preserved traditions is seen to be in itself untenable. What tradition would have preserved such objectless fragments as i. 40, 'They came and saw where He dwelt, and abode with Him that day'; ii. 12, 'After this He went down to Capernaum, He and His mother, and His brethren, and His disciples, and they continued there not many days'; iii. 23, 'And John also was baptizing in Aenon, near to Salim, because there was much water there : and they came and were baptized. . . . Then there arose a question between some of John's disciples and the Jews, about purifying'—(we hear nothing further about this dispute) ; vi. 23, 'Howbeit there came other boats from Tiberias ;' x. 40, 'He went away again beyond Jordan, unto the place where John at the first baptized ; and there He abode'; xi. 54, 'Jesus therefore went thence into a country near to the wilderness, into a city called Ephraim, and there continued with His disciples' ? Scraps of history like these have none of the appearance of invention, but they are just as little the kind of matter that is handed down to us by tradition. We see nothing like them in the true products of tradition, the Synoptic Gospels. Such isolated notices, if they had fallen from the lips of an Apostle, no disciple would have cared either to commit to memory or to take down in writing ; he would be intent upon the words of the Lord, and of the history

he would only retain so much as had a deeper significance in itself, or was the necessary framework to
anecdote or discourse. The same again holds in
regard to the numerous 'reflections,' many of which,
as we have seen, would have had no interest for the
second and third generation of Christians. The very
ease with which a passage like that of the 'woman
taken in adultery,' allows itself to be eliminated, is
sufficient proof that the same process cannot be applied
to the rest of the Gospel. A single mind is dominant
all through. Whether we look at style or matter, it is
the product 'to the very marrow' of one and the same
individuality. It is an organic whole, and will no
more bear to be dismembered than a living creature.

But the reasons which have led to such dismember-
ment are quite insufficient. No doubt the chief of
them has been the nature of the discourses. M.
Renan dismisses these too lightly for the interests of
science. And Dr. Weizsäcker, I cannot but think,
has formed a mistaken theory as to their composition.
He appears to regard them as *conscious* developments
of Synoptic matter [1]. But to me it is far more probable that they represent only the natural, spontaneous,
unconscious development that the original elements of
fact have undergone in the Apostle's mind. It cannot, I think, be denied that the discourses are to a
certain extent unauthentic, but this is rather in form
and disposition than in matter and substance. Our
analysis has detected nothing that could not have
proceeded from an Apostle, even from an Apostle who,
like St. John, had lain upon the bosom of the Lord.

[1] p. 279 foll.

The relation to the Synoptic narrative is similar. I cannot think that it proceeded from conscious manipulation of the Synoptic tradition or from the painful piecing together of discordant records. It can hardly be doubted that the Evangelist had seen the Synoptic Gospels, and that in their present form. But it can, I think, as little be doubted that he did not write with them actually before him. He writes with a plan and purpose of his own, partly perhaps with a view to supplement them, but that not in a petty or mechanical way. And when he presents a resemblance to them upon points of detail, it is because their statements fall in with his own recollections, recollections which they may have helped to revive, but which they did not in the first instance create. The Evangelist draws out of his treasure things old as well as new, but the treasure from which he draws is his own.

These are really the two most important grounds [1] which have led to the hypothesis of a mediate authorship ; but neither do they seem to require it, nor are the facts explained by it when it is there. The hypothesis raises more difficulties than it removes. And the same difficulties are equally removed by taking into account the play of ordinary psychological laws.

If we fix our attention firmly upon the history of the Apostle, and then look from that to the Gospel, we shall see the one reflected in the other. The

The Gospel reflects the history of the Apostle.

[1] Cf. Weizsäcker, pp. 298–300. The whole theory of mediate authorship is as yet represented by some five pages of Dr. Weizsäcker's work, and one of M. Renan's: it would therefore be disproportionate to contest it at greater length ; but I should be quite prepared to do so if necessary. It would simplify the issue, if Dr. Weizsäcker would point out definitely what portions of the Gospel he thinks non-Johannean.

Gospel contains, in outline at least, the autobiography of its author. It shows us first the youthful Jew penetrated with the Messianic hopes of his people, and brought up in the midst of a society in which they were eagerly canvassed, attaching himself to the Baptist, but leaving his first master for a second, whom he joined to leave no more. We see him during those three years receiving an indelible impression, in which the motions of the intellect were suspended by the absorbing power of love and devotion. When his Lord was taken away, we see him still in the midst of Jewish influences collecting and digesting his memories of the past ; but, as time wore on, suffering himself to move with it, and linking the train of his associations to the experiences of his own life and the history of the Church ; and finally, upon finding himself thrown into a different sphere, assimilating this too with his former consciousness. Thus when the Apostle came to pour forth the accumulated fruit of his life and reflection upon the world, he presents indeed a whole that is complex because of the variety of the experiences deposited in it, and yet is organically knit and bound together, and derives its essential features, not from the fluctuating elements of individual growth and expansion, but from the permanent basis of objective fact. The change is not in the subject matter, but in the relation of the Evangelist to it. He has looked at it as if from different points of view, and therefore shows it in different lights and in clearer relief.

Because such an individuality and such a history is rare, it is not therefore to be rejected as incredible. A rare and complex cause must be assumed to account

for rare and complex effects. And in the whole range
of literature there is not a work that presents such
varying and many-sided phenomena as the fourth
Gospel. The whole of these must be taken in, and
not a part of them. It is useless to account for the
unauthentic elements, and not for that far larger proportion that is authentic. It is useless to insist on
the marks of late composition, where the traces of a
contemporary and an eye-witness abound. It is useless to point to the culture of a Greek, when beneath
it there lies the indisputable stamp and character of
the Jew. And on the other hand, it is equally vain
to cramp that which lives and breathes in the iron
bands of an *à priori* theory. The Apostle is a man
of like passions with ourselves, more chastened, more
tender, more clothed with the spirit of his Lord,
more intimate with the world of the Unseen, and yet
not supernaturally withheld or withdrawn from the
ordinary laws to which flesh is heir; maturing
slowly and gradually, drawing upon the stores of his
experience, not wholly unforgetful, liable to mistakes,
unconsciously giving out the fruits of his own reflections as if they had been objective facts,—an Apostle,
and yet a man. If either side is lost, the picture is
destroyed; its humanity disappears; and a mechanical structure wanting in nature and vitality is set up
in its place. I can as little think of the author of the
fourth Gospel as a forger or even disciple laboriously
building upon other men's foundations, as see in him
a passive organ of infallibility. Both views equally
fail to explain the facts; and by the facts in this as
in all cases we must judge, certain that in the end
the interests of truth must accord with them.   In

this case they seem to give a clear verdict. The Gospel is the work of the Apostle, the son of Zebedee; it is the record of an eye-witness of the life of our Lord Jesus Christ; and its historical character is such as under the circumstances might be expected —it needs no adventitious commendation to make it higher.

THE END.

INDEX.

June 1874.

A Catalogue of Theological Books,
with a Short Account of their
Character and Aim,

Published by

MACMILLAN AND CO.

Bedford Street, Strand, London, W.C.

....

Abbott (Rev. E. A.)—Works by the Rev. E. A. ABBOTT, D.D., Head Master of the City of London School.

BIBLE LESSONS. Second Edition. Crown 8vo. 4*s.* 6*d.*

"*Wise, suggestive, and really profound initiation into religious thought.*" —Guardian. *The Bishop of St. David's, in his speech at the Education Conference at Abergwilly, says he thinks "nobody could read them without being the better for them himself, and being also able to see how this difficult duty of imparting a sound religious education may be effected.*"

THE GOOD VOICES: A Child's Guide to the Bible. With upwards of 50 Illustrations. Crown 8vo. cloth gilt. 5*s.*

"*It would not be easy to combine simplicity with fulness and depth of meaning more successfully than Mr. Abbott has done.*"—Spectator. *The* Times *says*—"*Mr. Abbott writes with clearness, simplicity, and the deepest religious feeling.*"

PARABLES FOR CHILDREN. Crown 8vo. cloth gilt. 3*s.* 6*d.*

"*They are simple and direct in meaning and told in plain language, and are therefore well adapted to their purpose.*"—Guardian.

I

4000. 6. 74.

Ainger (Rev. Alfred).—SERMONS PREACHED IN THE TEMPLE CHURCH. By the Rev. ALFRED AINGER, M.A. of Trinity Hall, Cambridge, Reader at the Temple Church. Extra fcap. 8vo. 6s.

This volume contains twenty-four Sermons preached at various times during the last few years in the Temple Church. "It is," the British Quarterly says, "the fresh unconventional talk of a clear independent thinker, addressed to a congregation of thinkers .... Thoughtful men will be greatly charmed by this little volume."

Alexander.—THE LEADING IDEAS of the GOSPELS. Five Sermons preached before the University of Oxford in 1870—71. By WILLIAM ALEXANDER, D.D., Brasenose College; Lord Bishop of Derry and Raphao; Select Preacher. Cr. 8vo. 4s. 6d.

"Eloquence and force of language, clearness of statement, and a hearty appreciation of the grandeur and importance of the topics upon which he writes characterize his sermons."—Record.

Arnold.—A BIBLE READING BOOK FOR SCHOOLS. THE GREAT PROPHECY OF ISRAEL'S RESTORATION (Isaiah, Chapters 40—66). Arranged and Edited for Young Learners. By MATTHEW ARNOLD, D.C.L., formerly Professor of Poetry in the University of Oxford, and Fellow of Oriel. Third Edition. 18mo. cloth. 1s.

The Times says—"Whatever may be the fate of this little book in Government Schools, there can be no doubt that it will be found excellently calculated to further instruction in Biblical literature in any school into which it may be introduced.... We can safely say that whatever school uses this book, it will enable its pupils to understand Isaiah, a great advantage compared with other establishments which do not avail themselves of it."

Baring-Gould.—LEGENDS OF OLD TESTAMENT CHARACTERS, from the Talmud and other sources. By the Rev. S. BARING-GOULD, M.A., Author of "Curious Myths of the Middle Ages," "The Origin and Development of Religious Belief," "In Exitu Israel," etc. In two vols. crown 8vo. 16s. Vol. I. Adam to Abraham. Vol. II. Melchizidek to Zechariah.

He has collected from the Talmud and other sources, Jewish and Mahommedan, a large number of curious and interesting legends concerning the principal characters of the Old Testament, comparing these frequently with similar legends current among many of the peoples, savage and civilised, all over the world. "These volumes contain much that is strange, and to the ordinary English reader, very novel."—Daily News.

Barry, Alfred, D.D.—The ATONEMENT of CHRIST. Six Lectures delivered in Hereford Cathedral during Holy Week, 1871. By ALFRED BARRY, D.D., D.C.L., Canon of Worcester, Principal of King's College, London. Fcap. 8vo. 2s. 6d.

In writing these Sermons, it has been the object of Canon Barry to set forth the deep practical importance of the doctrinal truths of the Atonement. "The one truth," says the Preface, "which, beyond all others, I desire that these may suggest, is the inseparable unity which must exist between Christian doctrine, even in its more mysterious forms, and Christian morality or devotion. They are a slight contribution to the plea of that connection of Religion and Theology, which in our own time is so frequently and, as it seems to me, so unreasonably denied." The Guardian *calls them "striking and eloquent lectures."*

Benham.—A COMPANION TO THE LECTIONARY, being a Commentary on the Proper Lessons for Sundays and Holydays. By the Rev. W. BENHAM, B.D., Vicar of Margate. Crown 8vo. 7s. 6d.

The Author's object is to give the reader a clear understanding of the Lessons of the Church, which he does by means of general and special introductions, and critical and explanatory notes on all words and passages presenting the least difficulty. "A very useful book. Mr. Benham has produced a good and welcome companion to our revised Lectionary. Its contents will, if not very original or profound, prove to be sensible and practical, and often suggestive to the preacher and the Sunday School teacher. They will also furnish some excellent Sunday reading for private hours."—Guardian.

Bernard.—THE PROGRESS OF DOCTRINE IN THE NEW TESTAMENT, considered in Eight Lectures before the University of Oxford in 1864. By THOMAS D. BERNARD, M.A., Rector of Walcot and Canon of Wells. Third and Cheaper Edition. Crown 8vo. 5s. (Bampton Lectures for 1864.)

"We lay down these lectures with a sense not only of being edified by sound teaching and careful thought, but also of being gratified by conciseness and clearness of expression and elegance of style."—Churchman.

Binney.—SERMONS PREACHED IN THE KING'S WEIGH HOUSE CHAPEL, 1829—69. By THOMAS BINNEY, D.D. New and Cheaper Edition. Extra fcap. 8vo. 4s. 6d.

"Full of robust intelligence, of reverent but independent thinking on the most profound and holy themes, and of earnest practical purpose."—London Quarterly Review.

Bradby.—SERMONS PREACHED AT HAILEYBURY. By E. H. BRADBY, M.A., Master. 8vo. 10s. 6d.

"He who claims a public hearing now, speaks to an audience accustomed to Cotton, Temple, Vaughan, Bradley, Butler, Farrar, and others...... Each has given us good work, several work of rare beauty, force, or originality; but we doubt whether any one of them has touched deeper chords, or brought more freshness and strength into his sermons, than the last of their number, the present Head Master of Haileybury."—Spectator.

Burgon.—A TREATISE on the PASTORAL OFFICE. Addressed chiefly to Candidates for Holy Orders, or to those who have recently undertaken the cure of souls. By the Rev. JOHN W. BURGON, M.A., Oxford. 8vo. 12s.

The object of this work is to expound the great ends to be accomplished by the Pastoral office, and to investigate the various means by which these ends may best be gained. Full directions are given as to preaching and sermon-writing, pastoral visitation, village education and catechising, and confirmation.—Spectator.

Butler (G.)—Works by the Rev. GEORGE BUTLER, M.A., Principal of Liverpool College :

FAMILY PRAYERS. Crown 8vo. 5s.

The prayers in this volume are all based on passages of Scripture—the morning prayers on Select Psalms, those for the evening on portions of the New Testament.

SERMONS PREACHED in CHELTENHAM COLLEGE CHAPEL. Crown 8vo. 7s. 6d.

Butler (Rev. H. M.)—SERMONS PREACHED in the CHAPEL OF HARROW SCHOOL. By H. MONTAGU BUTLER, Head Master. Crown 8vo. 7s. 6d.

"These sermons are adapted for every household. There is nothing more striking than the excellent good sense with which they are imbued." —Spectator.

A SECOND SERIES. Crown 8vo. 7s. 6d.

"Excellent specimens of what sermons should be,—plain, direct, practical, pervaded by the true spirit of the Gospel, and holding up lofty aims before the minds of the young."—Athenæum.

Butler (Rev. W. Archer).—Works by the Rev. WILLIAM ARCHER BUTLER, M.A., late Professor of Moral Philosophy in the University of Dublin :—

SERMONS, DOCTRINAL AND PRACTICAL. Edited, with a Memoir of the Author's Life, by THOMAS WOODWARD, Dean of Down. With Portrait. Ninth Edition. 8vo. 8s.

The Introductory Memoir narrates in considerable detail and with much interest, the events of Butler's brief life; and contains a few specimens of his poetry, and a few extracts from his addresses and essays, including a long and eloquent passage on the Province and Duty of the Preacher.

A SECOND SERIES OF SERMONS. Edited by J. A. JEREMIE, D.D., Dean of Lincoln. Seventh Edition. 8vo. 7s.

The North British Review *says, " Few sermons in our language exhibit the same rare combination of excellencies; imagery almost as rich as Taylor's; oratory as vigorous often as South's; judgment as sound as*

Butler (Rev. W. Archer.)—*continued.*

Barrow's; a style as attractive but more copious, original, and forcible than Atterbury's; piety as elevated as Howe's, and a fervour as intense at times as Baxter's. Mr. Butler's are the sermons of a true poet."

LETTERS ON ROMANISM, in reply to Dr. Newman's Essay on Development. Edited by the Dean of Down. Second Edition, revised by Archdeacon HARDWICK. 8vo. 10s. 6d.

These Letters contain an exhaustive criticism of Dr. Newman's famous "Essay on the Development of Christian Doctrine." "A work which ought to be in the Library of every student of Divinity."—BP. ST. DAVID'S.

LECTURES ON ANCIENT PHILOSOPHY. *See* SCIENTIFIC CATALOGUE.

Cambridge Lent Sermons. — SERMONS preached during Lent, 1864, in Great St. Mary's Church, Cambridge. By the BISHOP OF OXFORD, Revs. H. P. LIDDON, T. L. CLAUGHTON, J. R. WOODFORD, Dr. GOULBURN, J. W. BURGON, T. T. CARTER, Dr. PUSEY, Dean HOOK, W. J. BUTLER, Dean GOODWIN. Crown 8vo. 7s. 6d.

Campbell.—Works by JOHN M'LEOD CAMPBELL :—

THE NATURE OF THE ATONEMENT AND ITS RELATION TO REMISSION OF SINS AND ETERNAL LIFE. Fourth and Cheaper Edition, crown 8vo. 6s.

"Among the first theological treatises of this generation."—Guardian. *"One of the most remarkable theological books ever written."*—Times.

CHRIST THE BREAD OF LIFE. An Attempt to give a profitable direction to the present occupation of Thought with Romanism. Second Edition, greatly enlarged. Crown 8vo. 4s. 6d.

"Deserves the most attentive study by all who interest themselves in the predominant religious controversy of the day."—Spectator.

RESPONSIBILITY FOR THE GIFT OF ETERNAL LIFE. Compiled by permission of the late J. M'LEOD CAMPBELL, D.D., from Sermons preached chiefly at Row in 1829—31. Crown 8vo. 5s.

"There is a healthy tone as well as a deep pathos not often seen in sermons. His words are weighty and the ideas they express tend to perfection of life."—Westminster Review.

REMINISCENCES AND REFLECTIONS, referring to his Early Ministry in the Parish of Row, 1825—31. Edited with an Introductory Narrative by his Son, DONALD CAMPBELL, M.A., Chaplain of King's College, London. Crown 8vo. 7s. 6d.

These 'Reminiscences and Reflections,' written during the last year of his life, were mainly intended to place on record thoughts which might prove helpful to others. "*We recommend this book cordially to all who are interested in the great cause of religious reformation.*"—Times. "*There is a thoroughness and depth, as well as a practical earnestness, in his grasp of each truth on which he dilates, which make his reflections very valuable.*"—Literary Churchman.

Canterbury.—THE PRESENT POSITION OF THE CHURCH OF ENGLAND. Seven Addresses delivered to the Clergy and Churchwardens of his Diocese, as his Charge, at his Primary Visitation, 1872. By ARCHIBALD CAMPBELL, Archbishop of Canterbury. Third Edition. 8vo. cloth. 3s. 6d.

The subjects of these Addresses are, I. Lay Co-operation. II. Cathedral Reform. III. and IV. Ecclesiastical Judicature. V. Ecclesiastical Legislation. VI. Missionary Work of the Church. VII. The Church of England in its relation to the Rest of Christendom. There are besides, a number of statistical and illustrative appendices.

Cheyne.—Works by T. K. CHEYNE, M.A., Fellow of Balliol College, Oxford :—

THE BOOK OF ISAIAH CHRONOLOGICALLY ARRANGED. An Amended Version, with Historical and Critical Introductions and Explanatory Notes. Crown 8vo. 7s. 6d.

The object of this edition is to restore the probable meaning of Isaiah, so far as can be expressed in appropriate English. The basis of the version is the revised translation of 1611, *but alterations have been introduced wherever the true sense of the prophecies appeared to require it. The* Westminster Review *speaks of it as "a piece of scholarly work, very carefully and considerately done." The* Academy *calls it "a successful attempt to extend a right understanding of this important Old Testament writing."*

NOTES AND CRITICISMS on the HEBREW TEXT OF ISAIAH. Crown 8vo. 2s. 6d.

This work is offered as a slight contribution to a more scientific study of the Old Testament Scriptures. The author aims at completeness, independence, and originality, and constantly endeavours to keep philology distinct from exegesis, to explain the form without pronouncing on the matter.

Choice Notes on the Four Gospels, drawn from Old and New Sources. Crown 8vo. 4s. 6d. each Vol. (St. Matthew and St. Mark in one Vol. price 9s.).

These Notes are selected from the Rev. Prebendary Ford's Illustrations of the Four Gospels, the choice being chiefly confined to those of a more simple and practical character.

Church.—Works by the Very Rev. R. W. CHURCH, M.A., Dean of St. Paul's.

SERMONS PREACHED BEFORE the UNIVERSITY OF OXFORD. By the Very Rev. R. W. CHURCH, M.A., Dean of St. Paul's. Second Edition. Crown 8vo. 4s. 6d.

*Sermons on the relations between Christianity and the ideas and facts of modern civilized society. The subjects of the various discourses are:—"The Gifts of Civilization," "Christ's Words and Christian Society," "Christ's Example," and "Civilization and Religion." "Thoughtful and masterly . . . We regard these sermons as a landmark in religious thought. They help us to understand the latent strength of a Christianity that is assailed on all sides."—*Spectator.

ON SOME INFLUENCES OF CHRISTIANITY UPON NATIONAL CHARACTER. Three Lectures delivered in St. Paul's Cathedral, Feb. 1873. Crown 8vo. 4s. 6d.

"Few books that we have met with have given us keener pleasure than this. . . . . . . It would be a real pleasure to quote extensively, so wise and so true, so tender and so discriminating are Dean Church's judgments, but the limits of our space are inexorable. We hope the book will be bought."
—Literary Churchman.

THE SACRED POETRY OF EARLY RELIGIONS. Two Lectures in St. Paul's Cathedral. 18mo. 1s. I. The Vedas. II. The Psalms.

Clay.—THE POWER OF THE KEYS. Sermons preached in Coventry. By the Rev. W. L. CLAY, M.A. Fcap. 8vo. 3s. 6d.

In this work an attempt is made to shew in what sense, and to what extent, the power of the Keys can be exercised by the layman, the Church, and the priest respectively. The Church Review *says the sermons are "in many respects of unusual merit."*

Clergyman's Self-Examination concerning the APOSTLES' CREED. Extra fcap. 8vo. 1s. 6d.

Collects of the Church of England. With a beautifully Coloured Floral Design to each Collect, and Illuminated Cover. Crown 8vo. 12s. Also kept in various styles of morocco.

The distinctive characteristic of this edition is the coloured floral design which accompanies each Collect, and which is generally emblematical of the character of the day or saint to which it is assigned; the flowers which have been selected are such as are likely to be in bloom on the day to which the Collect belongs. The Guardian *thinks it "a successful attempt to associate in a natural and unforced manner the flowers of our fields and gardens with the course of the Christian year."*

Cotton.—Works by the late GEORGE EDWARD LYNCH COTTON, D.D., Bishop of Calcutta :—

SERMONS PREACHED TO ENGLISH CONGREGATIONS IN INDIA. Crown 8vo. 7s. 6d.

"The sermons are models of what sermons should be, not only on account of their practical teachings, but also with regard to the singular felicity with which they are adapted to times, places, and circumstances." —Spectator.

EXPOSITORY SERMONS ON THE EPISTLES FOR THE SUNDAYS OF THE CHRISTIAN YEAR. Two Vols. Crown 8vo. 15s.

These two volumes contain in all fifty-seven Sermons. They were all preached at various stations throughout India.

Cure.—THE SEVEN WORDS OF CHRIST ON THE CROSS. Sermons preached at St. George's, Bloomsbury. By the Rev. E. CAPEL CURE, M.A. Fcap. 8vo. 3s. 6d.

Of these Sermons the John Bull *says, " They are earnest and practical;" the* Nonconformist, *" The Sermons are beautiful, tender, and instructive;" and the* Spectator *calls them "A set of really good Sermons."*

Curteis.—DISSENT in its RELATION to the CHURCH OF ENGLAND. Eight Lectures preached before the University of Oxford, in the year 1871, on the foundation of the late Rev. John Bampton, M.A., Canon of Salisbury. By GEORGE HERBERT CURTEIS, M.A., late Fellow and Sub-Rector of Exeter College ; Principal of the Lichfield Theological College, and Prebendary of Lichfield Cathedral ; Rector of Turweston, Bucks. Third and Cheaper Edition, crown 8vo. 7s. 6d.

"Mr. Curteis has done good service by maintaining in an eloquent, temperate, and practical manner, that discussion among Christians is really an evil, and that an intelligent basis can be found for at least a proximate union."—Saturday Review *"A well timed, learned, and thoughtful book."*

Davies.—Works by the Rev. J. LLEWELYN DAVIES, M.A., Rector of Christ Church, St. Marylebone, etc. :—

THE WORK OF CHRIST ; or, the World Reconciled to God. With a Preface on the Atonement Controversy. Fcap. 8vo. 6s.

SERMONS on the MANIFESTATION OF THE SON OF GOD. With a Preface addressed to Laymen on the present Position of the Clergy of the Church of England; and an Ap-

Davies (Rev. J. Llewelyn)—*continued.*

pendix on the Testimony of Scripture and the Church as to the possibility of Pardon in the Future State. Fcap. 8vo. 6s. 6d.

"*This volume, both in its substance, prefix, and suffix, represents the noblest type of theology now preached in the English Church.*"—Spectator.

BAPTISM, CONFIRMATION, AND THE LORD'S SUPPER, as Interpreted by their Outward Signs. Three Expository Addresses for Parochial use. Fcap. 8vo., limp cloth. 1s. 6d.

The method adopted in these addresses is to set forth the natural and historical meaning of the signs of the two Sacraments and of Confirmation, and thus to arrive at the spiritual realities which they symbolize. The work touches on all the principal elements of a Christian man's faith.

THE EPISTLES of ST. PAUL TO THE EPHESIANS, THE COLOSSIANS, and PHILEMON. With Introductions and Notes, and an Essay on the Traces of Foreign Elements in the Theology of these Epistles. 8vo. 7s. 6d.

MORALITY ACCORDING TO THE SACRAMENT OF THE LORD'S SUPPER. Crown 8vo. 3s. 6d.

These discourses were preached before the University of Cambridge. They form a continuous exposition, and are directed mainly against the two-fold danger which at present threatens the Church—the tendency, on the one hand, to regard Morality as independent of Religion, and, on the other, to ignore the fact that Religion finds its proper sphere and criterion in the moral life.

THE GOSPEL and MODERN LIFE. Sermons on some of the Difficulties of the Present Day, with a Preface on a Recent Phase of Deism. Extra fcap. 8vo. 6s.

The "recent phase of Deism" examined in the preface to this volume is that professed by the "Pall Mall Gazette"—that in the sphere of Religion there are one or two "probable suppositions," but nothing more. Amongst other subjects examined are—"Christ and Modern Knowledge," "Humanity and the Trinity," "Nature," "Religion," "Conscience," "Human Corruption," and "Human Holiness."

WARNINGS AGAINST SUPERSTITION IN FOUR SERMONS FOR THE DAY. Extra fcap. 8vo. 2s. 6d

"*We have seldom read a wiser little book. The Sermons are short, terse, and full of true spiritual wisdom, expressed with a lucidity and a moderation that must give them weight even with those who agree least with their author....... Of the volume as a whole it is hardly possible to speak with too cordial an appreciation.*"—Spectator.

De Teissier.—Works by G. F. DE TEISSIER, B.D.:—

VILLAGE SERMONS, FIRST SERIES. Crown 8vo. 9s.

This volume contains fifty-four short Sermons, embracing many subjects of practical importance to all Christians. The Guardian *says they are* "*a little too scholarlike in style for a country village, but sound and practical.*"

VILLAGE SERMONS, SECOND SERIES. Crown 8vo. 8s. 6d.

"*This second volume of Parochial Sermons is given to the public in the humble hope that it may afford many seasonable thoughts for such as are Mourners in Zion.*" *There are in all fifty-two Sermons embracing a wide variety of subjects connected with Christian faith and practice.*

Donaldson.—THE APOSTOLICAL FATHERS: a Critical Account of their Genuine Writings and of their Doctrines. By JAMES DONALDSON, LL.D. Crown 8vo. 7s. 6d.

This book was published in 1864 *as the first volume of a 'Critical History of Christian Literature and Doctrine from the death of the Apostles to the Nicene Council.' The intention was to carry down the history continuously to the time of Eusebius, and this intention has not been abandoned. But as the writers can be sometimes grouped more easily according to subject or locality than according to time, it is deemed advisable to publish the history of each group separately. The Introduction to the present volume serves as an introduction to the whole period.*

Ecce Homo. A SURVEY OF THE LIFE AND WORK OF JESUS CHRIST. Eleventh Edition. Crown 8vo. 6s.

"*A very original and remarkable book, full of striking thought and delicate perception; a book which has realised with wonderful vigour and freshness the historical magnitude of Christ's work, and which here and there gives us readings of the finest kind of the probable motive of His individual words and actions.*"—Spectator. "*The best and most established believer will find it adding some fresh buttresses to his faith.*"—Literary Churchman. "*If we have not misunderstood him, we have before us a writer who has a right to claim deference from those who think deepest and know most.*"—Guardian.

Faber.—SERMONS AT A NEW SCHOOL. By the Rev. ARTHUR FABER, M.A., Head Master of Malvern College. Cr. 8vo. 6s.

"*These are high-toned, earnest Sermons, orthodox and scholarlike, and laden with encouragement and warning, wisely adapted to the needs of school-life.*"—Literary Churchman. "*Admirably realizing that combination of fresh vigorous thought and simple expression of wise parental counsel, with brotherly sympathy and respect, which are essential to the success of such sermons, and to which so few attain.*"—British Quarterly Review.

Farrar.—Works by the Rev. F. W. FARRAR, M.A., F.R.S., Head Master of Marlborough College, and Hon. Chaplain to the Queen :—

THE FALL OF MAN, AND OTHER SERMONS. Second and Cheaper Edition. Extra fcap. 8vo. 4s. 6d.

This volume contains twenty Sermons. No attempt is made in these Sermons to develope a system of doctrine. In each discourse some one aspect of truth is taken up, the chief object being to point out its bearings on practical religious life. The Nonconformist *says of these Sermons,—* "Mr. Farrar's Sermons are almost perfect specimens of one type of Sermons, which we may concisely call beautiful. The style of expression is beautiful—there is beauty in the thoughts, the illustrations, the allusions— they are expressive of genuinely beautiful perceptions and feelings." The British Quarterly *says,—*"Ability, eloquence, scholarship, and practical usefulness, are in these Sermons combined in a very unusual degree."

THE WITNESS OF HISTORY TO CHRIST. Being the Hulsean Lectures for 1870. New Edition. Crown 8vo. 5s.

The following are the subjects of the Five Lectures :—I. "The Antecedent Credibility of the Miraculous." II. "The Adequacy of the Gospel Records." III. "The Victories of Christianity." IV. "Christianity and the Individual." V. "Christianity and the Race." The subjects of the four Appendices are :—A. "The Diversity of Christian Evidences." B. "Confucius." C. "Buddha." D. "Comte."

SEEKERS AFTER GOD. The Lives of Seneca, Epictetus, and Marcus Aurelius. *See* SUNDAY LIBRARY at end of Catalogue.

THE SILENCE AND VOICES OF GOD : University and other Sermons. Crown 8vo. 6s.

*"We can most cordially recommend Dr. Farrar's singularly beautiful volume of Sermons...... For beauty of diction, felicity of style, aptness of illustration and earnest loving exhortation, the volume is without its parallel."—*John Bull. *"They are marked by great ability, by an honesty which does not hesitate to acknowledge difficulties and by an earnestness which commands respect."—*Pall Mall Gazette.

Fellowship : LETTERS ADDRESSED TO MY SISTER MOURNERS. Fcap. 8vo. cloth gilt. 3s. 6d.

*"A beautiful little volume, written with genuine feeling, good taste, and a right appreciation of the teaching of Scripture relative to sorrow and suffering."—*Nonconformist. *"A very touching, and at the same time a very sensible book. It breathes throughout the truest Christian spirit."—* Contemporary Review.

Forbes.—THE VOICE OF GOD IN THE PSALMS. By GRANVILLE FORBES, Rector of Broughton. Cr. 8vo. 6s. 6d.

Gifford.—THE GLORY OF GOD IN MAN. By E. H. GIFFORD, D.D. Fcap. 8vo., cloth. 3s. 6d.

Golden Treasury Psalter. *See* p. 27.

Hardwick.—Works by the Ven. ARCHDEACON HARDWICK :

CHRIST AND OTHER MASTERS. A Historical Inquiry into some of the Chief Parallelisms and Contrasts between Christianity and the Religious Systems of the Ancient World. New Edition, revised, and a Prefatory Memoir by the Rev. FRANCIS PROCTER, M.A. Two vols. crown 8vo. 15s.

After several introductory chapters dealing with the religious tendencies of the present age, the unity of the human race, and the characteristics of Religion under the Old Testament, the Author proceeds to consider the Religions of India, China, America, Oceanica, Egypt, and Medo-Persia. The history and characteristics of these Religions are examined, and an effort is made to bring out the points of difference and affinity between them and Christianity. The object is to establish the perfect adaptation of the latter faith to human nature in all its phases and at all times. "The plan of the work is boldly and almost nobly conceived. . . . . We commend the work to the perusal of all those who take interest in the study of ancient mythology, without losing their reverence for the supreme authority of the oracles of the living God."—Christian Observer.

A HISTORY OF THE CHRISTIAN CHURCH. Middle Age. From Gregory the Great to the Excommunication of Luther, Edited by WILLIAM STUBBS, M.A., Regius Professor of Modern History in the University of Oxford. With Four Maps constructed for this work by A. KEITH JOHNSTON. Third Edition. Crown 8vo. 10s. 6d.

For this edition Professor Stubbs has carefully revised both text and notes, making such corrections of facts, dates, and the like as the results of recent research warrant. The doctrinal, historical, and generally speculative views of the late author have been preserved intact. "As a Manual for the student of ecclesiastical history in the Middle Ages, we know no English work which can be compared to Mr. Hardwick's book."—Guardian.

A HISTORY of the CHRISTIAN CHURCH DURING THE REFORMATION. New Edition, revised by Professor STUBBS. Crown 8vo. 10s. 6d.

This volume is intended as a sequel and companion to the "History of the Christian Church during the Middle Age." The author's earnest wish has been to give the reader a trustworthy version of those stirring incidents which mark the Reformation period, without relinquishing his former claim to characterise peculiar systems, persons, and events according to the shades and colours they assume, when contemplated from an English point of view, and by a member of the Church of England.

Hervey.—THE GENEALOGIES OF OUR LORD AND SAVIOUR JESUS CHRIST, as contained in the Gospels of St. Matthew and St. Luke, reconciled with each other, and shown to be in harmony with the true Chronology of the Times. By Lord ARTHUR HERVEY, Bishop of Bath and Wells. 8vo. 10s. 6d.

Hymni Ecclesiæ.—Fcap. 8vo. 7s. 6d.

A selection of Latin Hymns of the Mediæval Church, containing selections from the Paris Breviary, and the Breviaries of Rome, Salisbury, and York. The selection is confined to such holy days and seasons as are recognised by the Church of England, and to special events or things recorded in Scripture. This collection was edited by Dr. Newman while he lived at Oxford.

Kempis, Thos. A.—DE IMITATIONE CHRISTI. LIBRI IV. Borders in the Ancient Style, after Holbein, Durer, and other Old Masters, containing Dances of Death, Acts of Mercy, Emblems, and a variety of curious ornamentations. In white cloth, extra gilt. 7s. 6d.

The original Latin text has been here faithfully reproduced. The Spectator *says of this edition, it "has many solid merits, and is perfect in its way." While the* Athenæum *says, "The whole work is admirable; some of the figure compositions have extraordinary merit."*

Kingsley.—Works by the Rev. CHARLES KINGSLEY, M.A., Rector of Eversley, and Canon of Westminster. (For other Works by the same author, *see* HISTORICAL and BELLES LETTRES CATALOGUES).

THE WATER OF LIFE, AND OTHER SERMONS. Second Edition. Fcap. 8vo. 3s. 6d.

This volume contains twenty-one Sermons preached at various places —Westminster Abbey, Chapel Royal, before the Queen at Windsor, etc.

VILLAGE SERMONS. Seventh Edition. Fcap. 8vo. 3s. 6d.

THE GOSPEL OF THE PENTATEUCH. Second Edition. Fcap. 8vo. 3s. 6d.

This volume consists of eighteen Sermons on passages taken from the Pentateuch. They are dedicated to Dean Stanley out of gratitude for his Lectures on the Jewish Church, under the influence and in the spirit of which they were written.

GOOD NEWS OF GOD. Fourth Edition. Fcap. 8vo. 3s. 6d.

This volume contains thirty-nine short Sermons, preached in the ordinary course of the author's parochial ministrations.

Kingsley (Rev. C.)—*continued*.

SERMONS FOR THE TIMES. Third Edition. Fcap. 8vo. 3*s*. 6*d*.

Here are twenty-two Sermons, all bearing more or less on the every-day life of the present day, including such subjects as these :—"Fathers and Children;" "A Good Conscience;" "Names;" "Sponsorship;" "Duty and Superstition;" "England's Strength;" "The Lord's Prayer;" "Shame;" "Forgiveness;" "The True Gentleman;" "Public Spirit."

TOWN AND COUNTRY SERMONS. Second Edition. Extra fcap. 8vo. 3*s*. 6*d*.

Some of these Sermons were preached before the Queen, and some in the performance of the writer's ordinary parochial duty. Of these Sermons the Nonconformist *says, "They are warm with the fervour of the preacher's own heart, and strong from the force of his own convictions. There is nowhere an attempt at display, and the clearness and simplicity of the style make them suitable for the youngest or most unintelligent of his hearers."*

SERMONS on NATIONAL SUBJECTS. Second Edition. Fcap. 8vo. 3*s*. 6*d*.

THE KING OF THE EARTH, and other Sermons, a Second Series of Sermons on National Subjects. Second Edition. Fcap. 8vo. 3*s*. 6*d*.

The following extract from the Preface to the 2nd Series will explain the preacher's aim in these Sermons :—" I have tried......to proclaim the Lord Jesus Christ, as the Scriptures, both in their strictest letter and in their general method, from Genesis to Revelation, seem to me to proclaim Him ; not merely as the Saviour of a few elect souls, but as the light and life of every human being who enters into the world; as the source of all reason, strength, and virtue in heathen or in Christian ;· as the King and Ruler of the whole universe, and of every nation, family, and man on earth ; as the Redeemer of the whole earth and the whole human race... His death, as a full, perfect, and sufficient sacrifice, oblation, and satis-faction for the sins of the whole world, by which God is reconciled to the whole human race."

DISCIPLINE, AND OTHER SERMONS. Fcp. 8vo. 3*s*. 6*d*.

Twenty-four Sermons preached on various occasions, some of them of a public nature—at the Volunteer Camp, Wimbledon, before the Prince of Wales at Sandringham, at Wellington College, etc. The Guardian *says, —"There is much thought, tenderness, and devoutness of spirit in these Sermons, and some of them are models both in matter and expression."*

DAVID. FOUR SERMONS : David's Weakness—David's Strength—David's Anger—David's Deserts. Fcap. 8vo. 2*s*. 6*d*.

These four Sermons were preached before the University of Cambridge,

Kingsley (Rev. C.)—*continued.*

and are specially addressed to young men. Their titles are,—"David's Weakness;" "David's Strength;" "David's Anger;" "David's Deserts."

WESTMINSTER SERMONS. 8vo. 10s. 6d.

These Sermons were preached at Westminster Abbey or at one of the Chapels Royal. Their subjects are:—The Mystery of the Cross: The Perfect Love: The Spirit of Whitsuntide: Prayer: The Deaf and Dumb: The Fruits of the Spirit: Confusion: The Shaking of the Heavens and the Earth: The Kingdom of God: The Law of the Lord: God the Teacher: The Reasonable Prayer: The One Escape: The Word of God: I: The Cedars of Lebanon: Life: Death: Signs and Wonders: The Judgments of God: The War in Heaven: Noble Company: De Profundis: The Blessing and the Curse: The Silence of Faith: God and Mammon: The Beatific Vision.

Lightfoot.—Works by J. B. LIGHTFOOT, D.D., Hulsean Professor of Divinity in the University of Cambridge; Canon of St. Paul's.

ST. PAUL'S EPISTLE TO THE GALATIANS. A Revised Text, with Introduction, Notes, and Dissertations. Fourth Edition, revised. 8vo. cloth. 12s.

While the Author's object has been to make this commentary generally complete, he has paid special attention to everything relating to St. Paul's personal history and his intercourse with the Apostles and Church of the Circumcision, as it is this feature in the Epistle to the Galatians which has given it an overwhelming interest in recent theological controversy. The Spectator *says "there is no commentator at once of sounder judgment and more liberal than Dr. Lightfoot."*

ST. PAUL'S EPISTLE TO THE PHILIPPIANS. A Revised Text, with Introduction, Notes, and Dissertations. Third Edition. 8vo. 12s.

The plan of this volume is the same as that of " The Epistle to the Galatians." "No commentary in the English language can be compared with it in regard to fulness of information, exact scholarship, and laboured attempts to settle everything about the epistle on a solid foundation."—Athenæum.

ST. CLEMENT OF ROME, THE TWO EPISTLES TO THE CORINTHIANS. A Revised Text, with Introduction and Notes. 8vo. 8s. 6d.

This volume is the first part of a complete edition of the Apostolic Fathers. The Introductions deal with the questions of the genuineness and authenticity of the Epistles, discuss their date and character, and analyse their contents. An account is also given of all the different epistles which bear the name of Clement of Rome. "By far the most copiously annotated

Lightfoot (Dr. J. B.)—*continued.*

edition of St. Clement which we yet possess, and the most convenient in every way for the English reader."—Guardian.

ON A FRESH REVISION OF THE ENGLISH NEW TESTAMENT. Second Edition. Crown 8vo. 6s.

The Author shews in detail the necessity for a fresh revision of the authorized version on the following grounds:—1. *False Readings.* 2. *Artificial distinctions created.* 3. *Real distinctions obliterated.* 4. *Faults of Grammar.* 5. *Faults of Lexicography.* 6. *Treatment of Proper Names, official titles, etc.* 7. *Archaisms, defects in the English, errors of the press, etc.* "*The book is marked by careful scholarship, familiarity with the subject, sobriety, and circumspection.*"—Athenæum.

Luckock.—THE TABLES OF STONE. A Course of Sermons preached in All Saints' Church, Cambridge, by H. M. LUCKOCK, M.A., Vicar. Fcap. 8vo. 3s. 6d.

Maclaren.—SERMONS PREACHED at MANCHESTER. By ALEXANDER MACLAREN. Third Edition. Fcap. 8vo. 4s. 6d.

These Sermons represent no special school, but deal with the broad principles of Christian truth, especially in their bearing on practical, every day life. A few of the titles are:—"*The Stone of Stumbling,*" "*Love and Forgiveness,*" "*The Living Dead,*" "*Memory in Another World,*" *Faith in Christ,*" "*Love and Fear,*" "*The Choice of Wisdom,*" "*The Food of the World.*"

A SECOND SERIES OF SERMONS. Second Edition. Fcap. 8vo. 4s. 6d.

The Spectator *characterises them as "vigorous in style, full of thought, rich in illustration, and in an unusual degree interesting.*"

A THIRD SERIES OF SERMONS. Second Edition. Fcap. 8vo. 4s. 6d.

Sermons more sober and yet more forcible, and with a certain wise and practical spirituality about them it would not be easy to find."—Spectator.

Maclear.—Works by G. F. MACLEAR, D.D., Head Master of King's College School:—

A CLASS-BOOK OF OLD TESTAMENT HISTORY. With Four Maps. Eighth Edition. 18mo. 4s. 6d.

"*The present volume,*" *says the Preface,* "*forms a Class-Book of Old Testament History from the Earliest Times to those of Ezra and Nehemiah. In its preparation the most recent authorities have been consulted, and wherever it has appeared useful, Notes have been subjoined illustrative of the Text, and, for the sake of more advanced students, references added to larger works. The Index has been so arranged as to form a concise Dictionary of the Persons and Places mentioned in the course of the*

Maclear (G. F.)—*continued.*

Narrative." The Maps, prepared by Stanford, materially add to the value and usefulness of the book. The British Quarterly Review *calls it "A careful and elaborate, though brief compendium of all that modern research has done for the illustration of the Old Testament. We know of no work which contains so much important information in so small a compass."*

A CLASS-BOOK OF NEW TESTAMENT HISTORY.
Including the Connexion of the Old and New Testament. Sixth Edition. 18mo. 5s. 6d.

The present volume forms a sequel to the Author's Class-Book of Old Testament History, and continues the narrative to the close of St. Paul's second imprisonment at Rome. The work is divided into three Books—I. The Connection between the Old and New Testaments. II. The Gospel History. III. The Apostolic History. In the Appendix are given Chronological Tables The Clerical Journal *says, "It is not often that such an amount of useful and interesting matter on biblical subjects, is found in so convenient and small a compass, as in this well-arranged volume."*

A CLASS-BOOK OF THE CATECHISM OF THE CHURCH OF ENGLAND. Third and Cheaper Edition.
18mo. 1s. 6d.

The present work is intended as a sequel to the two preceding books. "Like them, it is furnished with notes and references to larger works, and it is hoped that it may be found, especially in the higher forms of our Public Schools, to supply a suitable manual of instruction in the chief doctrines of our Church, and a useful help in the preparation of Candidates for Confirmation." The Literary Churchman *says, "It is indeed the work of a scholar and divine, and as such, though extremely simple, it is also extremely instructive. There are few clergy who would not find it useful in preparing candidates for Confirmation; and there are not a few who would find it useful to themselves as well."*

A FIRST CLASS-BOOK OF THE CATECHISM OF THE CHURCH OF ENGLAND, with Scripture Proofs for
Junior Classes and Schools. New Edition. 18mo. 6d.

This is an epitome of the larger Class-book, meant for junior students and elementary classes. The book has been carefully condensed, so as to contain clearly and fully, the most important part of the contents of the larger book.

A SHILLING-BOOK of OLD TESTAMENT HISTORY.
New Edition. 18mo. cloth limp. 1s.

This Manual bears the same relation to the larger Old Testament History, that the book just mentioned does to the larger work on the Catechism. It consists of Ten Books, divided into short chapters, and subdivided into

Maclear (G. F.)—*continued*.

sections, each section treating of a single episode in the history, the title of which is given in bold type.

A SHILLING-BOOK of NEW TESTAMENT HISTORY. New Edition. 18mo. cloth limp. 1s.

This bears the same relation to the larger New Testament History that the work just mentioned has to the large Old Testament History, and is marked by similar characteristics.

A MANUAL OF INSTRUCTION FOR CONFIRMATION AND FIRST COMMUNION, with Prayers and Devotions. 32mo. cloth extra, red edges. 2s.

This is an enlarged and improved edition of 'The Order of Confirmation.' To it have been added the Communion Office, with Notes and Explanations, together with a brief form of Self Examination and Devotions selected from the works of Cosin, Ken, Wilson, and others.

Macmillan.—Works by the Rev. HUGH MACMILLAN, LL.D., F.R.S.E. (For other Works by the same Author, see CATALOGUE OF TRAVELS and SCIENTIFIC CATALOGUE).

THE TRUE VINE; or, the Analogies of our Lord's Allegory. Second Edition. Globe 8vo. 6s.

This work is not merely an exposition of the fifteenth chapter of St. John's Gospel, but also a general parable of spiritual truth from the world of plants. It describes a few of the points in which the varied realm of vegetable life comes into contact with the higher spiritual realm, and shews how rich a field of promise lies before the analogical mind in this direction. The Nonconformist *says, " It abounds in exquisite bits of description, and in striking facts clearly stated." The* British Quarterly *says, " Readers and preachers who are unscientific will find many of his illustrations as valuable as they are beautiful."*

BIBLE TEACHINGS IN NATURE. Eighth Edition. Globe 8vo. 6s.

In this volume the author has endeavoured to shew that the teaching of nature and the teaching of the Bible are directed to the same great end; that the Bible contains the spiritual truths which are necessary to make us wise unto salvation, and the objects and scenes of nature are the pictures by which these truths are illustrated. " He has made the world more beautiful to us, and unsealed our ears to voices of praise and messages of love that might otherwise have been unheard."—British Quarterly Review. *" Mr. Macmillan has produced a book which may be fitly described as one of the happiest efforts for enlisting physical science in the direct service of religion."*—Guardian.

Macmillan (H.)—*continued*.

THE MINISTRY OF NATURE. Second Edition. Globe 8vo. 6*s.*

In this volume the Author attempts to interpret Nature on her religious side in accordance with the most recent discoveries of physical science, and to shew how much greater significance is imparted to many passages of Scripture and many doctrines of Christianity when looked at in the light of these discoveries. Instead of regarding Physical Science as antagonistic to Christianity, the Author believes and seeks to shew that every new discovery tends more strongly to prove that Nature and the Bible have One Author. "Whether the reader agree or not with his conclusions, he will acknowledge he is in the presence of an original and thoughtful writer."— Pall Mall Gazette. *"There is no class of educated men and women that will not profit by these essays."*—Standard.

M'Cosh.—For Works by JAMES MCCOSH, LL.D., President of Princeton College, New Jersey, U.S., *see* PHILOSOPHICAL CATALOGUE.

Maurice.—Works by the late Rev. F. DENISON MAURICE, M.A., Professor of Moral Philosophy in the University of Cambridge.

Professor Maurice's Works are recognized as having made a deep impression on modern theology. With whatever subject he dealt he tried to look at it in its bearing on living men and their every-day surroundings, and faced unshrinkingly the difficulties which occur to ordinary earnest thinkers in a manner that showed he had intense sympathy with all that concerns humanity. By all who wish to understand the various drifts of thought during the present century, Mr. Maurice's works must be studied. An intimate friend of Mr. Maurice's, one who has carefully studied all his works, and had besides many opportunities of knowing the Author's opinions, in speaking of his so-called "obscurity," ascribes it to "the never-failing assumption that God is really moving, teaching and acting; and that the writer's business is not so much to state something for the reader's benefit, as to apprehend what God is saying or doing." The Spectator *says—"Few of those of our own generation whose names will live in English history or literature have exerted so profound and so permanent an influence as Mr. Maurice."*

THE PATRIARCHS AND LAWGIVERS OF THE OLD TESTAMENT. Third and Cheaper Edition. Crown 8vo. 5*s.*

The Nineteen Discourses contained in this volume were preached in the chapel of Lincoln's Inn during the year 1851. *The texts are taken from the books of Genesis, Exodus, Numbers, Deuteronomy, Joshua, Judges, and Samuel, and involve some of the most interesting biblical topics discussed in recent times.*

Maurice (F. D.)—*continued.*

THE PROPHETS AND KINGS OF THE OLD TESTAMENT. Third Edition, with new Preface. Crown 8vo. 10s. 6d.

Mr. Maurice, in the spirit which animated the compilers of the Church Lessons, has in these Sermons regarded the Prophets more as preachers of righteousness than as mere predictors—an aspect of their lives which, he thinks, has been greatly overlooked in our day, and than which, there is none we have more need to contemplate. He has found that the Old Testament Prophets, taken in their simple natural sense, clear up many of the difficulties which beset us in the daily work of life; make the past intelligible, the present endurable, and the future real and hopeful.

THE GOSPEL OF THE KINGDOM OF HEAVEN. A Series of Lectures on the Gospel of St. Luke. Crown 8vo. 9s.

Mr. Maurice, in his Preface to these Twenty-eight Lectures, says,—"In these Lectures I have endeavoured to ascertain what is told us respecting the life of Jesus by one of those Evangelists who proclaim Him to be the Christ, who says that He did come from a Father, that He did baptize with the Holy Spirit, that He did rise from the dead. I have chosen the one who is most directly connected with the later history of the Church, who was not an Apostle, who professedly wrote for the use of a man already instructed in the faith of the Apostles. I have followed the course of the writer's narrative, not changing it under any pretext. I have adhered to his phraseology, striving to avoid the substitution of any other for his."

THE GOSPEL OF ST. JOHN. A Series of Discourses. Third and Cheaper Edition. Crown 8vo. 6s.

These Discourses, twenty-eight in number, are of a nature similar to those on the Gospel of St. Luke, and will be found to render valuable assistance to any one anxious to understand the Gospel of the beloved disciple, so different in many respects from those of the other three Evangelists. Appended are eleven notes illustrating various points which occur throughout the discourses. The Literary Churchman thus speaks of this volume: —"Thorough honesty, reverence, and deep thought pervade the work, which is every way solid and philosophical, as well as theological, and abounding with suggestions which the patient student may draw out more at length for himself."

THE EPISTLES OF ST. JOHN. A Series of Lectures on Christian Ethics. Second and Cheaper Edition. Cr. 8vo. 6s.

These Lectures on Christian Ethics were delivered to the students of the Working Men's College, Great Ormond Street, London, on a series of Sunday mornings. Mr. Maurice believes that the question in which we are most interested, the question which most affects our studies and our daily lives, is the question, whether there is a foundation for human morality,

Maurice (F. D.)—*continued.*

or whether it is dependent upon the opinions and fashions of different ages and countries. This important question will be found amply and fairly discussed in this volume, which the National Review *calls " Mr. Maurice's most effective and instructive work. He is peculiarly fitted by the constitution of his mind, to throw light on St. John's writings." Appended is a note on "Positivism and its Teacher."*

EXPOSITORY SERMONS ON THE PRAYER-BOOK. The Prayer-book considered especially in reference to the Romish System. Second Edition. Fcap. 8vo. 5s. 6d.

After an Introductory Sermon, Mr. Maurice goes over the various parts of the Church Service, expounds in eighteen Sermons, their intention and significance, and shews how appropriate they are as expressions of the deepest longings and wants of all classes of men.

LECTURES ON THE APOCALYPSE, or Book of the Revelation of St. John the Divine. Crown 8vo. 10s. 6d.

Mr. Maurice, instead of trying to find far-fetched allusions to great historical events in the distant future, endeavours to discover the plain, literal, obvious meaning of the words of the writer, and shews that as a rule these refer to events contemporaneous with or immediately succeeding the time when the book was written. At the same time he shews the applicability of the contents of the book to the circumstances of the present day and of all times. "Never," says the Nonconformist, *"has Mr. Maurice been more reverent, more careful for the letter of the Scripture, more discerning of the purpose of the Spirit, or more sober and practical in his teaching, than in this volume on the Apocalypse."*

WHAT IS REVELATION? A Series of Sermons on the Epiphany; to which are added, Letters to a Theological Student on the Bampton Lectures of Mr. Mansel. Crown 8vo. 10s. 6d.

Both Sermons and Letters were called forth by the doctrine maintained by Mr. Mansel in his Bampton Lectures, that Revelation cannot be a direct Manifestation of the Infinite Nature of God. Mr. Maurice maintains the opposite doctrine, and in his Sermons explains why, in spite of the high authorities on the other side, he must still assert the principle which he discovers in the Services of the Church and throughout the Bible.

SEQUEL TO THE INQUIRY, "WHAT IS REVELA-TION?" Letters in Reply to Mr. Mansel's Examination of "Strictures on the Bampton Lectures." Crown 8vo. 6s.

This, as the title indicates, was called forth by Mr. Mansel's Examination of Mr. Maurice's Strictures on his doctrine of the Infinite.

THEOLOGICAL ESSAYS. Third Edition. Crown 8vo. 10s. 6d.

"The book," says Mr. Maurice, "expresses thoughts which have been

Maurice (F. D.)—continued.

working in my mind for years; the method of it has not been adopted carelessly; even the composition has undergone frequent revision." There are seventeen Essays in all, and although meant primarily for Unitarians, to quote the words of the Clerical Journal, *" it leaves untouched scarcely any topic which is in agitation in the religious world; scarcely a moot point between our various sects; scarcely a plot of debateable ground between Christians and Infidels, between Romanists and Protestants, between Socinians and other Christians, between English Churchmen and Dissenters on both sides. Scarce is there a misgiving, a difficulty, an aspiration stirring amongst us now,—now, when men seem in earnest as hardly ever before about religion, and ask and demand satisfaction with a fearlessness which seems almost awful when one thinks what is at stake—which is not recognised and grappled with by Mr. Maurice."*

THE DOCTRINE OF SACRIFICE DEDUCED FROM THE SCRIPTURES. Crown 8vo. 7s. 6d.

Throughout the Nineteen Sermons contained in this volume, Mr. Maurice expounds the ideas which he has formed of the Doctrine of Sacrifice, as it is set forth in various parts of the Bible.

THE RELIGIONS OF THE WORLD, AND THEIR RELATIONS TO CHRISTIANITY. Fourth Edition. Fcap. 8vo. 5s.

These Eight Boyle Lectures are divided into two parts, of four Lectures each. In the first part Mr. Maurice examines the great Religious systems which present themselves in the history of the world, with the purpose of inquiring what is their main characteristic principle. The second four Lectures are occupied with a discussion of the questions, " In what relation does Christianity stand to these different faiths? If there be a faith which is meant for mankind, is this the one, or must we look for another?"

ON THE LORD'S PRAYER. Fourth Edition. Fcap. 8vo. 2s. 6d.

In these Nine Sermons the successive petitions of the Lord's Prayer are taken up by Mr. Maurice, their significance expounded, and, as was usual with him, connected with the every-day lives, feelings, and aspirations of the men of the present time.

ON THE SABBATH DAY; the Character of the Warrior, and on the Interpretation of History. Fcap. 8vo. 2s. 6d.

THE GROUND AND OBJECT OF HOPE FOR MANKIND. Four Sermons preached before the University of Cambridge. Crown 8vo. 3s. 6d.

In these Four Sermons Mr. Maurice views the subject in four aspects: —I. The Hope of the Missionary. II. The Hope of the Patriot. III. The Hope of the Churchman. IV. The Hope of Man. The Spectator

Maurice (F. D.)—*continued.*

says, "*It is impossible to find anywhere deeper teaching than this;*" *and* the Nonconformist, "*We thank him for the manly, noble, stirring words in these Sermons—words fitted to quicken thoughts, to awaken high aspiration, to stimulate to lives of goodness.*"

THE LORD'S PRAYER, THE CREED, AND THE COMMANDMENTS. A Manual for Parents and Schoolmasters. To which is added the Order of the Scriptures. 18mo. cloth limp. 1s.

This book is not written for clergymen, as such, but for parents and teachers, who are often either prejudiced against the contents of the Catechism, or regard it peculiarly as the clergyman's book, but, at the same time, have a general notion that a habit of prayer ought to be cultivated, that there are some things which ought to be believed, and some things which ought to be done. It will be found to be peculiarly valuable at the present time, when the question of religious education is occupying so much attention.

THE CLAIMS OF THE BIBLE AND OF SCIENCE. A Correspondence on some Questions respecting the Pentateuch. Crown 8vo. 4s. 6d.

This volume consists of a series of Fifteen Letters, the first and last addressed by a 'Layman' to Mr. Maurice, the intervening thirteen written by Mr. Maurice himself.

DIALOGUES ON FAMILY WORSHIP. Crown 8vo. 6s.

"*The parties in these Dialogues,*" *says the Preface,* "*are a Clergyman who accepts the doctrines of the Church, and a Layman whose faith in them is nearly gone. The object of the Dialogues is not confutation, but the discovery of a ground on which two Englishmen and two fathers may stand, and on which their country and their children may stand when their places know them no more.*"

THE COMMANDMENTS CONSIDERED AS INSTRUMENTS OF NATIONAL REFORMATION. Crown 8vo. 4s. 6d.

The author endeavours to shew that the Commandments are now, and ever have been, the great protesters against Presbyteral and Prelatical assumptions, and that if we do not receive them as Commandments of the Lord God spoken to Israel, and spoken to every people under heaven now, we lose the greatest witnesses we possess for national morality and civil freedom.

MORAL AND METAPHYSICAL PHILOSOPHY. Vol. I. Ancient Philosophy from the First to the Thirteenth Centuries. Vol. II. Fourteenth Century and the French Revolution, with a Glimpse into the Nineteenth Century. Two Vols. 8vo. 25s.

This is an edition in two volumes of Professor Maurice's History of

Maurice (F. D.)—*continued.*

Philosophy from the earliest period to the present time. It was formerly issued in a number of separate volumes, and it is believed that all admirers of the author and all students of philosophy will welcome this compact edition. In a long introduction to this edition, in the form of a dialogue, Professor Maurice justifies his own views, and touches upon some of the most important topics of the time.

SOCIAL MORALITY. Twenty-one Lectures delivered in the University of Cambridge. New and Cheaper Edition. Cr. 8vo. 10s. 6d.

"*Whilst reading it we are charmed by the freedom from exclusiveness and prejudice, the large charity, the loftiness of thought, the eagerness to recognise and appreciate whatever there is of real worth extant in the world, which animates it from one end to the other. We gain new thoughts and new ways of viewing things, even more, perhaps, from being brought for a time under the influence of so noble and spiritual a mind.*" —Athenæum.

THE CONSCIENCE: Lectures on Casuistry, delivered in the University of Cambridge. Second and Cheaper Edition. Crown 8vo. 5s.

In this series of nine Lectures, Professor Maurice, endeavours to settle what is meant by the word "Conscience," and discusses the most important questions immediately connected with the subject. Taking "Casuistry" in its old sense as being the "study of cases of Conscience," he endeavours to show in what way it may be brought to bear at the present day upon the acts and thoughts of our ordinary existence. He shows that Conscience asks for laws, not rules; for freedom, not chains; for education, not suppression. He has abstained from the use of philosophical terms, and has touched on philosophical systems only when he fancied "they were interfering with the rights and duties of wayfarers." The Saturday Review *says:* "*We rise from the perusal of these lectures with a detestation of all that is selfish and mean, and with a living impression that there is such a thing as goodness after all.*"

LECTURES ON THE ECCLESIASTICAL HISTORY OF THE FIRST AND SECOND CENTURIES. 8vo. 10s. 6d.

In the first chapter on "The Jewish Calling," besides expounding his idea of the true nature of a "Church," the author gives a brief sketch of the position and economy of the Jews; while in the second he points out their relation to "the other Nations." Chapter Third contains a succinct account of the various Jewish Sects, while in Chapter Fourth are briefly set forth Mr. Maurice's ideas of the character of Christ and the nature of His mission, and a sketch of events is given up to the Day of Pentecost. The remaining Chapters, extending from the Apostles' personal Ministry to the end of the Second Century, contain sketches of the character and

Maurice (F. D.)—*continued*.

work of all the prominent men in any way connected with the Early Church, accounts of the origin and nature of the various doctrines orthodox and heretical which had their birth during the period, as well as of the planting and early history of the Chief Churches in Asia, Africa and Europe.

LEARNING AND WORKING. Six Lectures delivered in Willis's Rooms, London, in June and July, 1854.—THE RELIGION OF ROME, and its Influence on Modern Civilisation. Four Lectures delivered in the Philosophical Institution of Edinburgh, in December, 1854. Crown 8vo. 5*s*.

SERMONS PREACHED IN COUNTRY CHURCHES. Crown 8vo. 10*s*. 6*d*.

"*Earnest, practical, and extremely simple.*"—Literary Churchman. "*Good specimens of his simple and earnest eloquence. The Gospel incidents are realized with a vividness which we can well believe made the common people hear him gladly. Moreover they are sermons which must have done the hearers good.*"—John Bull.

Moorhouse.—Works by JAMES MOORHOUSE, M.A., Vicar of Paddington :—

SOME MODERN DIFFICULTIES RESPECTING the FACTS OF NATURE AND REVELATION. Fcap. 8vo. 2*s*. 6*d*.

The first of these Four Discourses is a systematic reply to the Essay of the Rev. Baden Powell on Christian Evidences in "Essays and Reviews." The fourth Sermon, on "The Resurrection," is in some measure complementary to this, and the two together are intended to furnish a tolerably complete view of modern objections to Revelation. In the second and third Sermons, on the "Temptation" and "Passion," the author has endeavoured "to exhibit the power and wonder of those great facts within the spiritual sphere, which modern theorists have especially sought to discredit."

JACOB. Three Sermons preached before the University of Cambridge in Lent 1870. Extra fcap. 8vo. 3*s*. 6*d*.

THE HULSEAN LECTURES FOR 1865. Cr. 8vo. 5*s*.

"*Few more valuable works have come into our hands for many years... a most fruitful and welcome volume.*"—Church Review.

O'Brien.—AN ATTEMPT TO EXPLAIN and ESTABLISH THE DOCTRINE OF JUSTIFICATION by FAITH ONLY. By JAMES THOMAS O'BRIEN, D.D., Bishop of Ossory. Third Edition. 8vo. 12*s*.

This work consists of Ten Sermons. The first four treat of the nature and mutual relations of Faith and Justification; the fifth and sixth examine the corruptions of the doctrine of Justification by Faith only, and the objections which have been urged against it. The four concluding sermons deal with the moral effects of Faith. Various Notes are added explanatory of the Author's reasoning.

Palgrave.—HYMNS. By FRANCIS TURNER PALGRAVE. Third Edition, enlarged. 18mo. 1s. 6d.

This is a collection of twenty original Hymns, which the Literary Churchman *speaks of as "so choice, so perfect, and so refined,—so tender in feeling, and so scholarly in expression."*

Paul of Tarsus. An Inquiry into the Times and the Gospel of the Apostle of the Gentiles. By a GRADUATE. 8vo. 10s. 6d.

The Author of this work has attempted, out of the materials which were at his disposal, to construct for himself a sketch of the time in which St. Paul lived, of the religious systems with which he was brought in contact, of the doctrine which he taught, and of the work which he ultimately achieved. "Turn where we will throughout the volume, we find the best fruit of patient inquiry, sound scholarship, logical argument, and fairness of conclusion. No thoughtful reader will rise from its perusal without a real and lasting profit to himself, and a sense of permanent addition to the cause of truth."—Standard.

Picton.—THE MYSTERY OF MATTER; and other Essays. By J. ALLANSON PICTON, Author of "New Theories and the Old Faith." Crown 8vo. 10s. 6d.

Contents—The Mystery of Matter: The Philosophy of Ignorance: The Antithesis of Faith and Sight: The Essential Nature of Religion: Christian Pantheism.

Prescott.—THE THREEFOLD CORD. Sermons preached before the University of Cambridge. By J. E. PRESCOTT, B.D. Fcap. 8vo. 3s. 6d.

Procter.—A HISTORY OF THE BOOK OF COMMON PRAYER: With a Rationale of its Offices. By FRANCIS PROCTER, M.A. Eleventh Edition, revised and enlarged. Crown 8vo. 10s. 6d.

The Athenæum *says:—"The origin of every part of the Prayer-book has been diligently investigated,—and there are few questions or facts connected with it which are not either sufficiently explained, or so referred to, that persons interested may work out the truth for themselves."*

Procter and Maclear.—AN ELEMENTARY INTRODUCTION TO THE BOOK OF COMMON PRAYER. Re-arranged and Supplemented by an Explanation of the Morning

and Evening Prayer and the Litany. By F. PROCTER, M.A. and G. F. MACLEAR, D.D. New Edition. 18mo. 2s. 6d.

This book has the same object and follows the same plan as the Manuals already noticed under Mr. Maclear's name. Each book is subdivided into chapters and sections. In Book I. is given a detailed History of the Book of Common Prayer down to the Attempted Revision in the Reign of William III. Book II., consisting of four Parts, treats in order the various parts of the Prayer Book. Notes, etymological, historical, and critical, are given throughout the book, while the Appendix contains several articles of much interest and importance. Appended is a General Index and an Index of Words explained in the Notes. The Literary Church-man characterizes it as "by far the completest and most satisfactory book of its kind we know. We wish it were in the hands of every schoolboy and every schoolmaster in the kingdom."

Psalms of David CHRONOLOGICALLY ARRANGED.

An Amended Version, with Historical Introductions and Explanatory Notes. By FOUR FRIENDS. Second and Cheaper Edition, much enlarged. Crown 8vo. 8s. 6d.

One of the chief designs of the Editors, in preparing this volume, was to restore the Psalter as far as possible to the order in which the Psalms were written. They give the division of each Psalm into strophes, and of each strophe into the lines which composed it, and amend the errors of translation. The Spectator calls it "One of the most instructive and valuable books that have been published for many years."

Golden Treasury Psalter.—THE STUDENT'S EDITION.

Being an Edition with briefer Notes of the above. 18mo. 3s. 6d.

This volume will be found to meet the requirements of those who wish for a smaller edition of the larger work, at a lower price for family use, and for the use of younger pupils in Public Schools. The short notes which are appended to the volume will, it is hoped, suffice to make the meaning intelligible throughout. The aim of this edition is simply to put the reader as far as possible in possession of the plain meaning of the writer. "It is a gem," the Nonconformist says.

Ramsay.—THE CATECHISER'S MANUAL; or, the

Church Catechism Illustrated and Explained, for the Use of Clergymen, Schoolmasters, and Teachers. By ARTHUR RAMSAY, M.A. Second Edition. 18mo. 1s. 6d.

Rays of Sunlight for Dark Days. A Book of Selec-

tions for the Suffering. With a Preface by C. J. VAUGHAN, D.D. 18mo. New Edition. 3s. 6d. Also in morocco, old style.

Dr. Vaughan says in the Preface, after speaking of the general run of Books of Comfort for Mourners, "It is because I think that the little volume now offered to the Christian sufferer is one of greater wisdom and of deeper experience, that I have readily consented to the request that I would introduce it by a few words of Preface." The book consists of a series of very brief extracts from a great variety of authors, in prose and poetry, suited to the many moods of a mourning or suffering mind. "Mostly gems of the first water."—Clerical Journal.

Reynolds.—NOTES OF THE CHRISTIAN LIFE. A Selection of Sermons by HENRY ROBERT REYNOLDS, B.A., President of Cheshunt College, and Fellow of University College, London. Crown 8vo. 7s. 6d.

This work may be taken as representative of the mode of thought and feeling which is most popular amongst the freer and more cultivated Nonconformists. "It is long," says the Nonconformist, *"since we have met with any published sermons better calculated than these to stimulate devout thought, and to bring home to the soul the reality of a spiritual life."*

Roberts.—DISCUSSIONS ON THE GOSPELS. By the Rev. ALEXANDER ROBERTS, D.D. Second Edition, revised and enlarged. 8vo. 16s.

This volume is divided into two parts. Part I. "On the Language employed by our Lord and His Disciples," in which the author endeavours to prove that Greek was the language usually employed by Christ Himself, in opposition to the common belief that Our Lord spoke Aramæan. Part II. is occupied with a discussion "On the Original Language of St. Matthew's Gospel," and on "The Origin and Authenticity of the Gospels." "The author brings the valuable qualifications of learning, temper, and an independent judgment."—Daily News.

Robertson.—PASTORAL COUNSELS. Being Chapters on Practical and Devotional Subjects. By the late JOHN ROBERTSON, D.D. Third Edition, with a Preface by the Author of "The Recreations of a Country Parson." Extra fcap. 8vo. 6s.

These Sermons are the free utterances of a strong and independent thinker. He does not depart from the essential doctrines of his Church, but he expounds them in a spirit of the widest charity, and always having most prominently in view the requirements of practical life. "The sermons are admirable specimens of a practical, earnest, and instructive style of pulpit teaching."—Nonconformist.

Rowsell.—MAN'S LABOUR AND GOD'S HARVEST. Sermons preached before the University of Cambridge in Lent, 1861. Fcap. 8vo. 3s.

"We strongly recommend this little volume to young men, and especially to those who are contemplating working for Christ in Holy Orders."—Literary Churchman.

Salmon.—THE REIGN OF LAW, and other Sermons, preached in the Chapel of Trinity College, Dublin. By the Rev. GEORGE SALMON, D.D., Regius Professor of Divinity in the University of Dublin. Crown 8vo. 6s.

"Well considered, learned, and powerful discourses."—Spectator.

Sanday.—THE AUTHORSHIP AND HISTORICAL CHARACTER OF THE FOURTH GOSPEL, considered in reference to the Contents of the Gospel itself. A Critical Essay. By WILLIAM SANDAY, M.A., Fellow of Trinity College, Oxford. Crown 8vo. 8*s.* 6*d.*

The object of this Essay is critical and nothing more. The Author attempts to apply faithfully and persistently to the contents of the much disputed fourth Gospel that scientific method which has been so successful in other directions. "The facts of religion," the Author believes, "(i. e. the documents, the history of religious bodies, &c.) are as much facts as the lie of a coal-bed or the formation of a coral-reef." "The Essay is not only most valuable in itself, but full of promise for the future."—Canon Westcott in the *Academy.*

Selborne.—THE BOOK OF PRAISE : From the Best English Hymn Writers. Selected and arranged by Lord SELBORNE. With Vignette by WOOLNER. 18mo. 4*s.* 6*d.*

The present is an attempt to present, under a convenient arrangement, a collection of such examples of a copious and interesting branch of popular literature, as, after several years' study of the subject, have seemed to the Editor most worthy of being separated from the mass to which they belong. It has been the Editor's desire and aim to adhere strictly, in all cases in which it could be ascertained, to the genuine uncorrupted text of the authors themselves. The names of the authors and date of composition of the hymns, when known, are affixed, while notes are added to the volume, giving further details. The Hymns are arranged according to subjects. "There is not room for two opinions as to the value of the 'Book of Praise.'"—Guardian. *"Approaches as nearly as one can conceive to perfection."*—Nonconformist.

BOOK OF PRAISE HYMNAL. *See* end of this Catalogue.

Sergeant.—SERMONS. By the Rev. E. W. SERGEANT, M.A., Balliol College, Oxford ; Assistant Master at Westminster College. Fcap. 8vo. 2*s.* 6*d.*

Smith.—PROPHECY A PREPARATION FOR CHRIST. Eight Lectures preached before the University of Oxford, being the Bampton Lectures for 1869. By R. PAYNE SMITH, D.D., Dean of Canterbury. Second and Cheaper Edition. Crown 8vo. 6*s.*

The author's object in these Lectures is to shew that there exists in the Old Testament an element, which no criticism on naturalistic principles can either account for or explain away: that element is Prophecy. The author endeavours to prove that its force does not consist merely in its predictions. "These Lectures overflow with solid learning."—Record.

Smith.—CHRISTIAN FAITH. Sermons preached before the University of Cambridge. By W. SAUMAREZ SMITH, M.A., Principal of St. Aidan's College, Birkenhead. Fcap. 8vo. 3s. 6d.

"Appropriate and earnest sermons, suited to the practical exhortation of an educated congregation."—Guardian.

Stanley.—Works by the Very Rev. A. P. STANLEY, D.D., Dean of Westminster.

THE ATHANASIAN CREED, with a Preface on the General Recommendations of the RITUAL COMMISSION. Cr. 8vo. 2s.

The object of the work is not so much to urge the omission or change of the Athanasian Creed, as to shew that such a relaxation ought to give offence to no reasonable or religious mind. With this view, the Dean of Westminster discusses in succession—(1) *the Authorship of the Creed,* (2) *its Internal Characteristics,* (3) *the Peculiarities of its Use in the Church of England,* (4) *its Advantages and Disadvantages,* (5) *its various Interpretations, and* (6) *the Judgment passed upon it by the Ritual Commission. In conclusion, Dr. Stanley maintains that the use of the Athanasian Creed should no longer be made compulsory. "Dr. Stanley puts with admirable force the objections which may be made to the Creed; equally admirable, we think, in his statement of its advantages."*—Spectator.

THE NATIONAL THANKSGIVING. Sermons preached in Westminster Abbey. Second Edition. Crown 8vo. 2s. 6d.

These Sermons are (1) *" Death and Life," preached December* 10, 1871 ; (2) *" The Trumpet of Patmos," December* 17, 1871 ; (3) *" The Day of Thanksgiving," March* 3, 1872. *" In point of fervour and polish by far the best specimens in print of Dean Stanley's eloquent style."*—Standard.

Sunday Library. See end of this Catalogue.

Swainson.—Works by C. A. SWAINSON, D.D., Canon of Chichester :—

THE CREEDS OF THE CHURCH IN THEIR RE-LATIONS TO HOLY SCRIPTURE and the CONSCIENCE OF THE CHRISTIAN. 8vo. cloth. 9s.

The Lectures which compose this volume discuss, amongst others, the following subjects : " Faith in God," " Exercise of our Reason," "Origin and Authority of Creeds," and " Private Judgment, its use and exercise." " Treating of abstruse points of Scripture, he applies them so forcibly to Christian duty and practice as to prove eminently serviceable to the Church."—John Bull.

Swainson (C. A.)—*continued.*

THE AUTHORITY OF THE NEW TESTAMENT, and other LECTURES, delivered before the University of Cambridge. 8vo. cloth. 12*s.*

The first series of Lectures in this work is on " The Words spoken by the Apostles of Jesus," " The Inspiration of God's Servants," " The Human Character of the Inspired Writers," and " The Divine Character of the Word written." The second embraces Lectures on " Sin as Imperfection," " Sin as Self-will," "Whatsoever is not of Faith is Sin," " Christ the Saviour," and " The Blood of the New Covenant." The third is on "Christians One Body in Christ," " The One Body the Spouse of Christ," " Christ's Prayer for Unity," " Our Reconciliation should be manifested in common Worship," and " Ambassadors for Christ."

Taylor.—THE RESTORATION OF BELIEF. New and Revised Edition. By ISAAC TAYLOR, Esq. Crown 8vo. 8*s.* 6*d.*

The earlier chapters are occupied with an examination of the primitive history of the Christian Religion, and its relation to the Roman government; and here, as well as in the remainder of the work, the author shews the bearing of that history on some of the difficult and interesting questions which have recently been claiming the attention of all earnest men. The last chapter of this New Edition treats of " The Present Position of the Argument concerning Christianity," with special reference to M. Renan's Vie de Jésus.

Temple.—SERMONS PREACHED IN THE CHAPEL of RUGBY SCHOOL. By F. TEMPLE, D.D., Bishop of Exeter. New and Cheaper Edition. Extra fcap. 8vo. 4*s.* 6*d.*

This volume contains Thirty-five Sermons on topics more or less intimately connected with every-day life. The following are a few of the subjects discoursed upon :—"Love and Duty;" "Coming to Christ;" "Great Men;" "Faith;" " Doubts;" " Scruples;" "Original Sin;" "Friendship;" "Helping Others;" " The Discipline of Temptation;" "Strength a Duty;" "Worldliness;" "Ill Temper;" " The Burial of the Past."

A SECOND SERIES OF SERMONS PREACHED IN THE CHAPEL OF RUGBY SCHOOL. Second Edition. Extra fcap. 8vo. 6*s.*

This Second Series of Forty-two brief, pointed, practical Sermons, on topics intimately connected with the every-day life of young and old, will be acceptable to all who are acquainted with the First Series. The following are a few of the subjects treated of :—"Disobedience," "Almsgiving," " The Unknown Guidance of God," "Apathy one of our Trials," " High Aims in Leaders," "Doing our Best," " The Use of Knowledge," "Use of Observances," "Martha and Mary," "John the Baptist," "Severity

Temple (F., D.D.)—*continued*.

before Mercy," "Even Mistakes Punished," "Morality and Religion," "Children," "Action the Test of Spiritual Life," "Self-Respect," "Too Late," "The Tercentenary."

A THIRD SERIES OF SERMONS PREACHED IN RUGBY SCHOOL CHAPEL IN 1867—1869. Extra fcap. 8vo. 6s.

This third series of Bishop Temple's Rugby Sermons, contains thirty-six brief discourses, including the "Good-bye" sermon preached on his leaving Rugby to enter on the office he now holds.

Thring.—Works by Rev. EDWARD THRING, M.A.

SERMONS DELIVERED AT UPPINGHAM SCHOOL. Crown 8vo. 5s.

In this volume are contained Forty-seven brief Sermons, all on subjects more or less intimately connected with Public-school life. "We desire very highly to commend these capital Sermons which treat of a boy's life and trials in a thoroughly practical way and with great simplicity and impressiveness. They deserve to be classed with the best of their kind."— Literary Churchman.

THOUGHTS ON LIFE-SCIENCE. New Edition, enlarged and revised. Crown 8vo. 7s. 6d.

In this volume are discussed in a familiar manner some of the most interesting problems between Science and Religion, Reason and Feeling.

Tracts for Priests and People. By VARIOUS WRITERS.

THE FIRST SERIES. Crown 8vo. 8s.

THE SECOND SERIES. Crown 8vo. 8s.

The whole Series of Fifteen Tracts may be had separately, price One Shilling each.

Trench.—Works by R. CHENEVIX TRENCH, D.D., Archbishop of Dublin. (For other Works by the same author, *see* BIOGRAPHICAL, BELLES LETTRES, and LINGUISTIC CATALOGUES).

NOTES ON THE PARABLES OF OUR LORD. Twelfth Edition. 8vo. 12s.

This work has taken its place as a standard exposition and interpretation of Christ's Parables. The book is prefaced by an Introductory Essay in four chapters:—I. On the definition of the Parable. II. On Teaching by Parables. III. On the Interpretation of the Parables. IV. On other Parables besides those in the Scriptures. The author then proceeds to take up the Parables one by one, and by the aid of philology, history,

Trench—*continued.*

antiquities, and the researches of travellers, shews forth the significance, beauty, and applicability of each, concluding with what he deems its true moral interpretation. In the numerous Notes are many valuable references, illustrative quotations, critical and philological annotations, etc., and appended to the volume is a classified list of fifty-six works on the Parables.

NOTES ON THE MIRACLES OF OUR LORD.
Ninth Edition. 8vo. 12s.

In the 'Preliminary Essay' to this work, all the momentous and interesting questions that have been raised in connection with Miracles, are discussed with considerable fulness. The Essay consists of six chapters:—I. On the Names of Miracles, i. e. the Greek words by which they are designated in the New Testament. II. The Miracles and Nature—What is the difference between a Miracle and any event in the ordinary course of Nature? III. The Authority of Miracles—Is the Miracle to command absolute obedience? IV. The Evangelical, compared with the other cycles of Miracles. V. The Assaults on the Miracles—1. The Jewish. 2. The Heathen (Celsus etc.). 3. The Pantheistic (Spinosa etc.). 4. The Sceptical (Hume). 5. The Miracles only relatively miraculous (Schleiermacher). 6. The Rationalistic (Paulus). 7. The Historico-Critical (Woolston, Strauss). VI. The Apologetic Worth of the Miracles. The author then treats the separate Miracles as he does the Parables.

SYNONYMS OF THE NEW TESTAMENT. New
Edition, enlarged. 8vo. cloth. 12s.

The study of synonyms in any language is valuable as a discipline for training the mind to close and accurate habits of thought; more especially is this the case in Greek—" a language spoken by a people of the finest and subtlest intellect; who saw distinctions where others saw none; who divided out to different words what others often were content to huddle confusedly under a common term. . . . Where is it so desirable that we should miss nothing, that we should lose no finer intention of the writer, as in those words which are the vehicles of the very mind of God Himself?" This Edition has been carefully revised, and a considerable number of new synonyms added. Appended is an Index to the Synonyms, and an Index to many other words alluded to or explained throughout the work. "He is," the Athenæum *says, " a guide in this department of knowledge to whom his readers may intrust themselves with confidence. His sober judgment and sound sense are barriers against the misleading influence of arbitrary hypotheses."*

ON THE AUTHORIZED VERSION OF THE NEW
TESTAMENT. Second Edition. 8vo. 7s.

After some Introductory Remarks, in which the propriety of a revision is briefly discussed, the whole question of the merits of the present version is gone into in detail, in eleven chapters. Appended is a chronological list

Trench—*continued.*

of works bearing on the subject, an Index of the principal Texts considered, an Index of Greek Words, and an Index of other Words referred to throughout the book.

STUDIES IN THE GOSPELS.   Third Edition.   8vo.
   10s. 6d.

This book is published under the conviction that the assertion often made is untrue,—viz. that the Gospels are in the main plain and easy, and that all the chief difficulties of the New Testament are to be found in the Epistles. These "Studies," sixteen in number, are the fruit of a much larger scheme, and each Study deals with some important episode mentioned in the Gospels, in a critical, philosophical, and practical manner. Many references and quotations are added to the Notes. Among the subjects treated are:—The Temptation; Christ and the Samaritan Woman; The Three Aspirants; The Transfiguration; Zacchæus; The True Vine; The Penitent Malefactor; Christ and the Two Disciples on the way to Emmaus.

COMMENTARY ON THE EPISTLES to the SEVEN
   CHURCHES IN ASIA.   Third Edition, revised.   8vo.   8s. 6d.

The present work consists of an Introduction, being a commentary on Rev. i. 4—20, a detailed examination of each of the Seven Epistles, in all its bearings, and an Excursus on the Historico-Prophetical Interpretation of the Epistles.

THE SERMON ON THE MOUNT.   An Exposition
   drawn from the writings of St. Augustine, with an Essay on his
   merits as an Interpreter of Holy Scripture.   Third Edition, enlarged.   8vo.   10s. 6d.

The first half of the present work consists of a dissertation in eight chapters on "Augustine as an Interpreter of Scripture," the titles of the several chapters being as follow:—I. Augustine's General Views of Scripture and its Interpretation.   II. The External Helps for the Interpretation of Scripture possessed by Augustine.   III. Augustine's Principles and Canons of Interpretation.   IV. Augustine's Allegorical Interpretation of Scripture.   V. Illustrations of Augustine's Skill as an Interpreter of Scripture.   VI. Augustine on John the Baptist and on St. Stephen. VII. Augustine on the Epistle to the Romans.   VIII. Miscellaneous Examples of Augustine's Interpretation of Scripture.   The latter half of the work consists of Augustine's Exposition of the Sermon on the Mount, not however a mere series of quotations from Augustine, but a connected account of his sentiments on the various passages of that Sermon, interspersed with criticisms by Archbishop Trench.

SERMONS PREACHED in WESTMINSTER ABBEY.
   Second Edition.   8vo.   10s. 6d.

These Sermons embrace a wide variety of topics, and are thoroughly

Trench—*continued.*

practical, earnest, and evangelical, and simple in style. The following are a few of the subjects:—"Tercentenary Celebration of Queen Eliza- beth's Accession;" "Conviction and Conversion;" "The Incredulity of Thomas;" "The Angels' Hymn;" "Counting the Cost;" "The Holy Trinity in Relation to our Prayers;" "On the Death of General Have- lock;" "Christ Weeping over Jerusalem;" "Walking with Christ in White."

SHIPWRECKS OF FAITH. Three Sermons preached before the University of Cambridge in May, 1867. Fcap. 8vo. 2s. 6d.

These Sermons are especially addressed to young men. The subjects are "Balaam," "Saul," and "Judas Iscariot." These lives are set forth as beacon-lights, "to warn us off from perilous reefs and quick- sands, which have been the destruction of many, and which might only too easily be ours." The John Bull says, "they are, like all he writes, af- fectionate and earnest discourses."

SERMONS Preached for the most part in Ireland. 8vo. 10s. 6d.

This volume consists of Thirty-two Sermons, the greater part of which were preached in Ireland; the subjects are as follows:—Jacob, a Prince with God and with Men—Agrippa—The Woman that was a Sinner— Secret Faults—The Seven Worse Spirits—Freedom in the Truth—Joseph and his Brethren—Bearing one another's Burdens—Christ's Challenge to the World—The Love of Money—The Salt of the Earth—The Armour of God—Light in the Lord—The Jailer of Philippi—The Thorn in the Flesh —Isaiah's Vision—Selfishness—Abraham interceding for Sodom—Vain Thoughts—Pontius Pilate—The Brazen Serpent—The Death and Burial of Moses—A Word from the Cross—The Church's Worship in the Beauty of Holiness—Every Good Gift from Above—On the Hearing of Prayer—The Kingdom which cometh not with Observation—Pressing towards the Mark—Saul—The Good Shepherd—The Valley of Dry Bones —All Saints.

Tudor.—The DECALOGUE VIEWED as the CHRIST- IAN'S LAW. With Special Reference to the Questions and Wants of the Times. By the Rev. RICH. TUDOR, B.A. Crown 8vo. 10s. 6d.

The author's aim is to bring out the Christian sense of the Decalogue in its application to existing needs and questions. The work will be found to occupy ground which no other single work has hitherto filled. It is di- vided into Two Parts, the First Part consisting of three lectures on "Duty," and the Second Part of twelve lectures on the Ten Command- ments. The Guardian says of it, "His volume throughout is an outspoken and sound exposition of Christian morality, based deeply upon true founda- tions, set forth systematically, and forcibly and plainly expressed—as good a specimen of what pulpit lectures ought to be as is often to be found."

Tulloch.—THE CHRIST OF THE GOSPELS AND THE CHRIST OF MODERN CRITICISM. Lectures on M. RENAN'S "Vie de Jésus." By JOHN TULLOCH, D.D., Principal of the College of St. Mary, in the University of St. Andrew's. Extra fcap. 8vo. 4*s.* 6*d.*

Vaughan.—Works by CHARLES J. VAUGHAN, D.D., Master of the Temple :—

CHRIST SATISFYING THE INSTINCTS OF HUMANITY. Eight Lectures delivered in the Temple Church. New Edition. Extra fcp. 8vo. 3*s.* 6*d.*

The object of these Sermons is to exhibit the spiritual wants of human nature, and to prove that all of them receive full satisfaction in Christ. The various instincts which He is shewn to meet are those of Truth, Reverence, Perfection, Liberty, Courage, Sympathy, Sacrifice, and Unity. "We are convinced that there are congregations, in number unmistakeably increasing, to whom such Essays as these, full of thought and learning, are infinitely more beneficial, for they are more acceptable, than the recognised type of sermons."—John Bull.

MEMORIALS OF HARROW SUNDAYS. A Selection of Sermons preached in Harrow School Chapel. With a View of the Chapel. Fourth Edition. Crown 8vo. 10*s.* 6*d.*

"Discussing," says the John Bull, *" those forms of evil and impediments to duty which peculiarly beset the young, Dr. Vaughan has, with singular tact, blended deep thought and analytical investigation of principles with interesting earnestness and eloquent simplicity."* The Nonconformist *says " the volume is a precious one for family reading, and for the hand of the thoughtful boy or young man entering life."*

THE BOOK AND THE LIFE, and other Sermons, preached before the University of Cambridge. New Edition. Fcap. 8vo. 4*s.* 6*d.*

These Sermons are all of a thoroughly practical nature, and some of them are especially adapted to those who are in a state of anxious doubt.

TWELVE DISCOURSES on SUBJECTS CONNECTED WITH THE LITURGY and WORSHIP of the CHURCH OF ENGLAND. Fcap. 8vo. 6*s.*

Four of these discourses were published in 1860, *in a work entitled* Revision of the Liturgy; *four others have appeared in the form of separate sermons, delivered on various occasions, and published at the time by request; and four are new. The Appendix contains two articles,—one on "Subscription and Scruples," the other on the "Rubric and the Burial Service." The* Press *characterises the volume as " eminently wise and temperate."*

Vaughan (Dr. C. J.)—*continued.*

LESSONS OF LIFE AND GODLINESS. A Selection of Sermons preached in the Parish Church of Doncaster. Fourth and Cheaper Edition. Fcap. 8vo. 3s. 6d.

This volume consists of Nineteen Sermons, mostly on subjects connected with the every-day walk and conversation of Christians. They bear such titles as "The Talebearer," "Features of Charity," "The Danger of Relapse," "The Secret Life and the Outward," "Family Prayer," "Zeal without Consistency," "The Gospel an Incentive to Industry in Business," "Use and Abuse of the World." The Spectator *styles them "earnest and human. They are adapted to every class and order in the social system, and will be read with wakeful interest by all who seek to amend whatever may be amiss in their natural disposition or in their acquired habits."*

WORDS FROM THE GOSPELS. A Second Selection of Sermons preached in the Parish Church of Doncaster. Second Edition. Fcap. 8vo. 4s. 6d.

The Nonconformist *characterises these Sermons as " of practical earnestness, of a thoughtfulness that penetrates the common conditions and experiences of life, and brings the truths and examples of Scripture to bear on them with singular force, and of a style that owes its real elegance to the simplicity and directness which have fine culture for their roots.*

LESSONS OF THE CROSS AND PASSION. Six Lectures delivered in Hereford Cathedral during the Week before Easter, 1869. Fcap. 8vo. 2s. 6d.

The titles of the Sermons are:—I. "Too Late" (Matt. xxvi. 45). II. "The Divine Sacrifice and the Human Priesthood." III. "Love not the World." IV. "The Moral Glory of Christ." V. "Christ made perfect through Suffering." VI. "Death the Remedy of Christ's Loneliness." "This little volume," the Nonconformist *says, "exhibits all his best characteristics. Elevated, calm, and clear, the Sermons owe much to their force, and yet they seem literally to owe nothing to it. They are studied, but their grace is the grace of perfect simplicity."*

LIFE'S WORK AND GOD'S DISCIPLINE. Three Sermons. New Edition. Fcap. 8vo. 2s. 6d.

The Three Sermons are on the following subjects:—I. "The Work burned and the Workmen saved." II. "The Individual Hiring." III. "The Remedial Discipline of Disease and Death."

THE WHOLESOME WORDS OF JESUS CHRIST. Four Sermons preached before the University of Cambridge in November 1866. Second Edition. Fcap. 8vo. cloth. 3s. 6d.

Dr. Vaughan uses the word "Wholesome" here in its literal and original sense, the sense in which St. Paul uses it, as meaning healthy,

Vaughan (Dr. C. J.)—*continued.*

sound, conducing to right living; *and in these Sermons he points out and illustrates several of the "wholesome" characteristics of the Gospel, —the Words of Christ. The* John Bull *says this volume is "replete with all the author's well-known vigour of thought and richness of expression."*

FOES OF FAITH. Sermons preached before the University of Cambridge in November 1868. Fcap. 8vo. 3*s.* 6*d.*

The "Foes of Faith" preached against in these Four Sermons are:—I. "Unreality." II. "Indolence." III. "Irreverence." IV. "Inconsistency." "They are written," the London Review *says, "with culture and elegance, and exhibit the thoughtful earnestness, piety, and good sense of their author."*

LECTURES ON THE EPISTLE to the PHILIPPIANS. Third and Cheaper Edition. Extra fcap. 8vo. 5*s.*

Each Lecture is prefaced by a literal translation from the Greek of the paragraph which forms its subject, contains first a minute explanation of the passage on which it is based, and then a practical application of the verse or clause selected as its text.

LECTURES ON THE REVELATION OF ST. JOHN. Third and Cheaper Edition. Two Vols. Extra fcap. 8vo. 9*s.*

In this Edition of these Lectures, the literal translations of the passages expounded will be found interwoven in the body of the Lectures themselves. In attempting to expound this most-hard-to-understand Book, Dr. Vaughan, while taking from others what assistance he required, has not adhered to any particular school of interpretation, but has endeavoured to shew forth the significance of this Revelation by the help of his strong common sense, critical acumen, scholarship, and reverent spirit. "Dr. Vaughan's Sermons," the Spectator *says, "are the most practical discourses on the Apocalypse with which we are acquainted." Prefixed is a Synopsis of the Book of Revelation, and appended is an Index of passages illustrating the language of the Book.*

EPIPHANY, LENT, AND EASTER. A Selection of Expository Sermons. Third Edition. Crown 8vo. 10*s.* 6*d.*

The first eighteen of these Sermons were preached during the seasons of 1860, *indicated in the title, and are practical expositions of passages taken from the lessons of the days on which they were delivered. Each Lecture is prefaced with a careful and literal rendering of the original of the passage of which the Lecture is an exposition. The* Nonconformist *says that "in simplicity, dignity, close adherence to the words of Scripture, insight into 'the mind of the Spirit,' and practical thoughtfulness, they are models of that species of pulpit instruction to which they belong."*

THE EPISTLES OF ST. PAUL. For English Readers. PART I., containing the FIRST EPISTLE TO THE THESSALONIANS. Second Edition. 8vo. 1*s.* 6*d.*

Vaughan (Dr. C. J.)—*continued*.

It is the object of this work to enable English readers, unacquainted with Greek, to enter with intelligence into the meaning, connection, and phraseology of the writings of the great Apostle.

ST. PAUL'S EPISTLE TO THE ROMANS. The Greek Text, with English Notes. Fourth Edition. Crown 8vo. 7s. 6d.

This volume contains the Greek Text of the Epistle to the Romans as settled by the Rev. B. F. Westcott, D.D., for his complete recension of the Text of the New Testament. Appended to the text are copious critical and exegetical Notes, the result of almost eighteen years' study on the part of the author. The "Index of Words illustrated or explained in the Notes" will be found, in some considerable degree, an Index to the Epistles as a whole. Prefixed to the volume is a discourse on "St. Paul's Conversion and Doctrine," suggested by some recent publications on St. Paul's theological standing. The Guardian *says of the work,—"For educated young men his commentary seems to fill a gap hitherto unfilled. . . . As a whole, Dr. Vaughan appears to us to have given to the world a valuable book of original and careful and earnest thought bestowed on the accomplishment of a work which will be of much service and which is much needed."*

THE CHURCH OF THE FIRST DAYS.

Series I. The Church of Jerusalem. Third Edition.
" II. The Church of the Gentiles. Second Edition.
" III. The Church of the World. Second Edition.
Fcap. 8vo. cloth. 4s. 6d. each.

Where necessary, the Authorized Version has been departed from, and a new literal translation taken as the basis of exposition. All possible topographical and historical light has been brought to bear on the subject; and while thoroughly practical in their aim, these Lectures will be found to afford a fair notion of the history and condition of the Primitive Church. The British Quarterly *says,—"These Sermons are worthy of all praise, and are models of pulpit teaching."*

COUNSELS for YOUNG STUDENTS. Three Sermons preached before the University of Cambridge at the Opening of the Academical Year 1870-71. Fcap. 8vo. 2s. 6d.

The titles of the Three Sermons contained in this volume are:—I. "The Great Decision." II. "The House and the Builder." III. "The Prayer and the Counter-Prayer." They all bear pointedly, earnestly, and sympathisingly upon the conduct and pursuits of young students and young men generally.

NOTES FOR LECTURES ON CONFIRMATION, with suitable Prayers. Eighth Edition. Fcap. 8vo. 1s. 6d.

In preparation for the Confirmation held in Harrow School Chapel, Dr. Vaughan was in the habit of printing week by week, and distributing among the Candidates, somewhat full notes of the Lecture he purposed to

Vaughan (Dr. C. J.)—*continued.*

deliver to them, together with a form of Prayer adapted to the particular subject. He has collected these weekly Notes and Prayers into this little volume, in the hope that it may assist the labours of those who are engaged in preparing Candidates for Confirmation, and who find it difficult to lay their hand upon any one book of suitable instruction.

THE TWO GREAT TEMPTATIONS. The Temptation of Man, and the Temptation of Christ. Lectures delivered in the Temple Church, Lent 1872. Extra fcap. 8vo. 3*s.* 6*d.*

Vaughan.—Works by DAVID J. VAUGHAN, M.A., Vicar of St. Martin's, Leicester :—

SERMONS PREACHED IN ST. JOHN'S CHURCH, LEICESTER, during the Years 1855 and 1856. Cr. 8vo. 5*s.* 6*d.*

CHRISTIAN EVIDENCES AND THE BIBLE. New Edition, revised and enlarged. Fcap. 8vo. cloth. 5*s.* 6*d.*

"This little volume," the Spectator *says, "is a model of that honest and reverent criticism of the Bible which is not only right, but the duty of English clergymen in such times as these to put forth from the pulpit."*

Venn.—ON SOME OF THE CHARACTERISTICS OF BELIEF, Scientific and Religious. Being the Hulsean Lectures for 1869. By the Rev. J. VENN, M.A. 8vo. 6*s.* 6*d.*

These discourses are intended to illustrate, explain, and work out into some of their consequences, certain characteristics by which the attainment of religious belief is prominently distinguished from the attainment of belief upon most other subjects.

Warington.—THE WEEK OF CREATION ; OR, THE COSMOGONY OF GENESIS CONSIDERED IN ITS RELATION TO MODERN SCIENCE. By GEORGE WARINGTON, Author of "The Historic Character of the Pentateuch Vindicated." Crown 8vo. 4*s.* 6*d.*

*The greater part of this work is taken up with the teaching of the Cosmogony. Its purpose is also investigated, and a chapter is devoted to the consideration of the passage in which the difficulties occur. "A very able vindication of the Mosaic Cosmogony by a writer who unites the advantages of a critical knowledge of the Hebrew text and of distinguished scientific attainments."—*Spectator.

Westcott.—Works by BROOKE FOSS WESTCOTT, D.D., Regius Professor of Divinity in the University of Cambridge ; Canon of Peterborough :—

The London Quarterly, *speaking of Mr. Westcott, says,—"To a learning and accuracy which command respect and confidence, he unites what are not always to be found in union with these qualities, the no less valuable faculties of lucid arrangement and graceful and facile expression."*

Westcott (Dr. B. F.)—*continued.*

AN INTRODUCTION TO THE STUDY OF THE GOSPELS. Fourth Edition. Crown 8vo. 10s. 6d.

The author's chief object in this work has been to shew that there is a true mean between the idea of a formal harmonization of the Gospels and the abandonment of their absolute truth. After an Introduction on the General Effects of the course of Modern Philosophy on the popular views of Christianity, he proceeds to determine in what way the principles therein indicated may be applied to the study of the Gospels. The treatise is divided into eight Chapters:—I. The Preparation for the Gospel. II. The Jewish Doctrine of the Messiah. III. The Origin of the Gospels. IV. The Characteristics of the Gospels. V. The Gospel of St. John. VI. and VII. The Differences in detail and of arrangement in the Synoptic Evangelists. VIII. The Difficulties of the Gospels. The Appendices contain much valuable subsidiary matter.

A GENERAL SURVEY OF THE HISTORY OF THE CANON OF THE NEW TESTAMENT DURING THE FIRST FOUR CENTURIES. Third Edition, revised. Crown 8vo. 10s. 6d.

The object of this treatise is to deal with the New Testament as a whole, and that on purely historical grounds. The separate books of which it is composed are considered not individually, but as claiming to be parts of the apostolic heritage of Christians. The Author has thus endeavoured to connect the history of the New Testament Canon with the growth and consolidation of the Catholic Church, and to point out the relation existing between the amount of evidence for the authenticity of its component parts and the whole mass of Christian literature. "The treatise," says the British Quarterly, *"is a scholarly performance, learned, dispassionate, discriminating, worthy of his subject and of the present state of Christian literature in relation to it."*

THE BIBLE IN THE CHURCH. A Popular Account of the Collection and Reception of the Holy Scriptures in the Christian Churches. New Edition. 18mo. 4s. 6d.

The present volume has been written under the impression that a History of the whole Bible, and not of the New Testament only, would be required, if those unfamiliar with the subject were to be enabled to learn in what manner and with what consent the collection of Holy Scriptures was first made and then enlarged and finally closed by the Church. Though the work is intended to be simple and popular in its method, the author, for this very reason, has aimed at the strictest accuracy.

A GENERAL VIEW OF THE HISTORY OF THE ENGLISH BIBLE. Second Edition. Crown 8vo. 10s. 6d.

In the Introduction the author notices briefly the earliest vernacular versions of the Bible, especially those in Anglo-Saxon. Chapter I. is oc-

Westcott (Dr. B. F.)—*continued*.

cupied with an account of the Manuscript English Bible from the 14*th century downwards; and in Chapter II. is narrated, with many interesting personal and other details, the External History of the Printed Bible. In Chapter III. is set forth the Internal History of the English Bible, shewing to what extent the various English Translations were independent, and to what extent the translators were indebted to earlier English and foreign versions. In the Appendices, among other interesting and valuable matter, will be found "Specimens of the Earlier and Later Wycliffite Versions;" "Chronological List of Bibles;" "An Examination of Mr. Froude's History of the English Bible." The Pall Mall Gazette calls the work "A brief, scholarly, and, to a great extent, an original contribution to theological literature."*

THE CHRISTIAN LIFE, MANIFOLD AND ONE. Six Sermons preached in Peterborough Cathedral. Crown 8vo. 2s. 6d.

The Six Sermons contained in this volume are the first preached by the author as a Canon of Peterborough Cathedral. The subjects are:— I. "Life consecrated by the Ascension." II. "Many Gifts, One Spirit." III. "The Gospel of the Resurrection." IV. "Sufficiency of God." V. "Action the Test of Faith." VI. "Progress from the Confession of God." The Nonconformist *calls them "Beautiful discourses, singularly devout and tender."*

THE GOSPEL OF THE RESURRECTION. Thoughts on its Relation to Reason and History. Third Edition. Fcap. 8vo. 4s. 6d.

The present Essay is an endeavour to consider some of the elementary truths of Christianity, as a miraculous Revelation, from the side of History and Reason. The author endeavours to shew that a devout belief in the Life of Christ is quite compatible with a broad view of the course of human progress and a frank trust in the laws of our own minds. In the third edition the author has carefully reconsidered the whole argument, and by the help of several kind critics has been enabled to correct some faults and to remove some ambiguities, which had been overlooked before. He has not however made any attempt to alter the general character of the book.

ON THE RELIGIOUS OFFICE OF THE UNIVER-SITIES. Crown 8vo. 4s. 6d.

"There is certainly, no man of our time—no man at least who has obtained the command of the public ear—whose utterances can compare with those of Professor Westcott for largeness of views and comprehensiveness of grasp. . . . . . There is wisdom, and truth, and thought enough, and a harmony and mutual connection running through them all, which makes the collection of more real value than many an ambitious treatise."— Literary Churchman.

Wilkins.—THE LIGHT OF THE WORLD. An Essay, by A. S. WILKINS, M.A., Professor of Latin in Owens College, Manchester. Second Edition. Crown 8vo. 3s. 6d.

This is the Hulsean Prize Essay for 1869. The subject proposed by the Trustees was, "The Distinctive Features of Christian as compared with Pagan Ethics." The author has tried to show that the Christian ethics so far transcend the ethics of any or all of the Pagan systems in method, in purity and in power, as to compel us to assume for them an origin, differing in kind from the origin of any purely human system. "It would be difficult to praise too highly the spirit, the burden, the conclusions, or the scholarly finish of this beautiful Essay."—British Quarterly Review.

Wilson.—RELIGIO CHEMICI. With a Vignette beautifully engraved after a Design by Sir NOEL PATON. By GEORGE WILSON, M.D. Crown 8vo. 8s. 6d.

"George Wilson," says the Preface to this volume, "had it in his heart for many years to write a book corresponding to the Religio Medici *of Sir Thomas Browne, with the title* Religio Chemici. *Several of the Essays in this volume were intended to form chapters of it, but the health and leisure necessary to carry out his plans were never attainable, and thus fragments only of the designed work exist. These fragments, however, being in most cases like finished gems waiting to be set, some of them are now given in a collected form to his friends and the public."—"A more fascinating volume," the* Spectator *says, "has seldom fallen into our hands."*

Wilson.—THE BIBLE STUDENT'S GUIDE TO THE MORE CORRECT UNDERSTANDING of the ENGLISH TRANSLATION OF THE OLD TESTAMENT, BY REFERENCE TO THE ORIGINAL HEBREW. By WILLIAM WILSON, D.D., Canon of Winchester. Second Edition, carefully revised. 4to. 25s.

" The author believes that the present work is the nearest approach to a complete Concordance of every word in the original that has yet been made: and as a Concordance, it may be found of great use to the Bible student, while at the same time it serves the important object of furnishing the means of comparing synonymous words, and of eliciting their precise and distinctive meaning. The knowledge of the Hebrew language is not absolutely necessary to the profitable use of the work. The plan of the work is simple: every word occurring in the English Version is arranged alphabetically, and under it is given the Hebrew word or words, with a full explanation of their meaning, of which it is meant to be a translation, and a complete list of the passages where it occurs. Following the general work is a complete Hebrew and English Index, which is, in effect, a Hebrew-English Dictionary.

Worship (The) of God and Fellowship among Men. Sermons on Public Worship. By Professor MAURICE, and others. Fcap. 8vo. 3*s.* 6*d.*

This volume consists of Six Sermons preached by various clergymen, and although not addressed specially to any class, were suggested by recent efforts to bring the members of the Working Class to our Churches. The preachers were—Professor Maurice, Rev. T. J. Rowsell, Rev. J. Ll. Davies, Rev. D. J. Vaughan.

Yonge (Charlotte M.)—SCRIPTURE READINGS for SCHOOLS AND FAMILIES. By CHARLOTTE M. YONGE, Author of "The Heir of Redclyffe." Globe 8vo. 1*s.* 6*d.* With Comments. 3*s.* 6*d.*

SECOND SERIES. From Joshua to Solomon. Extra fcap. 8vo. 1*s.* 6*d.* With Comments. 3*s.* 6*d.*

THIRD SERIES. The Kings and Prophets. Extra fcap. 8vo., 1*s.* 6*d.*, with Comments, 3*s.* 6*d.*

Actual need has led the author to endeavour to prepare a reading book convenient for study with children, containing the very words of the Bible, with only a few expedient omissions, and arranged in Lessons of such length as by experience she has found to suit with children's ordinary power of accurate attentive interest. The verse form has been retained because of its convenience for children reading in class, and as more resembling their Bibles; but the poetical portions have been given in their lines. Professor Huxley at a meeting of the London School-board, particularly mentioned the Selection made by Miss Yonge, as an example of how selections might be made for School reading. "Her Comments are models of their kind."—Literary Churchman.

In crown 8vo. cloth extra, Illustrated, price 4*s.* 6*d.* each Volume; also kept in morocco and calf bindings at moderate prices, and in Ornamental Boxes containing Four Vols., 21*s.* each.

MACMILLAN'S SUNDAY LIBRARY.

A SERIES OF ORIGINAL WORKS BY EMINENT AUTHORS.

The Guardian *says*—"*All Christian households owe a debt of gratitude to Mr. Macmillan for that useful 'Sunday Library.'*"

THE FOLLOWING VOLUMES ARE NOW READY:—

The Pupils of St. John the Divine.—By CHARLOTTE M. YONGE, Author of "The Heir of Redclyffe."

The author first gives a full sketch of the life and work of the Apostle himself, drawing the material from all the most trustworthy authorities, sacred and profane; then follow the lives of his immediate disciples, Ignatius,

Quadratus, Polycarp, and others; which are succeeded by the lives of many of their pupils. She then proceeds to sketch from their foundation the history of the many churches planted or superintended by St. John and his pupils, both in the East and West. In the last chapter is given an account of the present aspect of the Churches of St. John,—the Seven Churches of Asia mentioned in Revelations; *also those of Athens, of Nîmes, of Lyons, and others in the West. "Young and old will be equally refreshed and taught by these pages, in which nothing is dull, and nothing is far-fetched."—*Churchman.

The Hermits.—By CANON KINGSLEY.

*The volume contains the lives of some of the most remarkable early Egyptian, Syrian, Persian, and Western hermits. The lives are mostly translations from the original biographies. "It is from first to last a production full of interest, written with a liberal appreciation of what is memorable for good in the lives of the Hermits, and with a wise forbearance towards legends which may be due to the ignorance, and, no doubt, also to the strong faith of the early chroniclers."—*London Review.

Seekers after God.—LIVES OF SENECA, EPICTETUS, AND MARCUS AURELIUS. By the Rev. F. W. FARRAR, M.A., F.R.S., Head Master of Marlborough College.

*In this volume the author seeks to record the lives, and gives copious samples of the almost Christ-like utterances of, with perhaps the exception of Socrates, "the best and holiest characters presented to us in the records of antiquity." The volume contains portraits of Aurelius, Seneca, and Antoninus Pius. "We can heartily recommend it as healthy in tone, instructive, interesting, mentally and spiritually stimulating and nutritious."—*Nonconformist.

England's Antiphon.—By GEORGE MACDONALD.

*This volume deals chiefly with the lyric or song-form of English religious poetry, other kinds, however, being not infrequently introduced. The author has sought to trace the course of our religious poetry from the 13th to the 19th centuries, from before Chaucer to Tennyson. He endeavours to accomplish his object by selecting the men who have produced the finest religious poetry, setting forth the circumstances in which they were placed, characterising the men themselves, critically estimating their productions, and giving ample specimens of their best religious lyrics, and quotations from larger poems, illustrating the religious feeling of the poets or their times. "Dr. Macdonald has very successfully endeavoured to bring together in his little book a whole series of the sweet singers of England, and makes them raise, one after the other, their voices in praise of God."—*Guardian.

Great Christians of France: ST. LOUIS and CALVIN. By M. GUIZOT.

From among French Catholics, M. Guizot has, in this volume, selected

Louis, King of France in the 13*th century, and among Protestants, Calvin the Reformer in the* 16*th century, "as two earnest and illustrious representatives of the Christian faith and life, as well as of the loftiest thought and purest morality of their country and generation." In setting forth with considerable fulness the lives of these prominent and representative Christian men, M. Guizot necessarily introduces much of the political and religious history of the periods during which they lived. "A very interesting book,"* says the Guardian.

Christian Singers of Germany. — By CATHERINE WINKWORTH.

In this volume the authoress gives an account of the principal hymnwriters of Germany from the 9*th to the* 19*th century, introducing ample specimens from their best productions. In the translations, while the English is perfectly idiomatic and harmonious, the characteristic differences of the poems have been carefully imitated, and the general style and metre retained. "Miss Winkworth's volume of this series is, according to our view, the choicest production of her pen."*—British Quarterly Review.

Apostles of Mediæval Europe.—By the Rev. G. F. MACLEAR, D.D., Head Master of King's College School, London.

In two Introductory Chapters the author notices some of the chief characteristics of the mediæval period itself; gives a graphic sketch of the devastated state of Europe at the beginning of that period, and an interesting account of the religions of the three great groups of vigorous barbarians— the Celts, the Teutons, and the Sclaves—who had, wave after wave, overflowed its surface. He then proceeds to sketch the lives and work of the chief of the courageous men who devoted themselves to the stupendous task of their conversion and civilization, during a period extending from the 5*th to the* 13*th century; such as St. Patrick, St. Columba, St. Columbanus, St. Augustine of Canterbury, St. Boniface, St. Olaf, St. Cyril, Raymond Sull, and others. "Mr. Maclear will have done a great work if his admirable little volume shall help to break up the dense ignorance which is still prevailing among people at large."*—Literary Churchman.

Alfred the Great.—By THOMAS HUGHES, Author of " Tom Brown's School Days." Third Edition.

" The time is come when we English can no longer stand by as interested spectators only, but in which every one of our institutions will be sifted with rigour, and will have to shew cause for its existence. . . . . As a help in this search, this life of the typical English King is here offered." Besides other illustrations in the volume, a Map of England is prefixed, shewing its divisions about 1000 A.D., *as well as at the present time. "Mr. Hughes has indeed written a good book, bright and readable we need hardly say, and of a very considerable historical value."*— Spectator.

Nations Around.—By Miss A. KEARY.

This volume contains many details concerning the social and political life, the religion, the superstitions, the literature, the architecture, the commerce, the industry, of the Nations around Palestine, an acquaintance with which is necessary in order to a clear and full understanding of the history of the Hebrew people. The authoress has brought to her aid all the most recent investigations into the early history of these nations, referring frequently to the fruitful excavations which have brought to light the ruins and hieroglyphic writings of many of their buried cities. "Miss Keary has skilfully availed herself of the opportunity to write a pleasing and instructive book."—Guardian. *"A valuable and interesting volume."*— Illustrated Times.

St. Anselm.—By the Very Rev. R. W. CHURCH, M.A., Dean of St. Paul's. Second Edition.

In this biography of St. Anselm, while the story of his life as a man, a Christian, a clergyman, and a politician, is told impartially and fully, much light is shed on the ecclesiastical and political history of the time during which he lived, and on the internal economy of the monastic establishments of the period. The author has drawn his materials from contemporary biographers and chroniclers, while at the same time he has consulted the best recent authors who have treated of the man and his time. "It is a sketch by the hand of a master, with every line marked by taste, learning, and real apprehension of the subject."—Pall Mall Gazette.

Francis of Assisi.—By Mrs. OLIPHANT.

The life of this saint, the founder of the Franciscan order, and one of the most remarkable men of his time, illustrates some of the chief characteristics of the religious life of the Middle Ages. Much information is given concerning the missionary labours of the saint and his companions, as well as concerning the religious and monastic life of the time. Many graphic details are introduced from the saint's contemporary biographers, which shew forth the prevalent beliefs of the period; and abundant samples are given of St. Francis's own sayings, as well as a few specimens of his simple tender hymns. "We are grateful to Mrs. Oliphant for a book of much interest and pathetic beauty, a book which none can read without being the better for it."—John Bull.

Pioneers and Founders; or, Recent Workers in the Mission Field. By CHARLOTTE M. YONGE, Author of "The Heir of Redclyffe." With Frontispiece, and Vignette Portrait of BISHOP HEBER.

The missionaries whose biographies are here given, are—John Eliot, the Apostle of the Red Indians; David Brainerd, the Enthusiast; Christian F. Schwartz, the Councillor of Tanjore; Henry Martyn, the Scholar-Missionary; William Carey and Joshua Marshman, the Serampore Missionaries; the Judson Family; the Bishops of Calcutta,—Thomas Middleton, Reginald Heber, Daniel Wilson; Samuel Marsden, the Australian Chaplain and Friend of the Maori; John Williams, the Martyr of Erromango; Allen Gardener, the Sailor Martyr; Charles Frederick Mackenzie, the Martyr of Zambesi. "*Likely to be one of the most popular of the 'Sunday Library' volumes.*"—Literary Churchman.

Angelique Arnauld, Abbess of Port Royal. By
FRANCES MARTIN.   Crown 8vo.   4s. 6d.

This new volume of the 'Sunday Library' contains the life of a very remarkable woman founded on the best authorities.   She was a Roman Catholic Abbess who lived more than 200 years ago, whose life contained much struggle and suffering.   But if we look beneath the surface, we find that sublime virtues are associated with her errors, there is something admirable in everything she does, and the study of her history leads to a continual enlargement of our own range of thought and sympathy.

THE "BOOK OF PRAISE" HYMNAL,
COMPILED AND ARRANGED BY
LORD SELBORNE.

In the following four forms :—

A. Beautifully printed in Royal 32mo., limp cloth, price 6d.
B.   „   „   Small 18mo., larger type, cloth limp, 1s.
C. Same edition on fine paper, cloth, 1s. 6d.
Also an edition with **Music**, selected, harmonized, and composed by **JOHN HULLAH**, in square 18mo., cloth, 3s. 6d.

The large acceptance which has been given to "The Book of Praise" by all classes of Christian people encourages the Publishers in entertaining the hope that this Hymnal, which is mainly selected from it, may be extensively used in Congregations, and in some degree at least meet the desires of those who seek uniformity in common worship as a means towards that unity which pious souls yearn after, and which our Lord prayed for in behalf of his Church.   "The office of a hymn is not to teach controversial Theology, but to give the voice of song to practical religion.   No doubt, to do this, it must embody sound doctrine ; but it ought to do so, not after the manner of the schools, but with the breadth, freedom, and simplicity of the Fountain-head."   On this principle has Sir R. Palmer proceeded in the preparation of this book.

The arrangement adopted is the following :—

PART I. *consists of Hymns arranged according to the subjects of the Creed—"God the Creator," "Christ Incarnate," "Christ Crucified," "Christ Risen," "Christ Ascended," "Christ's Kingdom and Judgment," etc.*

PART II. *comprises Hymns arranged according to the subjects of the Lord's Prayer.*

PART III. *Hymns for natural and sacred seasons.*

There are 320 Hymns in all.

CAMBRIDGE :—PRINTED BY J. PALMER.